LEAVE IT TO THE PEOPLE

Quentin Reynolds

Leave It to the People

Random House
NEW YORK

FIRST PRINTING

Copyright, 1948, 1949, by Quentin Reynolds

*All rights reserved under International
and Pan-American Copyright Conventions
Published in New York by Random House, Inc.,
and simultaneously in Toronto, Canada, by
Random House of Canada, Limited.*

*Manufactured in the United States of America
By H. Wolff, New York
Designed by Marshall Lee*

To Ginny,

without whom, etc.

My thanks for the help given to me by:
Moshe Brilliant in Tel Aviv; Franca Danesi
in Rome; Apostoulos Koskinides in Athens;
Jacqueline de Moduit in Paris; F. M. S. Donders
in The Hague; Kenneth Downs in Berlin; Bernt
Balchen in Oslo; and, above all, to Belle Becker,
Random House editor, for her drastic but skillful
surgery in editing this book.

Q. R.

This is a book about people. It is about people I listened to in what was Palestine when I reached there and Israel when I left. It is about people in Italy and Greece and France and Holland and Germany and Norway. To me, people are more fascinating than historic monuments, cathedrals, or factories. I met the important people of Europe: the cab drivers and farmers and fighters and tavern keepers and workers and chorus girls and horse trainers, and if now and then a cabinet member or prime minister manages to insert himself into the following pages it is only because I found him to be too interesting or colorful to exclude.

The first few chapters are on the people of Israel, but they could never be called "Middle East Dilemma Solved," or anything as pretentious as that. But, if you really like people, you might enjoy meeting Zeev Unna and his wife Leah, who are farmers, or soft-eyed "Big Isaac" Sadeh, leader of the Palestinian Commandos (Palmach), one of the greatest warriors of our age, or Reuben Rubin, the new country's leading painter, or Paul Blauner, waiter by day and fighter by night, or a thirteen-year-old lad named Michael Cegla who squealed with delight and excitement as he watched Egyptian planes drop their bombs on Tel Aviv, or Colonel David "Mickey" Marcus, who once played football for West Point then became one of Israel's greatest military commanders. Of course we'll meet David Ben-

Gurion and Menachem Beigin, head of the Irgun Zvai Leumi. And we'll see the tiny nation born.

I went to the land of Israel and found the people there were very much like ourselves, with the same passion for freedom and a hatred of being pushed around. I found, too, that democracy (our brand—not the shoddy Russian substitute which is offered under the same label) was no experiment in Israel; it was a fierce, vital force that dominated the whole land.

From Palestine I went to Italy, and again, although I met several of the cabinet ministers, I spent most of my time with people like Giovanni Croccolino, a mechanic in the Fiat plant, and Roberto Rossellini, who made *Open City* and *Paisan,* and dozens of others whose names would mean nothing to you—but people of some interest. I found out, too, how the Communists had almost captured Italy and how some smart Yankee salesmanship had prevented it. I discovered that democracy was far from dead in Italy; that something had emerged from the smoldering ashes of Fascism, and that something seemed to be a new awareness of democracy and a willingness to work for it and sacrifice for it which Italy had not shown during the years of Mussolini's dictatorship.

I spent some time in Greece, but you will find no solution in the following pages to the horrible conflict between Communism and a miserable government which we support as the lesser of two evils. I met Dwight Griswold, head of the American Mission, and Lieutenant General James A. van Fleet and Georges Melas, Greek Minister of Justice, and I have written a little of the problems which confront them in what is most assuredly a country under sentence of death. But I met the real Greeks far from Athens, in villages without water or fuel or food. I met men like Apostolos Koskinides, the miracle worker, who prays each fall to Hercules, ancient God of Sport, and asks him to help the football fortunes of North Carolina State University; and Father Constantin Kokiniotis, the hawk-nosed, bearded priest of Magoula; and Filea Economu, the schoolteacher; and Spiros Nikos, a carpenter, and a doctor named Spiros Rhodopoulos and dozens of others, and through them I managed to see Greece as they know it. In these people, too, the democratic spirit still lives, despite the efforts of political factions which have done their best for so long not only to destroy each other but to kill independent thought and action in the country.

In France I never even saw a cabinet minister. But backstage at the Folies Bergère I met a girl named Yvonne Menard whom you might like to know. And I met Souverain, the best-loved horse in the world, who was born on the Normandy battlefield and he spent his yearling days with the sound of diving planes and screaming shells in his ears. Souverain eventually pulled the greatest upset in racing history to make his owner, known as "Lulu the Chestnut," a millionaire and a man of distinction. I found Souverain much more interesting than any cabinet minister. Besides, in the summer of 1948, France was changing cabinets more often than the St. Louis Browns were changing pitchers at home, and you might make an appointment with the Minister of Defense only to find when you arrived that he was no longer a Minister of Defense but a grower of mushrooms in a village near Bordeaux. But I met a wisp of a nun, Sister Claire, in Dunkerque, and a doctor named André Rommel and an old man in a wheel chair named Jules Beck (a cousin of de Gaulle); and many others who seemed worth telling about. I spent some time with Averell Harriman and he gave me an honest, clear-cut picture of how ERP was working in Europe and a little (but not much) of that is included in the chapters on France.

In Holland I met Mynheer Frans van Heuven, a tavern owner; Gerald Rutton, renowned as a resistance fighter; huge Sergeant Johannes Krabber, bodyguard to Queen Wilhelmina, and a Communist named Jan Reyndorp who told me that his party was making no headway at all in Holland. The people just didn't want it.

Then I drove to Germany with two old friends and a French poodle named Peter. I rode the air lift from Frankfort to Berlin and talked with General LeMay and General Lucius Clay. In Berlin, something very similar to democracy was sprouting from the debris and rubble of the city. Men like Ernst Reuter and Franz Neumann, and a calm-eyed woman, Frau Louise Schroeder, were actually risking their lives to oppose the Soviet masters of the Russian sector in Germany. And I met a very amiable and very tough cop named Ray Carlucci (Director of Criminal Investigation) in Berlin and, so help me, I met a man who calmly admitted that he had been a Nazi.

One night in Norway, Bernt Balchen told me of a shooting contest he had held at four o'clock one morning with Hermann Goering in the Berlin apartment of the great flier, Ernst Udet. I met Torborg Lavik who had been condemned to death three times by the Germans, and I learned a great deal about an airport called Sola, which is near Stavanger. But the greatest thing I met in Norway was a spirit of fierce and militant democracy.

Now I am back and each day I read in our newspapers stern warnings of what Russia will do in Western Europe. I see dire prophecies that one day all of Europe will go Communist, and when I read these things I think of the hundreds of people I met in a dozen countries and I am not alarmed. I know now that democracy is stronger than we realize; you can kick it around and suppress it temporarily, but democracy has more lives than a cat. Democracy is too tough to kill and if there is one conviction in this book that is it.

I did not consciously set out to build a case for democracy; I set out only to write about people I found of interest. Gradually, through the eyes of those people, I saw democracy as a growing force in Europe and not as a doormat for the use of Communists. Democracy has one great and wonderful secret weapon which, I believe, will never be duplicated by any totalitarian state. The secret weapon? People. That's all—just people. And if you'd like to meet them—come on along.

LEAVE IT TO THE PEOPLE

CHAPTER ONE

T*he miracle* occurred on a cool, crisp, slightly over-
cast day early in April, 1948. At three o'clock that afternoon
I was in New York. Actually I was sitting in a huge Air
France Constellation at La Guardia Field—one of fifty-two
passengers bound for Europe. The cabin door of the plane
slammed shut, a voice called pleasantly, *"Serrez votre ceinture
de sauvetage,"* and in the time it took the trim, blue-uniformed
stewardess to say those five words, everyone of us in that huge
plane had been transported to France.

We all fastened our safety belts as she had ordered, and
then the stewardess, wearing the automatic, well-lacquered
smile worn by airplane stewardesses the world over, went from
passenger to passenger, helping. She was assisted by a steward
who wore the same smile. Both kept murmuring soothing
French phrases and nearly all of the passengers answered in
French; some casually, some gaily, and some, who had the

perception to realize that a miracle had just taken place, a bit tremulously. The big Constellation, breaking every accepted rule of take-off behavior, purred gently down the runway.

It was so quiet that I heard the faintly puzzled and slightly disappointed voice of a child three seats ahead of me asking his mother, *"Sommes-nous pas encore dans l'air?"* which, I think, meant, "Are we in the air yet?" I felt like telling the child not to be such a little fool. We had been in France ever since that door slammed forty seconds before. Since then not a word of English had been spoken by anyone. The fifty-two passengers seemed, by some strange alchemy, to have changed appearance. Their very clothing seemed to have taken on a French accent.

We had been out an hour or so when a steward came along with a tray of cocktails. *"Apéritif?"* he asked. There were martinis (but the dark color betrayed their sweetness) and there was dubonnet and vermouth. I picked the dubonnet and found it cold and pleasant.

Then the steward handed each of us a menu. I blinked when I saw it, and then remembered that we were in France. It seemed natural to have *galantine de volaille Périgourdine,* and *entrecôte* with *purée de pommes Mousseline,* and *fonds d'artichauts Châtelaine.* There was a salad too, and with this a small bottle of Bordeaux. A feeling of warmth and friendliness filled the plane. There was Gruyere, Roquefort, and Camembert cheese and I was surprised to see that all three were American made. There was fruit too, and ice cream and pastry and a small bottle of champagne for each passenger. It was as good a meal as I'd ever had in Paris.

I hadn't had time to read the New York papers before I left, and now they went well with the coffee. Not that there was much in the way of news to make a Europe-bound traveler happy. "General Assembly Opens in Flushing Meadow in Atmosphere of Pessimism and Bafflement," one headline read. Another said, "Police Amass 100,000 Men Northern Italy Against Communist Uprising." Another tidbit from Italy

4

shrieked, "One Hour Nationwide General Strike Called by Togliatti." In Austria, too, it looked as though democracy was getting kicked around a bit. "Russians Start Applying Restrictions to Travelers to and from Vienna," the *Herald Tribune* said, and the *Times* had a story from France telling of plans made by the Central Committee of the Communist Party to create a Communist-led government by popular, not parliamentary action. This was to combat what the Communist leaders called "the menace of American imperialist expansion."

There was an editorial in the *New York Post* denying that there was any Soviet influence behind the Palestinian provisional government. Two nights ago at a dinner I had sat next to an Englishman who was an employee of an oil company. When I told him I was leaving for Palestine in a few days he shook his head. "It's a horrible mess over there. It isn't generally known, but the Palestinian fighters are nearly all Communists. Practically every armed man captured so far by the British carried a Communist Party membership card in his pocket." This contradicted every report I had heard from Palestine, but this was one of the questions I was carrying to Europe with me.

Our plane slipped quietly between the earth and the stars and the monotonous drone of the motors seemed to have put everyone to sleep. A plane filled with sleeping people is a good place for reflection. Nearly every European story I looked at in the papers presented a question without giving an answer. I might, I thought, be able to find the answers to some of these questions during the next six months. At least I could try.

There was a story from Moscow saying that Robert Magidoff of NBC and the McGraw-Hill publications had been expelled from Russia for "collecting information on Soviet atomic activity and smuggling that information to the United States." I smiled at that because I had lived with gentle Bob Magidoff for many months in Russia and the thought of Magidoff being an agent was more than a trifle absurd.

5

Every bit of news from Europe indicated that the Russians were winning on all diplomatic fronts. The impression the papers gave you was that virtually all of Europe was becoming more and more receptive to Soviet overtures; more and more eager to embrace Communism. What, I wondered, had happened to the democratic spirit in Europe? Was it lying dormant? Was democracy looked upon with such disdain that no one was bothering to fight for it? Was it dead? You couldn't find answers to such questions in the papers. Columnists here at home were quick with their opinions but, after all, they were only interviewing themselves. The correspondents abroad were, for the most part, factual reporters, and they were too busy writing of events to explain their cause and effect. Czechoslovakia had fallen into the Soviet net a few weeks before, but as yet I hadn't read one story that satisfactorily explained the tragic death of democracy in what we had all thought to be a truly democratic country.

The stories from Europe all seemed to indicate that the people of Czechoslovakia had been the authors of their own destruction. I had known Benes and Jan Masaryk and had always thought of Czechoslovakia in terms of these two men; in terms of their courage and intense passion for democracy. They thought that their country could be a bridge connecting the East and the West; they never envisioned it as an integral part of the East. Masaryk had been in New York a few months before and we had talked of Soviet efforts to infiltrate into what we were by then thinking of as "Western" countries. Masaryk and I had started to reminisce about the time we'd been together in London. Once he had given a party at the Savoy Hotel for some Czech pilots who had escaped from the Germans and had formed a fighter squadron attached to the R.A.F. I reminded Masaryk of that night.

"You're lucky to have men like that now in Prague," I told him, with the complacence of ignorance. "As long as you have a nucleus of those war veterans behind your party, Russia can never take over Czechoslovakia." Jan Masaryk never answered softly. He always exploded. And he never used temperate language when profanity would serve, but somehow it seemed to fit him because there was nothing dirty about his profanity—it was merely the manifestation of an angry, militant spirit that found it difficult to express itself in conventional, polite English. When I said that about the Czech pilots his eyes opened wide and he threw up his hands.

"Damn it, Reynolds, you think like a child. For the love of God," he stormed, "look at the map. Just look at the map."

That's all he said. I didn't bother looking at the map. The thought of Czechoslovakia going Communist was as absurd as the thought of Maine voting Democratic. It was only after the blow had fallen in Prague that I remembered what Jan had said about the map—and I remembered, too, that Maine had voted Democratic once or twice.

I hesitate to write further about Masaryk, because when you write of your friendship for a great man who is dead, you are really boasting of that friendship and forcing his perhaps reluctant spirit in an inverted way to pay tribute to you. To write familiarly of the great ones who are dead is a shoddy device, because there is no one to contradict you and repudiate your claims to a friendship that might have existed only in your own exalted ego. I will never forget the day we heard that Masaryk had died. And I know I can be forgiven for adding one epitaph to his memory. Robert Low, who had been in Prague for *Time Magazine,* had been summoned to New York. He stayed with us. He talked a great deal about Masaryk, whom he had known in London during the early days of the war and whom, of course, he had seen a great deal of in Prague. When Masaryk had left Prague for a United Nations session he had lent Bob and his wife his apartment.

Low returned to Europe, but his office had transferred him to Istanbul. En route he cabled me that he had left a bunch of keys in the top drawer of my desk. He asked me to air mail them to Masaryk in Prague. The cable arrived late one afternoon. I found the keys. Attached to them was a tag on which

Bob had written, "Keys to Jan Masaryk's apartment." I walked into our living room with them. Ginny (my wife) was there reading the afternoon papers which had just arrived.

"Bob left the keys to Jan Masaryk's apartment here," I told her. "He wants us to send them to him in Prague."

"Jan won't need them," she said in a low voice. She held up the papers. The headlines all cried: "Jan Masaryk Dead."

Was democracy, too, now dead in Czechoslovakia? Reading the gloomy newspaper reports, you wondered if democracy in Europe was not a corpse merely waiting for decent interment. As a correspondent, I had worked under every political system, and how intelligent men could voluntarily reject democracy in favor of either Fascist or Communist totalitarianism was something I couldn't understand. Yet I had seen intelligent men choose Fascism back in the early thirties when I was stationed in Berlin. I remember men in Berlin hailing a cold, impersonal state in which they would no longer exist as individuals. The German Fascist sales force was a clever group. It was selling the shoddy religion of materialism, but so disguising it with slogans that many who should have known better accepted it as a healthy revival of patriotism or, at worst, nationalism.

Now Moscow was sending out a fairly clever group of salesmen who were peddling a product which offered the individual much the same opportunity for self-destruction that was once offered by the dear, dead salesmen of Fascism. They too were disguising their product. Every speech that Vishinsky made, every bit of propaganda that the Kremlin had pumped into European countries, stressed the fact that Communism was actually democracy in its purest form. It seemed incredible that a nation with only one political party; with no unions except state unions; with a police force that cracked down on anyone whose speech, actions, thinking (or even musical composition) did not conform to the line laid down by the State; with not even an approximation of a Bill of Rights (except a constitution that had never been put into effect) could be

8

able to sell itself as a democracy. But apparently millions in Europe were buying the idea that Communism and democracy were synonymous. They didn't realize that there was more of Alice in Wonderland than there was of Karl Marx in the sales presentation.

"When I use a word," Humpty Dumpty said scornfully to Alice, "it means just what I choose it to mean."

Stalin's salesmen were using the same technique. Could this apparent inclination to choose Communism over democracy be due to the fact that democracy was content to rest on its record, that it wasn't bothering to sell its product? More than one industrial organization producing a fine product has gone broke because it believed with Ralph Waldo Emerson that if a man builds a better mousetrap the world will beat a pathway to his door. That is one of the most absurd untruths ever to attain the dubious dignity of a platitude. Professor Emerson obviously knew nothing about mousetraps, nor did he know anything about marketing or selling a product. It is true that the world is always receptive to a better mousetrap, a better automobile, a better radio or a better political philosophy, but often the builders of inferior products and inferior political philosophies are so loud and persuasive in their selling methods that the world never gets a chance to hear about the superior product.

The Western world talks smugly of its "proud, democratic birthright," but does it shout this pride from the housetops so that all shall know, or does it merely whisper it? In the war of "ideas" that Russia has been waging, what weapons have we used to combat the Soviet offensive? Have we been too proud to use salesmanship as a weapon?

Christ wasn't too proud to urge his followers to spread his gospel of the fatherhood of God, the brotherhood of man, the forgiveness of sin and life everlasting. Had he depended on the historians, his life, his death and his teachings might well have survived only as legends, or they might well have been destroyed by the forces of status quo. But happily there were

9

twelve great salesmen among his followers, and today, two thousand years later, millions listen and believe their testimony as contained in the Gospels.

"Serrez votre ceinture de sauvetage," a voice called, waking me from a half-sleep. *"Nous arrivons à Gander."* Lights came on and people began to yawn and stretch. The plane settled, but you wouldn't know it in this pressurized cabin. A few moments later the plane kissed the concrete runway delicately and came gently to a stop. We were told that sandwiches and drinks awaited us inside. Air France certainly didn't want any of its passengers to lose weight on this trip. We would be here only half an hour, which was good news. Gander is a place of dreary memory to those of us who did a lot of commuting to Europe during the war. It is a place where we invariably waited for weather to clear.

But now I saw that someone had done a face-lifting job on Gander. It wasn't knee-deep in mud, and its hangars and big administration building were gleaming with fresh paint. It was cheerful and well lighted inside, and a group of passengers from a westbound plane were sitting in comfortable armchairs having coffee and drinks. One of the passengers was seated apart from the others. He looked rather forlorn. I walked up behind him and said, *"Zdrastvuite, Gospadin Magidoff,"* which was about the sum total of all the Russian I knew.

"Zdra——" he began, and then jerked his head around. It was Robert Magidoff coming home from Moscow.

"I should have known it was you," he said in his soft, hesitant voice. "We never had anyone in Moscow who could mispronounce *zdrastvuite* the way you do. Where are you bound for?"

We went to the bar. I asked him if he'd like a vodka and he shuddered. I'd spent ten months in Moscow with Magidoff and I'd never seen him drink anything stronger than Russian beer, a watery concoction that not only has the taste but the strength of warm dishwater. Magidoff had spent twelve years in Moscow and had never drunk a glass of vodka, a great tribute to his sound judgment and good taste. I managed to persuade him to have a glass of Canadian ale which he sipped at first tentatively and then with growing appreciation. I told him that he had been a page-one story in the New York papers, and the unassuming Magidoff almost choked on his ale.

"I stopped in Berlin," he said in worried tones, "and saw the boys at the Press Club but, my God, I never dreamed . . ."

"You'll be landing at La Guardia in about eight hours, Bob," I told him. "There will be a lot of the boys there to get your story."

"I haven't got a story," he said miserably. "They just gave me the air. God knows why. Every story I sent, every letter I sent, all went through regular channels. I can't figure it out yet."

"You're a spy, chum. You may as well face it. Have you got the papers with you?"

"I wouldn't know an atomic bomb if I fell over one," he said mournfully. "Maybe we have agents in Europe. I don't even know that. But if we do, I hope there are smarter men than me on the job." He shook his head, puzzled. "Imagine me a spy?"

"You think Russia is looking for war, Bob?" I asked him.

"No," he said in a puzzled tone. "Why should Russia be looking for war?"

"You better know the facts of life before you reach home," I said. "Practically every newspaper, every radio commentator, every disc jockey and every man running for alderman is shouting that Russia is all set to attack us."

"You know the Russians," he said. "They're nice people—real nice people. They have no quarrel with us."

"If you go around talking like that you'll be accused of being a Soviet agent. It is very unfashionable to like the Russians these days."

"Well, there are some Russian censors I don't like much. They have the same bunch there you were always fighting with," he smiled. "And it's difficult to work up any liking for the Kremlin mob. But I've got nothing against the Russian people."

"Between now and the time you reach La Guardia, work up a big hatred against them and you'll be the hottest thing in the business. But if you as much as order Russian dressing for a salad you'll end up right in front of the House Committee on un-American Activities, as a subversive agent intent upon overthrowing our government by force."

"First I'm an American agent; now I'm a Communist agent," Magidoff moaned. "I didn't know things were as screwy as that back home. Can't a man be just a correspondent any more?"

We sat and talked of our colleagues in Moscow and in Berlin, and then Magidoff mentioned Ambassador Bedell Smith and his eyes grew bright with enthusiasm. "What a wonderful man," Bob said. "As soon as he heard how they were accusing me he asked me to stay at the Embassy as his guest. He's one Ambassador who doesn't mind sticking his neck out for a correspondent."

They called Bob's plane then and we shook hands and he walked toward the gate, a perplexed and rather unhappy man. I have never been able to get over the sheer stupidity of Soviet officials in Moscow.

Even during the war, when we were sending out nothing but enthusiastic reports on how the Red Army was fighting, how magnificently the Russian people were working, we were looked upon with grave suspicion by the Soviet Foreign Office. Official Russia seemed to look upon all American and British correspondents as subversive agents trying to undermine the faith of the Russian people in their government. Now they accused the transparently honest, guileless Magidoff of plotting against them; Magidoff, who in stories and broadcasts had always been meticulously fair to the Soviet Union.

The accusation was so absurd that Magidoff couldn't even work up any anger about it. It is difficult to get really angry at stupidity; you can get impatient and disgusted, but anger is too vital an emotion to waste on stupidity. I don't mean that the fourteen members of the Politburo are stupid, but the lower echelons in the Soviet government service are filled by incompetent, suspicious, fear-dominated men. Once you got away from them and came in contact with the Russian farmer, worker, or scientist, you meet the Russians Magidoff meant when he said, "They're nice people—real nice people."

Our plane was called and I climbed aboard and fell asleep. Eight hours later the stewardess awoke us by saying simply, "Paris." Her automatic smile had survived the long trip. When girls are selected for the job they must be sent to some institution where permanent smiles are lacquered on their faces and where a permanently cheerful note is grafted in their throats. They all look alike, smile alike, talk alike. But they look good and they smile pleasantly and they talk soothingly, and who can quarrel with that?

Fifty-two of us climbed out of the plane. We hadn't lost a single passenger.

Waiting for a connecting plane at Orly Airfield is like standing outside the ball park while the game is being played. You can hear and sense the excitement of what is going on inside but you can't see it or be a part of it. Orly is only about thirty-five minutes from the Champs Élysées. We were close enough to sense the peculiar excitement which only Paris seems to generate, but we were still outside the ball park enjoying the game vicariously.

However, it was only a two-hour wait and then my Palestine-bound plane was announced. It was another Constellation, but we had a brand-new crew and a different group of passengers. We took off quietly, this time bound for Rome. Planes on this run have to climb quite high to go over some mountains called the Alps, and today there were a lot of huge cotton balls hanging up there which we had to travel through, so we never did see the pretty things. And because Rome was shrouded in heavy rain we landed at the Ciampino airport without getting a glimpse of the capital. The chief characteristics of the Ciampino airport are lack of charm, lack of heating and bad coffee. Air France, as usual, had several thousand calories waiting for each passenger, but Air France couldn't do anything about that coffee. It reminded me of the coffee we used to get in Moscow. That came in a can on which was pictured a large acorn. It was the Russian way of boasting, "This is not the ordinary coffee the capitalist countries are forced to drink. This is very special. It is made of acorns." It certainly tasted as though it were made of very old tired acorns. So did this Italian version, but it was wet and it was warm.

One of our passengers looked familiar to me. We introduced ourselves and it developed that we'd met before. He was a New Yorker, Sidney Green, en route to Palestine to do "a little work for the Jewish Agency." In New York, Green was a public accountant. We talked for an hour or so and then our plane was called. The rain slanted down persistently and the big Constellation looked awfully heavy and soggy standing there on the steel mesh which served as a runway at Ciampino. This airfield had taken a real shellacking during the war; its hangars were grotesquely twisted skeletons. We climbed into the plane and it took off easily. The next stop would be Lydda Airport ten miles outside Tel Aviv. There was an air of subdued excitement among the passengers now. Most of them were big men with ruddy faces. They looked like a group of New England farmers. It was difficult to judge their nationality. Green was sitting with me now and I asked him if he knew. He not only knew their nationality; he knew the name and status of nearly all of the passengers. Most of them were Palestinians, he told me. They had been in England or Switzerland or New York on government missions. Some of them, Green added dryly, had been buying "agricultural equipment." Green smiled but didn't enlarge on the subject.

"Most of these men are either in the army or hold government positions," he told me. "Some of them are fairly important in their own country."

We talked of Palestine as the plane, impervious to the rain that was beating a rat-tat-tat on the small windows, hurried over Southern Italy and then struck out over the Mediterranean. I dozed off for a couple of hours and then the stewardess awoke us. It was still dark. I peered out of the window and found that the rain had stopped and that a white moon was giving light to the calm water below. We were landing at Tunis, the stewardess told us. Why? She wasn't sure. Perhaps the weather ahead was bad. Perhaps the pilot didn't like the way an engine was behaving. We flew low over Tunis and the moonlight drenching the city gave it a spurious appearance of cleanliness. The whitewashed city gleamed brightly, and if you hadn't been in Tunis before you might have believed the lie the moonlight was telling. But I'd spent some weeks in and around Tunis in 1943 and hoped now that we wouldn't have to spend too much time in the place. Since the war ended I've often heard G.I.'s talk nostalgically of England or Italy or France or even Germany, but I never heard any G.I. become wistful over returning to North Africa. From the air the Tunis landing field seemed to be merely an extension of the Mediterranean. We landed smoothly and were brought into the inevitable dining room. Our crew had undoubtedly radioed ahead to expect guests for breakfast. The white marble-topped tables were set and waiters started to bring in fried eggs and bottles of Algerian wine, North African beer and, finally, coffee. Rather incredibly, the coffee was good. There would be quite a delay, we were told. We sat and talked and the passengers began to emerge as individuals. The huge smiling man was Shimon Hacohen; the middle-aged man with the twinkling eyes who chatted easily in several languages was Attorney Jacob Shapiro of Haifa. There was an eighteen-year-old boy whom they all called David. The good-looking woman with the large blue eyes and lovely complexion who talked with a slight English accent was "Mrs. Wingate." The others seemed to have a great

16

affection for her; their attitude was almost paternal. Our stewardess came in to tell us that it would be several hours before we could leave, and that we were to be taken to various hotels in Tunis to wait. Eight of us who had been assigned to the Palace Hotel climbed into a small bus and headed for the city. Now and then we'd pass a depot filled with wrecks of planes, trucks, even tanks, and they were a reminder that a war was fought here not so long ago. I recalled the weeks I'd spent here in 1943.

General Carl Spaatz had lived in a beautifully equipped villa, and Air Chief Marshal Tedder, with whom Spaatz worked, had his headquarters outside Tunis. It was here that they planned the softening up of Sicily, the raid on Rome, and the air operations that covered the invasion at Salerno. Tunis had been a busy place in 1943 and you saw more khaki and R.A.F. blue than you did dirty white cotton and red fezzes. Back of Tunis were our airfields where B-26's and B-17's and their escorting P-38's were based. The one bright spot in those days was the Officers' Club on the beach at La Marsa, only a few miles from Tunis. One of the great unsung heroes of the war presided here, a British mess sergeant who had found the secret of transforming American and British rations into really tasty food. That club, which was for both American and British officers, really demonstrated how successful a combined operation could be. Officers pooled their food and liquor rations and the club became known up and down the coast as the only real oasis in North Africa. Often pilots who had been standing at the bar too long would suddenly remember that they were scheduled for a night operation. The club was geographically situated to take care of such emergencies. The pilot would merely walk a few yards to the edge of the Mediterranean, slip out of his clothes and plunge into the water. A few immersions were usually enough to banish the hazy dream world induced by too many drinks. Pilots had one great advantage over the rest of the armed forces. Once in their aircraft, all they had to do was to "check the oxygen." A few

17

whiffs of oxygen would kill or severely cripple the worst of hangovers. Some of our pilots used a great deal more oxygen on the ground, just before taking off, than they did up in that wild blue yonder. Many of them thought that oxygen was too precious to be wasted at 20,000 feet. To some of them it was strictly a medicinal commodity.

But today as we entered the city and drove down the busy, noisy Avenue de France, we didn't see a single uniform; only dirty white cotton. The streetcar bells clanged loudly, everyone seemed to be shouting, and the driver of every automobile kept sounding his horn or siren. There is a strong taboo not only in Africa but throughout the Middle East against using your brakes. Instead of slowing as you approach a street intersection, you grip the wheel tightly, jam your foot down on the accelerator and start blowing your horn. This custom has been so hallowed by age that it is now the accepted way of driving. If, by any chance, you hit another car and have any breath left, the ritual is to start screaming imprecations at the driver of the other car. Victory invariably goes to the driver who yells the loudest.

Our bus driver showed himself to be no novice at the game. He swung to the left of trolley cars; he bumped against trucks, yelling happily as fender grazed fender, and then he tore into the rue d'Italie with a triumphant jerk and stopped short in front of the hotel. Across from the hotel was a moving picture house with a huge poster that cried, "Paul Muni in *Scarface*."

There were no rooms ready but there was a pleasant lounge and coffee waiting for us. A slight, almost imperceptible air of tension seemed to have settled around our group of eight. I was puzzled by it and wondered if I were imagining it, and then Shimon Hacohen, his face serious now, spoke to Attorney Shapiro.

"I heard at the airport," he said, "that the plane might go to Cairo first before heading for Palestine. I'm afraid that might prove awkward for several of us."

"It might prove to be more than awkward," Shapiro said solemnly. "I suggest that we get a guarantee from the pilot before we leave that under no circumstances will he land at Cairo until he delivers us to Lydda Airport."

"Most certainly," Mrs. Wingate said sharply. "You are all too well known to risk landing there in Cairo. We all know that several Palestinians have been detained for questioning at the Cairo Airport, and we know that several of them have not been heard from since. Why not be our spokesman, Jacob?"

"Very well," he nodded, and went looking for a telephone. This seemed to me to be a little over-dramatic and perhaps my skepticism showed on my face. Shimon Hacohen apparently saw it and he smiled.

"Our country is at war, you know," he said softly. "A nasty, bloody war. We are short of weapons, short of trucks and tanks and aircraft, and short, too, of personnel. Each of us, in one way or another, is useful to the conduct of our war effort. The Egyptians know who we are. If we stopped at Cairo I am afraid that several of us would be taken from the plane. I spent three years in a German prison camp during the last war. I am afraid," he added, "that I have developed an allergy to military prisons."

"Yes," Mrs. Wingate nodded, "and Jacob would be certain to be taken. And, of course, young David." She smiled at the handsome blond youngster. "David has been in school in Sweden but he is on his way home to join the Haganah. No, the Egyptians would not allow anyone of his age to proceed to Palestine."

Shapiro returned. "I got hold of the Air France officials. They were very understanding," he said. "We can't leave, however, for several hours."

"Isn't there another air line that could take us into Palestine?" I asked.

Shapiro shook his head. "No, they have all pulled out but Air France. Lydda Airport is in rather an exposed spot. It is commanded by a plateau where there is an Arab village, and there is some sniping. Then the trip into Tel Aviv is partly through Arab-dominated territory. It is not always an easy trip. Your American commercial pilots demanded a considerable raise in pay to take their planes into Lydda, so the company stopped the service. Now only Air France continues to operate."

The room clerk bustled in to announce that he had one room ready. Would the lady like to go up now? The lady said she would finish her coffee. The clerk said he would like her name so he could register her.

"Lorna Wingate," she said, and then for the first time I realized who she was. Lorna Wingate was the widow of the leader of Wingate's Raiders. Major General Orde Wingate had been a military commander in Palestine during the thirties. In 1936 the Arabs began to attack Jewish settlements and Wingate organized the Palestinians into mobile units known as Wingate's Night Squads. They were successful in putting down the Arab disturbances. Wingate's close association with the people of Palestine convinced him that their cause was just, and although a non-Jew, he became one of them in spirit. General Wingate was a deeply religious man who was outraged by the way his own government and the world was handling the Palestine question. To him it was a human problem; not a political or economic problem. When war came and he was sent to Burma, he kept his Palestine contacts alive. He wrote letters constantly to his old friends in Jerusalem, Tel Aviv and the Negeb, and he always ended his letters with the Biblical quotation (Psalm 137): "If I forget thee, O Jerusalem, may my right hand fail; may my tongue cleave to the roof of my mouth." But Wingate never forgot Jerusalem. I had heard all this when I had been in Palestine during the war. I had read, too, that when General Wingate was killed in Burma his widow had pledged herself to continue his work for a free, independent Palestine. And now she sat with us, beautiful, charming, witty, talking of the country which she had learned to love because she saw it through the eyes of her dead husband. She spoke of Ernest Bevin's anti-Semitism as evidenced in virtually every speech he had ever made on the subject of Palestine.

One of the others who had just come from London said that everyone was talking of a tea recently given by Mrs. Bevin. She had invited about sixty women. Mrs. Bevin, infected by her husband's almost pathological hatred of Jews, was careful not to ask any Jewess to her tea, but, unknown to her, several of the women present were entirely in sympathy with the Jews in Palestine and violently opposed to the official policy as established by Bevin and the British and American oil companies. Some of those present at the tea brought up the question, but Mrs. Bevin promptly put an end to the discussion of the Jews by saying angrily, "If my Ernie had his way they all would have been exterminated long ago."

"I heard that story in London myself from a dozen sources," Lorna Wingate said, "but I wasn't at the tea so I can't vouch for it."

"Do you believe it?" I asked her.

"Good heavens, yes!" she said.

It seemed reasonable. After all, Ernest Bevin has done his best to exterminate the Jews of Palestine. There is probably nobody in the world as arrogant as a powerful labor leader, and Ernest Bevin, before he became a minister of the Crown, was the leader of the world's largest and most powerful labor group, the Transport Workers' Union. He was intolerant even then of anyone who disagreed with his labor policies and he was indignant at other labor groups which did not conform to his line. Bevin always hated Communist labor groups in England, not for any ideological reasons but because they had the effrontery to break from his union and oppose his policies. As Foreign Minister, his arrogance had increased. He treated countries which did not follow his line as though they were recalcitrant unions which had broken away from his own organization. Palestine had gone ahead, ignoring his orders, and Bevin, like John L. Lewis, is a man who doesn't like to be ignored. Bevin is a complete captive of his own prejudices; a man who seems proud of his insularity and ignorance and who wears a cloak of arrogance which so many mistake for honest conviction.

We had arrived at the picture-showing stage now and Lorna Wingate proudly displayed a snapshot of her four-year-old son.

"I am going to bring him up in a settlement in Palestine," she said. "I want him to study Hebrew and to learn of the greatness of the people his father loved. I want him to be a good Palestinian and a good Englishman. I want him to be his father's son."

She left us then to rest. Shimon Hacohen said thoughtfully, "A wonderful wife of a great man. Of course, we can never pay the debt we owe to General Wingate. When things were darkest in Palestine it was Wingate who saved us. From him we learned the type of military tactics suited to the defense of a land like ours. Today his military teachings are embodied in the methods used by the Palmach."

"Palmach?" This word was new to me.

"Palmach means striking force," he explained. "The Palmach is the equivalent of the Commandos. They are specially trained for assault operations. They travel fast, strike quickly, and then disappear to strike somewhere else. Their leader is a man we just call 'Big Isaac.'"

"What's his real name?"

Hacohen laughed. "Until May 15th, when we are accepted formally as a sovereign nation, our military leaders must remain underground."

"Will there be real trouble after May 15th?" I asked.

There was a heavy silence for a moment. "Yes," Shimon Hacohen said slowly. "There will be real trouble. Five nations are poised ready to attack us on that date. The Egyptians have planes; the forces of Trans Jordan have the well-trained, well-equipped Arab Legion under Major Glubb Pasha, and they have tanks and British twenty-five pounders and experienced British officers. We have very little to combat this. Oh, we'll win all right, but the cost will be frightful. I—I'm afraid we'll lose at least twenty thousand of our finest young men."

I looked at young David. His eyes were shining as he listened.

"Maybe," he said respectfully, "we will prove to be better fighters than you think."

"I had forgotten for the moment you were listening, young David," Shimon smiled. "If I keep on talking you may regret you left your quiet school in Sweden."

David laughed. "Who could study philosophy and mathematics when his country is being invaded?"

The room clerk came in again to tell us that rooms were now ready for all of us. Sidney Green and I doubled up in a room with two white-painted iron beds. It was difficult to sleep, not only because the mattresses were filled with something related to crushed cement but because so many disturbing things had been said downstairs. An hour before, these fellow passengers of mine had been an anonymous group and at best my only interest in them had been a mild curiosity. What they thought or felt or what had happened or was about to happen to them was none of my concern. But now I had met them and each was an individual in his or her own right; this was no longer an impersonal group—they were people I was beginning to know. Young David, who might have been anybody's kid brother, was on his way toward possible death. Lorna Wingate was no longer just a beautiful, rather patrician-looking woman; she was a vital, intense, highly intelligent person building a monument to the memory of her dead hero-husband, the only kind of monument she felt he would have liked. Her militant stand on Palestine must have meant the loss of old friendships and bitter enmity back in London. Huge Shimon Hacohen had been introduced to me as a farmer; now he was revealed as a former British officer who had spent three horrible years in a German prison camp and as a man whose mind was tortured by the knowledge that thousands and thousands of young Davids would soon be dead. Jacob Shapiro was not merely a pleasant, middle-aged man of obvious culture; he was a Palestinian whose brains and experience were in some manner serving his country.

"You get a different perspective as you get close to Palestine, don't you?" Sidney Green in the next bed had noticed that I wasn't asleep. I agreed that you did.

"Back in New York you think of Palestine as a difficult, complex question," he went on. "Oh, you're in sympathy with the people of the country but you give a few dollars to help them and let it go at that. It's hard to think of Palestine in terms of people, and until you do you can't understand why they fight."

We lay there, both thinking aloud, and then we slept. Some time later a knocking on the door awoke us and a voice told us that the bus would be ready in a few minutes. It was dark now and I had no idea what time it was. My watch was still on New York time and, half-asleep, I tried to figure out what time it would be in Tunis. But for the moment I had forgotten whether you lose or gain hours traveling east and I gave up the hopeless struggle which any eighth-grade kid could have resolved without trouble in twenty seconds. Green suggested that we might as well shave; we were both beginning to look a bit mangy. He walked toward the bathroom carrying his toilet kit.

"We'll feel better after a shave, a hot bath and a cold shower," Green said heartily.

"I will make you a small bet that there is no hot water, no tub and maybe no shower. You're in Tunis, chum."

There was no hot water, there was no tub, but there was a hesitant, vacillating shower that dripped cold water in a way that made one wonder if it hadn't once been used by the Chinese as an instrument of torture. Green went through the agonizing routine and shamed me into following him. The bus was waiting. There was a long line at the ticket booth in front of the theatre across the street. A lot of Tunisians were going to learn about our American way of life from Paul Muni and *Scarface* tonight.

Our plane was ready and now everyone seemed to be in a holiday mood. They were going home and you could sense their happiness. We even had a tail wind now to speed us along. The stewardess told us that we were traveling about 325 miles an hour, but inside our warm cabin there was not the slightest sensation of motion or speed. We seemed to be outracing the night, leaving it behind us, and soon we flew into that undecided gray hour that is neither night nor day, and caught up with the dawn. We slipped into a huge bank of clouds, bumping easily over them, much as a toboggan bumps over small uneven contours of snow and ice as it glides downhill. And then we slid smoothly off the top of the last great cloud, and now there was nothing below but the blue of the Mediterranean; pale aquamarine, shading into dark indigo, according to the depth of the water. There was nothing above but the lighter blue and dazzling gold of the sky, for we had outdistanced the clouds, and then someone cried out, "There it is!" Far ahead, there was a break in the smooth sea and, beyond that, vague, undefinable patches of white and dark. Palestine. The land seemed hurrying to meet us. The dark patches grew larger and, as we settled down, we could see that they were cultivated areas, and the white patches, sand. We sped over the white city of Tel Aviv and beyond, to Lydda Airport. We circled it once and then landed.

As the passengers set foot on the land, each seemed to grow in stature. Each seemed to take on a new confidence and each seemed to laugh more readily. They were foreigners everywhere else in the world; here they were Palestinians and this was their home. The rest of us were the foreigners now. We walked toward the administration building. Four sleepy-eyed British soldiers stood guard at the entrance to the building. They were handsome lads, bronzed and healthy-looking, and they wore the uniform of the Argyll and Sutherland Highlanders, khaki shirts open at the neck and green kilts. But there were naked bayonets in their rifles.

I stood on the steps looking out across the airport. Ours

was the only plane there. No more peaceful scene could be imagined. The airport was in the midst of a farming area. Green fields stretched as far as the eye could see. Crossing the perimeter of the field beyond the plane was a slowly moving caravan. There were a dozen camels and each looked as though it had a stiff neck. From a distance camels look rather stately. They move with great dignity and now, with the early morning sun behind them, they looked clean and majestic. There were a dozen small donkeys in the caravan ridden by Arabs whose feet almost touched the ground. A dozen women walked.

"They are Arab farmers on their way to the fields," Shimon Hacohen said.

"Looks like a picture postcard," I said.

A young British immigration official looked at our passports rather intently before stamping them. Porters were bringing our baggage to the room where the customs men waited behind a long counter. The customs men were Palestinians, but employees of the British. There was nothing perfunctory about their examination. I had a half dozen pair of nylon stockings with me, a gift to the wife of an old friend, Gershon Agronsky, editor of the *Palestine Post*. In England a customs officer would have said, "These are to be used as gifts? Right? Well, now, we can't charge a man duty on a little gift like that." Customs officials all over the world (except the British) have the knack of making you feel guilty even if you have nothing but a flock of dirty laundry in your luggage. These Palestinians were no exception. Virtually every passenger had to pay duty on gifts he had brought home. The customs men had a conference over my six pairs of stockings. Finally one of them asked what I had paid for them. I had absolutely no idea. My wife had bought them and packed them in my bag. Had anyone tapped me on the shoulder, I would have said meekly, "All right, officer, I'll go quietly." I had never bought a pair of nylon stockings in my life. I looked at them. What

26

could these absurdly fragile things cost? One dollar? Ten dollars? I had no idea.

"About two dollars a pair," I said timidly. The man in charge looked dubious and then he took out a pencil and did some figuring.

"That will be 100 piastres duty," he said sternly. I had forgotten the value of a piastre and, besides, I had nothing but traveler's checks and a few dollar bills with me. He would be glad to take dollars, he said. I gave him four dollars and everyone seemed to breathe a sigh of relief. Arab porters grabbed our bags and carried them outside to a waiting bus. Our baggage was lashed to the top of the bus and then I looked more closely and saw that this wasn't a bus. It was, in fact, an armored truck. We climbed into it. It was much like the patrol wagon used in most American cities, except the sides were half-inch steel plate. There were two wooden benches running the length of the truck; hardly enough room for the sixteen of us. Lorna Wingate sat on Shimon Hacohen's lap, and young David, grinning happily, squatted on the floor. Two young lads in khaki shorts climbed aboard. One got behind the wheel; the other sat beside him. Sidney Green sat next to me and we looked at each other blankly. Our fellow passengers were all quiet. The truck began to move. We only went about two hundred yards and then it swerved sharply to the right and stopped. Then the driver backed skillfully and stopped at the entrance of a wooden shed. Three tanned youngsters in khaki shorts and shirts smiled a greeting and hopped aboard. A dozen or so others came out of the shed, each carrying something. Several carried blanket rolls, and the boys inside our truck grabbed these and pushed them under the benches. Others passed cardboard cartons into the truck and still others wooden boxes which seemed heavy. Everything was loaded now. The driver turned his head and cried out something in Hebrew.

"He is in a hurry to get off," Shapiro said, as though amused by some secret joke.

Now the lads who had been loading the truck started to climb inside. They laughed as they jostled each other and us. They crowded behind the driver. They sprawled on the floor of the truck and others sprawled over them, but they didn't mind the crowding; they all laughed and chatted good-naturedly. Finally twelve of them were inside.

"What's this all about?" I asked Shapiro.

"These boys may come in handy later on," he said, and then we were off. We drove about half a mile and stopped at a road block. Two young British Tommies stuck their heads inside. "Everyone got passes?" one of them called, and the driver grinned and said, "Sure, everyone has a pass." The second Tommy said, "All air-line passengers, I presume," and the driver grinned again and said, "Sure—just a load of passengers." "Cheerio, then," the Tommy called out, and several of the youngsters waved at him. The truck started to move. It hadn't gone a hundred yards before the man sitting next to the driver called out, "Okay," and each of the lads moved. They reached under the benches and brought out the blanket rolls. Inside each roll was a Sten gun, the equivalent of what our movie gangsters once called tommy guns. Laughing, kidding each other, the boys assembled the guns quickly (it takes about eighteen seconds to put a Sten gun together). They dipped into the cartons and brought out clips of bullets and slid these into the guns. The truck stopped for a moment and four of the boys hopped out. No one, apparently, had to give orders; evidently they had all done this many times before. We heard them climbing up to the roof of the truck and then they yelled to go ahead. The steel doors at the back of the truck slammed shut and the truck headed toward Tel Aviv.

The boys, who seemed to look older now cradling the Sten guns, reached up and opened the narrow slits cut into the sides of the truck. There was no windshield up front; merely a steel plate with thin horizontal openings.

"There are two bad stretches of road between here and

Tel Aviv," Shimon Hacohen confided to me. "The Arabs control that territory."

Two of the youngsters started to sing and the others joined in. Soon all were singing and then Shapiro and Shimon Hacohen and young David and the others joined in. It sounded like a marching song, militant, exciting, and the young voices hit the steel sides of our truck and bounced back.

"That's the 'Song of the Negeb,' " Shapiro explained. "The Negeb is our desert. Although these are not desert troops."

"These kids regular troops?" None of them looked more than eighteen.

"Yes," he said, and added dryly, "you'll notice that they handle those guns with the familiarity that comes with experience. These boys are part of the Haganah. Six months ago they were all at school or working on farms. Now they are trained soldiers."

"You said they weren't from the desert?"

"These boys are clean-shaven. The troops who fight in the Negeb wear beards. It isn't an affectation with them. They wear beards in the desert because water is too scarce to waste on shaving."

There was a cry from the boys on top of the trucks. The driver slammed on the brakes, and the voices stopped abruptly. The steel doors at the back opened quickly, four boys tumbled out and the doors slammed again. Inside, the youngsters shoved the short barrels of their guns through the slits. The driver reached under his seat and picked up a Sten gun. Three of the boys moved to the front. They crouched and peered through the slits. It was very quiet now inside the truck, but no one seemed perturbed. Lorna Wingate had a quiet smile on her face. Three sharp reports muffled by the steel sides of the truck seemed to come from a long way off.

Our boys didn't return the fire. I wondered if they had anything on the roof of the truck heavier than Sten guns, which had an accurate range of only sixty yards or so. I asked Shimon Hacohen about that.

"I imagine they have," he said. "But these are useful little weapons. We make them here in cellars, in apartments, in the back rooms of shops. They're fine for close work. You can spray a lot of lead if they come at you in close formation. The Dieppe raid taught us something about these little guns. A great many men stumbled walking into the beach at Dieppe. It wasn't sand, you know; it was a beach of rock and shale. The guns hitting the rocks when the boys lost their footing went off, causing several casualties. We have added a safety catch to the gun. Quite an improvement."

"I thought you were a farmer," I told him.

"In our country even farmers must know something about weapons," Shimon said.

The doors at the back opened and the lads hopped in again. We started to move toward Tel Aviv. Three times during the next half hour the armored truck stopped and the boys leaped out to reconnoiter, but there was no more firing and then the driver called something cheerful over his shoulder, and the boys slipped the clips from the guns and dismantled them. Back the guns went into the blanket rolls. The boys looked younger once they had shoved them under the benches. They looked like members of a high-school football team on the way home after winning a game. They began to sing again and then they started something that seemed familiar. The words were Hebrew, but no one could mistake the tune. It was the "Anniversary Song."

"They stole that from Al Jolson," I said to Green.

"That song was old when Jolson was young," Green remarked.

"Nothing was old when Jolson was young," I reminded him.

We stopped at another road block and once again two British sergeants exchanged pleasantries, looked perfunctorily inside the truck and waved us on. What amazed me was this spirit of camaraderie existing between these British soldiers and the young Haganah men. Before May 15th the Haganah was tolerated by the British as a sort of defensive National

Guard, and the British allowed it enough small-caliber weapons to carry out the military duties usually associated with a National Guard outfit. Neither of these two "inspections" had been anything but casual ones and the truck might have carried a dozen mortars, Bren guns or dozens of grenades. Obviously some "arrangement" had been reached with the British guards, for such slipshod inspections were not the usual routine with any British army group I had ever seen in action.

Finally our truck entered Tel Aviv. Sidney Green was going to the Kaete Dan Hotel and I decided to go with him. I had stayed there when I had been in Palestine in 1941 and 1943. We climbed into a cab and within a few moments were in front of the lovely little hotel. When I was here before the hotel had been owned by a charming, youthful-looking white-haired man named Joseph Rosenblueth and his wife, Kaete. The Kaete Dan is on the Mediterranean and nearly every bedroom has a terrace. A young, dark, smiling man with a shock of black hair was behind the desk. He was Samuel Federman, and he told me that he and his brother now owned the Kaete Dan. Rosenblueth had bought a half interest in Piltz', a restaurant night club down the street.

"But everything is the way it was when Joseph ran the place," Federman said anxiously. "We haven't changed anything."

"Then it's still good," I said.

The phone behind the desk had been ringing. Federman picked it up and listened and the smile left his face. Finally he hung up.

"I guess you'll both be staying with us for some time," he said slowly. "The Arabs just captured Lydda Airport."

"We just came from there," I protested.

"I know," he said. "They moved in a few minutes after you left the field. It is wholly in their hands now and so is the Lydda Road. That means we're completely cut off from the outside world. There will be no more incoming or outgoing mail."

"Well, I was going right on to Jerusalem anyhow," I told him.

Samuel Federman laughed shortly. "Jerusalem? There is only one road to Jerusalem. We managed to get a food convoy through the other day, but now the road is closed. The Arabs have built huge road blocks across it. They control the road now and it is impossible to get through to Jerusalem."

I thought of Gershon Agronsky. If I could phone him I felt sure he could get me to Jerusalem. I asked Sam to get Gershon on the phone. He smiled and shook his head.

"You don't understand," he said. "Agronsky is in Jerusalem, and Jerusalem is in a state of siege. The telephone wires have been cut. There has been no communication with Jerusalem for several days. I'm afraid you're stuck here with us for awhile," he said apologetically, as though he were responsible. "But we'll try to make you comfortable. We're short of meat. It all goes to the front. But we have plenty of chicken and veal and fish and fresh vegetables. We'll do our best."

He showed us to our rooms. Mine on the first floor opened on a rather large terrace that overlooked the beach and the sea. The room was immaculately clean. In fact, the first thing that strikes you when you reach Tel Aviv is the fantastic cleanliness of the city. One reason for this is that the wind usually blows in from the Mediterranean, and it carries no soot or grime with it.

"Henry Wallace had this room when he was here a couple of months ago," Sam said suddenly. "You know Henry Wallace."

"Nobody knows Henry Wallace," I said.

"Very nice, he was, but not what we expected," Federman laughed. "I remember his first night here. I was on duty all that night."

"On duty?"

There was a note of surprise in Federman's answer. "Of course. All of us are in the Home Guard or in some branch of the army. Some of us, the cooks and the waiters and myself, are on part-time service. We serve three or four nights a week guarding the roads into the city or driving. But we're all

32

trained, and when they attack Tel Aviv, as they probably will after May 15th, we'll be on full duty."

"Where did you get your training?" I asked.

"Well, I served in the British Army all during the war," he said. "Most of us did, you know. . . . But about Henry Wallace. I came off duty about 5:30 A.M. and came back here. There was Henry Wallace sitting on the front steps talking to the milkman. The milkman didn't know who he was. The two of them were having a big discussion about milk; butter and cream content, and the best way to keep milk fresh in the absence of refrigeration. Five-thirty in the morning! Mr. Wallace seemed to know a lot about milk and about crops. As a matter of fact, their discussion got so technical that they lost me. I couldn't follow them so I went to bed."

A white-coated waiter came into the room carrying a tray. "Please—please," he said, "you'd like some coffee? And the cook made some pastry yesterday. I brought you a piece. You know pastry is always better the next day. Right, Mr. Federman?"

"Sure, Paul," he laughed. "This is Paul Blauner, your waiter. Any time you want anything, pick up the phone and ask for Paul."

He left, and Paul tried to persuade me to have some eggs or maybe a piece of broiled fish. The coffee was enough, I told him. He poured me a cup and added hot milk. I walked out on the terrace. The terrace jutted out so that you had a clear view of the Tel Aviv port to the right. To the left, perhaps half a mile away, was Jaffa, the Arab city.

"You sure you want to stay out here?" Paul asked a little anxiously.

"Sure, the sun feels good. It's quiet here. Maybe you could set up a table for me sometime. This would be a nice place to work."

"Of course," he said a little doubtfully. "I'll be . . ."

I jerked my head back instinctively as a hornet buzzed by my face. The shrill high zzzzzz sound was followed by a dull thud. Paul was looking at a large stucco house some fifty yards to the right.

"It hit there in the wall," he said.

"What was it?" I was completely bewildered.

"A high-powered rifle," he said calmly. "Very high-powered. Look toward Jaffa. You see that tower that stands out? That is their mosque. They do their sniping from there. In the past three months they have killed about two hundred of our people. This terrace is right in their line of fire. I do not think they aim at anyone. The whole city is their target."

"Why doesn't the Haganah do something about it?"

"The British are in Jaffa with their twenty-five pounders and their machine guns and their mortars," Paul said grimly. "If we attacked Jaffa they would consider it an act of aggression against them and it would give them an excuse to retaliate. Or if we infiltrated into Jaffa and took over the mosque, the word would go out all over the Arab world that we were destroying their shrines and that would result in what the Arab leaders want—a holy war."

"And they'll keep on shooting?"

Paul nodded. "Of course. I will give you my glasses sometime. Train them on the tower; the minaret of the mosque. You will notice a flash every few minutes. They can silence the rifles but they cannot hide the flash. But when you do this, hug the wall here. Do not stand out there. A great many bullets whiz over this terrace every day. They may be aiming at the port which is over to the right. Or perhaps they just shoot at random. In any case," he added gravely, "you would not feel comfortable working out here. I can fix up a table in your room."

"Tel Aviv seems to be a pretty exciting place these days," I said.

"Exciting? No, I would not say that. But interesting." He brightened up. "Yes, it is an interesting place. After all, a nation is being born here these days. You will not find it dull, I hope."

34

CHAPTER THREE

I *spent* a couple of weeks getting acquainted with Tel Aviv, and it was a rewarding experience. I was helped a great deal by Moshe Brilliant, Tel Aviv correspondent for the *Palestine Post*. I had heard a great deal about Moshe Brilliant from Ed Morgan and Frank Gervasi, both of *Collier's Weekly*. They had worked long stretches in the Middle East and before I had left home both had urged me to look him up. They said he was not only one of the finest newspapermen in the Middle East, he was one of the finest men. Although a Palestinian, he had, they said, managed to retain his sense of objectivity. Morgan had shown me a brilliant article that Moshe had done for *Harper's Magazine,* the only objective, informative article I had ever read on the Irgun Zvai Leumi and the Fighters for Freedom (The Stern Group); the two underground military organizations operating independently and usually in direct opposition to the Palestine national administration, headed by David Ben-Gurion.

I found Moshe Brilliant to be a dark-haired, good-looking man of thirty-five. He had been brought up in Brooklyn and had gone to Palestine in 1933 with his parents for a visit. He had met a girl named Sylvia who was also visiting Palestine with her parents. They had married, and Moshe, liking Tel Aviv, suggested that they stay around awhile. It wasn't long before they both fell in love with Palestine; it's an easy place to fall in love with.

Smart Gershon Agronsky had hired Brilliant to work on the *Post*. When we entered the war, Moshe tried to enlist in the American army. He was sent to a Middle East camp for his physical examination and spent several days there.

"They were wonderful guys," Moshe said thoughtfully, telling me about it, "but somehow I felt like an outsider. It's hard to explain. Mind you, there wasn't a trace of anti-Semitism among those men. They were great to me, but, damn it, I just felt as though I were an outsider. I was a Jew. They accepted me, all right, but there was some barrier between us that neither they nor I could explain. I remembered how it had been back home in New York. If someone asked a man what he was, he would say, 'I am a Jew,' but he would say it either defiantly or apologetically. In Palestine, being a Jew is nothing to get emotional about. It is a fact that you accept as casually as, say, a man at home who is born a Methodist or an Episcopalian. He doesn't go around shouting it defiantly or admitting it sheepishly. So I decided to become a citizen of Palestine. I haven't regretted it."

Palestine didn't regret it either. He seemed to know everyone from David Ben-Gurion to the waiters at the Kaete Dan, and everyone seemed to like him. Life at the Kaete Dan was interesting. Goldie Myerson, of Jerusalem, a magnificent, American-born woman, revered by everyone in Palestine for her courage and wisdom, was there. Industrialists like Moshe Bejerano, who, with his brothers, owned cigarette and canning factories, dropped in often and he and David Horowitz, Palestine's leading economist, would discuss the economic future of their country brilliantly. My particular friend was Franz Winkler, a banker in Jerusalem. Like most Palestinians he seemed to talk every known language, all of them without accent. He had come from Jerusalem on a two-day business trip. The road had closed behind him and now he was an exile from Jerusalem, desperately worried about his family there. The only way he could get in touch with them was to cable banking friends in New York City who then cabled Jerusalem. Each morning Franz woke me and we'd run down to the beach for a swim.

The Armon Hotel across from the Kaete Dan was press headquarters. Kenneth Bilby of the *Herald Tribune* and his lovely, nineteen-year-old bride, Helen; Gene Currivan of the *New York Times;* quiet, thoughtful Richard Mowrer of the New York Post Syndicate; ebullient Izzy Stone of what was then *PM;* Jim Long of the A.P. and Bob Mullen and Eliav Simon of U.P., and a couple of British correspondents lived here. Mr. Erich Braun, a tall, soft-spoken man, managed and owned the hotel. He actually liked having correspondents living with him, which made him unique among hotel men in Europe. Not that correspondents are objectionable or troublesome tenants. Far from it. American correspondents abroad are engaged in a business as highly competitive as the selling of soap, and a man who neglects his work will soon find himself back on a police beat or (with luck) on a rewrite desk. The thing that makes most hotel men abroad unhappy about having a group of correspondents as guests is a little thing called Greenwich Mean Time. Correspondents must live and work not by the local clock but by the time in New York. There was a seven-hour differential between Palestine and New York time. Kilby and Currivan, for instance, could send stories up to five A.M. in Tel Aviv with a reasonable chance of catching their last editions in New York. The U.P. and A.P. men, of course, were on duty twenty-four hours a day.

Before Jerusalem was bottled up, that city had been press headquarters for Palestine, but now the government was in Tel Aviv, all military communiqués were issued in Tel Aviv, and cable facilities (washed out in Jerusalem) were still good in Tel Aviv. Covering the Palestine story during the fighting of Spring, 1948, was not an easy job for a press association or daily newspaper correspondent. There was no static front, in the technical sense of the word. There was no one spot (except Jerusalem) where you could go and be sure that you would get the important story of the day. You might go to Haifa, eighty miles north, and then find that the big story was the capture of the Lydda Airport ten miles from the Armon Hotel. You might hear a rumor that Gaza was about to be attacked and you might, with great difficulty, get transportation to that part of Palestine, but while you were on the way, Haifa might fall or Tel Aviv be attacked. Men like Kilby and Currivan had to be all over the place. They as well as the press-association men had "stringers," local reporters who covered the routine news, and, in addition, they had tipsters who were constantly rushing in and out of the Armon.

They sometimes did this rushing at two or three in the morning, which threw the whole well-ordered routine of the Armon out of kilter. Tel Aviv is a city that goes to bed early. Most hotels, following the Middle East custom, locked their doors around eleven. You could always wake the night clerk if you came home later than that.

Owner Braun had to start living by New York time, but it didn't seem to bother the good-natured hotel man. He told his bartender, a fair-haired, soft-spoken genius named Richard Strauss, to remain open as long as the boys needed him, and he always had his cook leave a plate of sandwiches in the ice box. Richard had a peculiar obsession. He loved ships. When he wasn't behind the bar he was out on the beach or sitting on the terrace of the Kaete Dan Hotel watching the ships come into the harbor. About once a year the urge would be too overwhelming to resist and Richard would ship out as a steward or bartender. Braun was getting a little worried. Richard had been with him for nearly two years now and he was afraid that his bartender would soon be getting the wanderlust. The correspondents were a little apprehensive too, because by now Richard knew the individual taste of each of his clients. He knew that this one wanted his martini with two olives and only a drop of vermouth; that this one liked his whisky sour on the sweet side and that a third insisted upon a drop of grenadine in his Tom Collins. Richard was one of the most sensitive practitioners of the art of drink mixing I have ever seen. He also had a passion for cleanliness. His little bar glistened from constant polishing and his glasses sparkled. Richard also had an uncanny knack for figures. Seven or eight of the boys might burst into the bar at once, thirsty after a foray into the dusty, sandswept territory outside the city. They would have a few drinks and ask for the bill.

"I put one round on your bill, Mr. C.," he would say calmly. "Another on Mr. L's bill and I split the third round between Mr. F. and Mr. D. I didn't put Mr. S. down for a round. He paid for three rounds last night."

I was surprised to find that most correspondents and Palestinians had a high regard for the native products. The Rishon wines made in Palestine were excellent, dry and with a bouquet highly reminiscent of the wines of Burgundy. The vermouth and the brandy were good. The Palestinian brandy is not nearly as strong as French cognac but is a lot smoother. Palestine beer, while it lacked the sparkle of American beer, was adequate. And then there was Palestine gin. It looked like gin. It came in a bottle labeled "Gin" and it had the strength of gin. Richard wouldn't serve it at the Armon bar. When conversation lagged at the bar you could always take up the question of Palestinian gin. One night there was a discussion as to what was the world's worst-tasting drink. Some voted for Irish whisky; a group put forth slivovitz and there was a school of thought that held grappa to be the most revolting of all. But Richard held out for Palestinian gin.

39

"You only have to taste it," he said reasonably, "to settle the question." I tasted it. It had the elusive, subtle charm of one-day-old Georgia white mule; the fragrance of a water-soaked sock and the bouquet of a breeze that has passed slowly over a sulphurous swamp.

"Two thousand years of persecution and now this," I said to Richard. "A country that can survive this stuff should find the Arabs easy to beat."

"Oh, we'll beat the Arabs all right," Richard said casually. That was the attitude of Tel Aviv.

No one in the city made flamboyant speeches about victory or about the necessity of sacrifice and work; these were taken for granted. All roads leading out of Tel Aviv were closed and closely guarded by the military. Only those with essential business were allowed to leave the city. Once Tel Aviv and adjacent Jaffa on the south were one city; Jaffa remained as it was, but Tel Aviv mushroomed to the north and east and became a separate all-Jewish municipality, while Jaffa remained an all-Arab city.

Tel Aviv was built on sand, but it was built of steel and concrete, and its citizens seemed to have taken on the enduring qualities of steel and concrete. Today Tel Aviv is the commercial and cultural center of the country. Tel Aviv has the same sun-washed look that some Southern California cities have.

When the city was about fifteen years old it was given a coat-of-arms consisting of a beacon of light to the Jews of the world and a gate of entry into Palestine. It has been just that for many years. If you ask a citizen of Tel Aviv what the city's chief imports are, he says laughingly, "People." Thousands of the immigrants who have come to Palestine during the past fifteen years have come through the port of Tel Aviv. Quite often (much more often than the British realized) the immigrants entered quite informally, without benefit of visa. They came by night in small boats which pushed their noses into the white sand of the Tel Aviv beaches, and they waded ashore while their children were carried in the arms of the people of Tel Aviv. The city made it a point to be well equipped to care for those seeking haven in Palestine.

Children were immediately taken to one of the hospitals in the city or to children's villages outside Tel Aviv. One of the finest children's homes is a large modern building on what is still known as King George V Street. This, like many others, is supported by the Women's International Zionist Organization. Only the youngest babies are brought here. Each ward holds twenty cribs. The name of each child is written on a card and attached to the foot of the crib. The nurse who showed me through the wards seemed to know the history of each baby in the hospital.

"This is Dan," she said, picking up a chuckling one-year-old. "He was born on Cyprus. His mother died and he was brought to us. Here in the next crib is Deborah. . . . She's big for six months. Deborah, too, came from Cyprus. Her parents? We don't know. Now here's a little boy named Uri. Uri is a refugee from the Jaffa border. When the sniping began, we took in all of the children from that area. Uri is a Yemenite, and Uri has seven sisters and six brothers. That's right—fourteen in all, and Uri's mother is only thirty-four. She married when she was fourteen. Now here's Jacob, only three weeks old. He was born on the boat coming from Cyprus. And little Miriam is seven months old; no, she has no parents."

The older children who are sent to the children's villages outside the city sometimes present a problem. Those who are ten or twelve have lived haunted lives, and their experiences show in their wide, troubled eyes and quick nervous reactions. Many of the villages are supported by an organization of American women known as the Mizrachi.

"Our main job," one of the men in charge of the children at Raanana said, "is to get the new boys interested in something. Thousands of these children have had to steal food to live, and many of them stole to keep their parents alive. At first they can't believe that they can have all they want to eat.

They sneak bread into their beds at night. We put newly arrived children in rooms with those who have been here some time, and gradually they thaw out; the suspicion and hardness leave them. They have absolutely no moral values at first. It is mainly the example of the other children which gives them a sense of right and wrong. They have never played—these children. We have to teach them how to play. Most kids love to work on the farm or the gardens. It's strange how these newly arrived boys are thrilled when vegetables or flowers they have planted actually appear. It takes months to banish the horrible memories they carry with them, and sometimes," he added sadly, "it takes years. Now they are often awakened by the shots from Arab snipers. The old terror they knew comes back to them."

But there was no terror among the children who were born in Tel Aviv and went to school in the city. One of the favorite targets of the Jaffa marksmen and snipers from the near-by Arab village of Salameh seemed to be the Bialik School on Levinsky Street, not far from the Jaffa border. Neither the Jaffa nor Salameh snipers could miss the big modern stucco building which housed a thousand school children. Every day a dozen bullets from high-powered rifles crashed into the school. It is a three-story building, and one day I stood outside and counted ninety-two bullet holes on the right wing of the school. The school authorities had piled sandbags behind every window. By some miracle not a single child was killed. I met the principal of the school and he seemed unconcerned about the danger, but filled with pride when he talked about his charges.

"Sometimes in the middle of a lesson there will be a sharp noise and the kids will laugh and say, 'Another one.' They've become so accustomed to the thought of bullets hitting the building that it hardly distracts them any more. They are safe as long as they are in school, but my worries begin when they leave," he sighed. "They collect bullets the way kids once collected marbles. Once school is out they run to the front of the building, hoping to find bullets that hit the school and then dropped to the ground. One of the youngsters has collected forty of them. That makes him the most popular kid in school."

"How many of the kids dropped out of school?" I asked.

"Not one," he said proudly. "We left it to the parents and they had a meeting. Not one parent took his child out of school. Actually they're safer in school than they'd be on the streets. And they're completely without fear."

And there was no fear among the citizens of Tel Aviv. There was discomfort and overcrowding because hundreds had been evacuated from the Jaffa border area and from settlements outside the city. Every apartment lobby held eight or ten, and those who lived in the buildings furnished cots, sheets and blankets for them. However, in spite of the abnormal conditions, the citizens of Tel Aviv insisted upon living as close to normal lives as possible. Every night they trooped into the Opera Mograbi on the Second of November Square (named to commemorate the date of the signing of the Balfour Declaration) to watch the Kaufman-Hart play, *You Can't Take It With You*, which was playing in the Chamber Theatre occupying the lower part of the big building. If their tastes ran to something different, the Mograbi Cinema above was showing the film, *Forever Amber*, and if the knowledgeable audience occasionally laughed at the wrong moments—well, that happened when the picture was shown in New York and Boston and Des Moines. As you went in, Haganah soldiers (women) asked you for identification cards. If you were a soldier you had to convince them that you weren't A.W.O.L. The Palestinian Orchestra never stopped giving concerts. One night the organization gave a concert only for Haganah men and women. If Director Jasha Horenstein had any feeling of trepidation playing for 1,500 uniformed soldiers nearly all of whom carried either side arms or Sten guns, it didn't show in his masterly direction of Beethoven's *Egmont Overture*, nor did the frail-looking soloist, lovely, Palestine-born Pina Salzman, seem any more nervous playing a Beethoven piano concerto than she had been when she played the same number at London's Albert Hall.

It was a common sight to see the musicians hurry from the stage and pile into buses on their way to give a late concert for troops somewhere on the Jerusalem Road. And always leading the convoy of buses, as a rather grim reminder that there was more than music in the air, there would be an armored car with uniformed armed men, and trailing them would be one of the large white ambulances of the Mogen Dovid Adom (Red Shield of David).

Night life as it is known in New York or Paris never really existed in Tel Aviv, but what there was of it centered in the hotels on Hayarkon Street, which borders the beach. The food was universally good, whether you stayed at the Kaete Dan Hotel or the Gat-Rimmon or Armon Hotel, or the Park.

One night there was a mild celebration in the cocktail lounge of the Gat-Rimmon. Young Herbert Brun who played the piano there had received word that he had won a Koussevitsky scholarship to study in America, one of the most coveted of musical awards. There were no planes or ships leaving Tel Aviv and it was impossible for Brun to get to Boston, and for all anyone knew an Arab army might crash into the city tomorrow—but everyone was happy because Brun had been chosen.

That was the night that Meyer Weisgal, of the famed Weizmann Institute of Rehovoth, his wife, and several of the physicists, chemists, and mathematicians who work at the Institute some thirty miles away, had started off blithely for Tel Aviv to spend the night. The scientists were too engrossed discussing such problems as producing nylon-type stockings from the bean of the castor tree (which they have done) or of various unexplored ways of utilizing the cheapest raw material in the world (the sun's rays) to realize that they were driving through territory infested with bands of Arab snipers. It wasn't until several bullets slammed against the outside

44

of their jeep station wagon and one had crashed through the window to narrowly miss the head of Doctor Ernest Bergmann, scientific head of the Institute, that the great brains realized that the war was not as remote as it might seem to scientific minds. After a few hectic hours, Haganah men eliminated the Arabs and a dozen of them escorted the scientists the few remaining miles to Tel Aviv. When they reached the Gat-Rimmon Hotel the relieved Weisgal insisted upon inviting the Haganah men in for a glass of beer. It had been a warm trip and the men were not averse to slaking their thirst. With Mrs. Weisgal acting as hostess, the men sat at tables in the cocktail lounge. They had been in action for so long and had been so dependent on their guns that it seemed natural to retain them.

The headwaiter was very unhappy. He apologized profusely to Mrs. Weisgal, to her husband, to Doctor Bergmann and to the soldiers.

"Revolvers we don't mind," he said almost tearfully. "Everyone carries a revolver. But gentlemen—Sten guns and Bren guns are too much. They really detract from the otherwise pleasant atmosphere here. Would you gentlemen mind checking the guns in the cloakroom?"

Next to the Gat-Rimmon is the night spot known merely as Piltz.' It has a fine orchestra whose leader, Menashke Baharoff, had written the "Song of the Haganah," which became extremely popular in the army. Every night a hundred or so uniformed Haganah men and their girls came to Piltz' to dine and dance. My old friend, the popular Joseph Rosenblueth, for years one of the best-liked and most successful hotel men in Tel Aviv, was half-owner. Rosenblueth was only fifty, so he had to give ten hours a day to army duties and most of the work of running Piltz' fell to Manager Albert Meyer. Meyer had been a banker in Berlin. He managed to get out in 1936. He was forty when he arrived in Tel Aviv. He had never liked banking and he decided to spend all of his time at what had merely been a banker's hobby—cooking. He soon became a really expert cook, and now he supervised the cuisine at Piltz'. There had been fierce fighting for weeks in upper Galilee, but now it had been completely cleared of Arabs and a few members of the Palmach had been given a few days' rest in Tel Aviv.

Several of them were in Piltz' one night when I dropped in. I stood at the bar with genial Meyer, who greeted them all, many by name.

"Look at this boy." Meyer pointed to a tall, bronzed, uniformed lad who had just walked in with a girl, also in uniform. Both of them blinked at the brightness of the lights.

"See his beard?" Meyer laughed. "A very blond, new, young beard. He's about eighteen. Obviously he's been fighting with the Palmach in the desert. The kid seems to be bewildered by the lights and music. Probably never been in a night club before. The girl is just as shy; she would probably be very confident with a Sten gun in her hand. She's undoubtedly with the Palmach, too."

Meyer greeted the two youngsters breezily. He said he'd put them at a table away from the music. The boy asked if one could buy dinner at Piltz'. Meyer nodded. Then the boy took some money out of his pocket.

"This is all the money I have left," he blurted out. "What can we have for this money?"

Meyer counted it carefully. "You have twelve piastres here. For that you can each have an entire duck dinner and four bottles of beer each."

The smiles that illuminated the faces of the two youngsters were wonderful to see. Meyer conducted them to a table and I watched him giving precise orders to the waiter. First there would be Meyer's specialty, a chopped-chicken-liver omelet, slightly flavored with the juice of an onion. Then there would be *canard à l'orange* and French-fried potatoes and a salad. The soldier could have beer if he wished, but Meyer said that he had some excellent Rishon wine which would cost no more. The couple deliberated and then decided on the wine.

"Leave the dessert to me," Meyer pleaded. "Let me make you something special."

They agreed, and Meyer told the waiter to bring out the ingredients to make *crêpe suzettes*. He then told the waiter (in German) to bring him the bill. I watched the two completely happy youngsters devour the best dinner that the genius of Meyer could provide. And it cost them twelve piastres. A piastre is four cents.

"Suppose I bought that meal, what would it cost me?" I asked.

Meyer laughed. "About six pounds."

Six Palestinian pounds amounts to twenty-four American dollars. Food is expensive in Tel Aviv because so much of it has to be imported. But men like Meyer (and he is by no means an exception) manage to see to it that boys in uniform get the very best at the very lowest rates. There are no war profiteers in Tel Aviv.

Although Piltz' was usually filled with laughing young men and women, occasionally the war crept into its bright, gay atmosphere. One night a Haganah officer, David Weiss, came in and went directly to the bar. His face was tight with anger and his eyes were cold and empty. I had known Weiss first when he was fighting as a machine gunner with the British Army in Libya in 1941, and I'd run into him the week I arrived in Tel Aviv. He was usually a gay, happy-go-lucky man, proud of only one thing—his accuracy with a machine gun.

"They got him," he said without expression. "My sergeant, Kaplan. You knew him. We served five years together in the British Army. He and six others were out on reconnaissance last night. They didn't come back. Today we found them all— all dead. Kappie was dead as a stone. They hadn't shot him. They had burned his feet until they were black. They had cut long gashes in his legs. They had slashed his thighs and his stomach. He lived through all that, the medico said. They cut him as only Arabs and Ethiopians know how to cut a man.

47

Finally they cut his throat. He was dead as a stone when I found him—when I found what was left of him."

The Arab Legion of King Abdullah in the main conformed to the accepted rules of warfare in regard to prisoners; the so-called Arab Army of Liberation under Fawzi el-Kawukji did not.

Tel Aviv, which gets up very early, usually goes to bed before midnight. This was true even before the blackout which went into effect May 14th. The midday heat is severe during the summer months, so business usually comes to a standstill from one until four. But the businessman with a shop on Allenby Road, and the butcher, the baker, and the candlestickmaker, whose stores are on Ben Yehuda Road, are invariably at work by seven in the morning. There is only one late spot in Tel Aviv, which is open practically all night. That is the Kassitt, on Dizengoff Street. This is a sidewalk café within a few minutes' walk of the theatres, and for years the actors, musicians, composers and writers have made it their headquarters. They go there for coffee and sandwiches after the night's work is done and they talk about symphonies to be written and dream of plays to be produced.

Many who went into the army kept up the old custom. Even when the fighting fortunes of Israel were at their lowest ebb, the Kassitt was packed each night with soldiers on leave and with the theatrical crowd. There were always willing singers or comedians happy to put on impromptu acts for the men in khaki.

They would keep some real star like Shoshana Damari on her feet singing until she was drooping with exhaustion, and actors like Raphael Klatchkin and Joseph Sukeinik never received the whole-hearted applause in theatres that they received in the early-morning hours from entertainment-hungry Haganah men just in from the fighting. Usually the sessions would end with someone starting a song which would be picked up by everyone else.

Tel Aviv never allowed the months of sniping from adjacent

48

Jaffa, or the all-out bombing which began May 15th, to stop her building program. Construction of apartment houses on the outskirts of the city never stopped, and essential workers were refused by the Haganah. Building was as vitally important as bullets. The building program was designed especially for the benefit of men who had served in the last war, and already a great many have been completed. The apartments are modern in every way, designed to take full advantage of the sun. Every apartment (practically every room) has its own balcony. These apartments were constructed by the city at a cost of about $4,000 for a unit of four rooms. Tenants were charged the construction cost plus 3½ percent. An ex-service man could "buy" such an apartment for $600 down and monthly payments of $20. The same apartment on fashionable Hayarkon Street, built and owned by private contractors, would cost the tenant about four times that amount.

Tel Aviv began to have growing pains a few years ago. The kid had just grown too fast, but fortunately the city fathers called in Jacob Ben Sira, a specialist in such disorders. As Municipal Engineer, Ben Sira has charge of all planning and construction. His theory was that the city grow out—instead of up. There are no ugly sun-eclipsing skyscrapers in Tel Aviv. There are few office or apartment houses higher than six stories, and none can be built which will shut out the sun from its neighbor.

Tel Aviv will really come of age when its port is enlarged. It is not a deep-water port. The ships anchor a quarter of a mile offshore and their cargo has to be lowered into lighters which then are towed to the docks and unloaded—a long, laborious process. However, if it hadn't been for the port, Israel would never have been born. All of the guns (except Sten guns, which were all made secretly in Palestine) and ammunition which enabled the country to fight, passed through the port of Tel Aviv. And nearly all the immigrants who have found happiness in the country came in through the port of Tel Aviv.

The port was managed by soft-spoken, handsome Alexander Zipstein. I had heard of Zipstein. In fact any time you were served Turkish coffee in Tel Aviv and you commented appreciatively on it, someone was sure to say, "Wait until you taste the Turkish coffee Zipstein serves at his office. He has a pet Arab there who makes it better than anyone in the Middle East."

I finally went to Zipstein's office at the port to find out for myself. It was all true. A huge, middle-aged, smiling Arab was there at a table making the thick, sweet coffee which is called Turkish. It was dangerous for an Arab to keep on working for a Jew during May, 1948, because the Iraquis and the Trans-Jordan leaders had decreed death for any Arab who did not fight against Palestine.

"My boy just won't leave," Zipstein said, smiling. "However, I make him sleep here in the office and the men who work here at the port are all so fond of him, I doubt if any Arabs could get close enough to hurt him. He does make great coffee, doesn't he?"

"Ah, yes, thank you," the grinning "boy" bowed happily.

"That's all he does," Zipstein said. "I'll tell you a secret. I have him down on the payroll as secretary. Quite often ships come in during the night or early morning. My boy is on duty here twenty-four hours a day making coffee. That's all he wants to do—make coffee."

Weeks later when the port became the chief target for Egyptian bombers, Zipstein and his pet Arab never left the unsubstantial wooden office. They remained there all during the bombings, but although bombs fell all around the port, killing and wounding a great many, neither was injured.

Tel Aviv is a young city, but she already has her traditions. The people of Tel Aviv have always been forced to fight. At first it was against the shifting sands, the hot sun and the blistering heat of a wind which invariably blows fifty days each year. Then the city had to fight in two wars not of her making and a third war for survival. But Tel Aviv has survived.

Thousands of those who come to Tel Aviv from displaced persons camps arrive well equipped to find places for themselves in the economic life of the country. Several times I stood on the wharf watching the lighters bringing people in from the ships which usually anchored a quarter of a mile or so out to sea. As their feet finally touched the soil of the new land many broke down completely. It seemed indecent to watch their naked emotion. Six million of their sons and brothers had been exterminated and they had survived. Fear, hunger, disease, torture had been their constant companions for years, and now for the first time they were free and wanted. They were greeted with soft cries of *"Shalom."* In Tel Aviv people say *"shalom"* as we say "hello" or "good morning." *Shalom* means "peace." And they are greeted by everyone at the port with cries of *"Bruchim Ha' baim,"* which means "welcome."

Every time I stood there watching this new blood being pumped into the arteries of the country I thought of the people who had made it possible: the Jews of America. Each year the United Jewish Appeal raises a huge sum from the five million Jews of America, and it is this money which has kept the homeless, stateless Jews of Europe alive. Every American who made some sacrifice in order to contribute each year would have felt that the sacrifice was worth it, if he could have seen the faces of these families reaching the only land in the world where they are honestly wanted and welcomed.

The money contributed by American Jews did more than merely keep these unfortunate victims of the world's cruelty alive. As soon as camps were organized for displaced persons, the Joint Distribution Committee (an agency of the U.J.A.) began a program of practical education, looking ahead to the day when the displaced persons would be able to find refuge in Palestine or some other country. Many of these men and women had never been given an opportunity to learn a trade.

51

The Joint Distribution Committee assigned teachers and material to the camps, and during the past three years thousands have learned trades. They came to the new country well equipped to contribute something to its progress—not as burdens.

To thousands and thousands of Jews in America the thought of Zionism and a nation of Jews is unwelcome; if they remember their faith at all it is on holidays. They feel about Judaism, in fact, as most non-Jewish Americans feel about their religion. But even those American Jews who disapprove of Zionism contribute each year to the United Jewish Appeal, and in recent years thousands of non-Jews (notably in Dallas and Little Rock) have helped swell the huge total that has kept the Jews of Europe alive. It has turned out to be a great investment in humanity, and if one wishes to think of it in terms of ideology it is resulting in the growth of the only strong democratic nation in the Middle East. The Arab countries are feudal states, and they proved in World War II that they were ready at all times to sell out to the highest bidder. But Palestine is a democracy in its purest form. The people of the country have a fierce hatred for any kind of totalitarianism. They were its first victims and they, more than anyone else, know how diabolical is the regimentation of ideas and thoughts. Russia has made an earnest effort to woo Palestine, and the country was grateful for the support the Soviet Union gave it during United Nations' sessions, but the thought of living under Communism is as abhorrent to the people of Palestine as is the thought of living under Fascism.

The oil-company man who told me so emphatically that "Nearly every Palestinian captured by the British carried a Communist Party card" was telling a deliberate lie. When I inquired in Tel Aviv about what he said I was met with incredulous stares. I asked bankers, military leaders, industrialists, American and British correspondents and local Tel Aviv newspapermen.

"Communists in uniform?" Moshe Brilliant laughed. "Someone has been kidding you. We have one Communist newspaper in the whole country. It has a circulation of 1,800. Who are the uniformed men with Communist cards captured by the British? They captured and executed a great many members of Irgun Zvai Leumi, but the Irgun politically is very much to the right. Many of them are fanatically religious, especially the Yemenites, all of them are fervent Zionists and, heaven knows, Communism and Zionism are as far apart as Communism and Catholicism. To say the Irgun is communistic is as absurd as saying that the Knights of Columbus is communistic. The Haganah is composed of men of all political parties, but most of them follow Ben-Gurion and his Mapai Party, which is a right-wing Socialist party. It is about as communistic as the liberal wing of the Republican Party in America. The Palmach is political in addition to being a fighting unit, but its politics are those of the agricultural settlements out of which the Palmach originated. You've been in the settlements before when you were here. Visit them again and see if you can find any Communists. The Stern Group? There may be Communists among them but, frankly, I don't know. And I doubt if there are more than five hundred men in the Stern Group."

I decided to visit one of the settlements. Years before I'd spent a few days at Givat Brenner, one of the largest of them. At that time the guiding spirit of the settlement was Enzo Sereni, a brilliant Italian Jew who had come to Palestine to escape the Fascism of Mussolini. Sereni was a man of culture and charm, and I was anxious to see him again. Although Givat Brenner was only about thirty miles from Tel Aviv, I arranged for a car and when we set off I was a little surprised to notice that the driver had a revolver and a Sten gun on the seat beside him.

"Been a lot of sniping on that road," he said.

We were stopped several times by road blocks and each time women in Haganah uniforms asked for credentials. By now, Reuben Zaslani, chief security officer in Tel Aviv, had provided me with papers good anywhere the Haganah operated. About five miles from the settlement we were told that we couldn't go any farther alone. My driver explained that our errand was important and we were given an escort of a dozen armed men who hopped into a truck and told us to follow them. They took us right up to the entrance of the settlement. My driver dropped me at the office of the director and I walked in, asking casually for Doctor Sereni. The three men who were there in the office looked shocked, and one of them asked gently, "Haven't you heard what happened to him?"

Sereni's knowledge of Italy made him a valuable man to the Allied side, and, in 1943, he went to work for a joint American-British unit which was directing psychological warfare from Cairo. It was he who had written the pamphlets which had been dropped over Sicily and Italy. He felt that he could organize anti-Fascist forces in Italy to fight actively against the Germans if he could contact them personally, and he finally persuaded British military authorities to parachute him behind the enemy lines. They dropped him in Northern Italy and he did organize sabotage and intelligence units, and for weeks he reported regularly via the radio which had been dropped with him. Then all reports stopped.

Six weeks after V-E Day, British officers, going over the list of those who had died or been killed at Dachau, came across the brief epitaph: "Enzo Sereni, died November, 1944." That was the story they told me. Sereni's picture was on the wall. He looked as I remembered him, a face full of intelligence and warm expressive eyes. I tried not to think of what my old friend had gone through at Dachau before he had died.

I walked around the settlement with the present director. There were half a dozen posts where khaki-clad men with rifles watched the surrounding country for signs of Arabs. I asked if these were Haganah men.

"We are part of it," the director said. "We guard the settlement ourselves. A great many of our young men, of course, are with the Palmach, and some are in Haganah, but we have a sort of Home Guard of our own. They have all had military training and are capable of guarding the settlement, unless we have a major attack. But our intelligence is excellent. We have many good friends among the Arabs and we will have advance news of any big attack. Then we'll call for the Haganah field units."

We climbed to the tower atop the administration building. Once Sereni had brought me here. The tower commanded the whole surrounding country. You could see men and women working in the fields. You couldn't see the mine fields that had been laid in strategic areas, nor could you see the Bren guns held by guards in well-camouflaged spots in the groves. The director had to leave, and I began to chat with a slim, dark-haired guard whose name was Zeev Unna. He was married and had two children. His wife, Leah, was out in the fields, he said. Perhaps I'd like to have coffee with his wife and himself later and perhaps I'd like to meet his children? He would be off duty in an hour or so. He suggested that I meet them in the room he and Leah shared. I arrived a little early, but Zeev had sent a message to Leah and she was waiting with a friendly smile of welcome.

Leah had brought an armful of flowers in with her, and when she put them in vases the vivid red of the hibiscus and the deep blue of the cornflowers brightened the room and gave it a festive air. Leah Unna had been working in the fields since six that morning. Now she had changed into a neat blue dress with white trimming and had tied a blue ribbon around her tumbling dark hair. Her husband came in and her eyes lit up for a moment; then she took the gun from him and placed it on top of a tall wardrobe.

Zeev laughed and said earnestly, "She is always afraid the children will get hold of the gun. But I always take the bullets out before I come home."

Zeev Unna ordinarily worked in the fields here at Givat

55

Brenner (Brenner Hill) but he is now one of those picked to guard the community.

Today was a special occasion. Their seven-year-old daughter, Tamar, was to come out of the hospital and that was why Leah had brought the flowers. "Tamar only had a cold," Leah explained in precise English, "but they kept her there four days and we couldn't see her. We might have caught it and passed it on to Gad."

There was a squealing outside and then the room was full of Tamar and Gad and they were hurling themselves at their mother, and dark-eyed Tamar was telling of the chocolate they'd given her in the hospital, and Gad, like any four-year-old boy the world over, was climbing all over his father. The Unna family was at home and reunited. They would stay reunited until it was time for Tamar and Gad to go to the children's dormitory where they sleep each night.

Life in an agricultural settlement in Israel seems hard to an outsider but Leah and Zeev only look puzzled when you mention it. To them life is full and exciting and the work in the fields is work they have chosen for themselves because both have a great love for the land. Leah came from Germany as a child. Zeev left his native Hamburg when he was sixteen to find his destiny in Palestine. And he found it here at Givat Brenner, which is only thirty miles from Tel Aviv.

Leah sent the children out to play and we sat down over coffee to talk of life as lived by a typical farming family. Givat Brenner is the largest communal settlement in Israel. It is a community of a thousand people and all but the children work, either on the land or in the factory which cans the tomatoes and the fruit which is grown by the settlement. In every sense the settlement is communal—but it is not at all communistic, for there is complete freedom of thought and speech there and no police force to regiment either.

"But we are not much interested in politics," Zeev Unna laughed. "We have our work and our children and sometimes we go on a holiday. These are our main interests."

The day begins early for the Unna family, as it does for everyone in the settlement. They are up at five-thirty and after breakfast in the huge community-operated dining hall they go to the fields. Once these hundreds of acres were desert, but the land wasn't dead; it was merely asleep. It needed only irrigation and fertilization, and when these were supplied the land became fertile. Today there are trees heavy with oranges and lemons and endless rows of tomato plants, carrots, beans, and acres of wheat. Zeev and Leah have grown up with this land and have watched it change and their pride in it is intense.

At eleven-thirty each morning work stops for an hour. Lunch is brought to those who are working in the more distant fields and the others again meet in the dining hall. All morning Tamar and Gad are at school. Gad is still in kindergarten. Tamar with the other older children is learning reading, writing and arithmetic as well as English, which is taught in all the schools of Israel. When a child is thirteen he starts to learn a trade. At Givat Brenner he usually learns farming, but some children are taught blacksmithing and others are taught to be mechanics. Nearly all remain to work at Givat Brenner, although some occasionally leave to find industrial work in Tel Aviv or Haifa.

"But we are farmers at heart," Zeev said earnestly. "We never could have survived and made a nation had it not been for the land. Leah and I hope that our two children will stay here and work on the land as we are doing. We feel we are contributing something to the country when we look at our crop each season."

It is only when the day's work is done that Zeev and Leah see their children. Children of the settlement all sleep and have their meals in a separate house. But this separation seems to increase rather than diminish the affection between children and parents. And there is always Saturday to look forward to. On Saturday Zeev and Leah have the two children to themselves. Sometimes they pack a picnic lunch and take them to the orange groves for the day. And before the war, Zeev occasionally took his family to the beach in Tel Aviv for an outing.

"We have everything anyone could ask for," Leah said earnestly. "We even have a radio."

"Yes," Zeev said with a laugh, "during the war I joined the British Army. For the first time in many years I had money in my pocket. So after I was demobilized I bought a radio. However, I was glad to come back here where I belong."

The people of the community-run settlements do not draw wages. Each year Zeev and Leah are allowed two weeks' vacation and they are given sixty-four dollars. Usually they take the children to the seashore. They always stop at the homes of friends, so the sixty-four dollars are ample to cover their expenses. During the rest of the year they have no need for money.

"What would we do with money?" Zeev asked. "If Leah or I need new clothes we go to our group-owned store and get them. If we want some chocolate for the children we have only to ask for it. All of our food is given to us. No, we don't work for money."

At Givat Brenner and at the other group settlements the output of fruit and vegetables is higher than it is on the farms owned by individuals. Every economic report has shown that to be a fact. People like Zeev and Leah have a deep love for their country and a fervent sense of gratitude to it. Had it not been Palestine, it would undoubtedly have been the gas chamber or the crematorium. When they work nine hours a day six days a week they feel that in a small measure they are paying a debt to the country which gave them asylum.

"I have an uncle in America," Zeev said, smiling. "He writes me quite often. He told me he had read in an American paper that our settlements were communistic. This is really foolish. Here we have complete political freedom. We think as we wish and talk as we wish. Each year our settlement makes a profit. We elect a director and a council each year and they decide what to do with the money we have earned. Last year we built a moving-picture theatre and we have pictures every week. Each year we improve our hospital and our children's house, and build additional barracks for those who come from abroad."

"There is another thing." Leah brushed the dark hair back from her forehead. "We can leave whenever we wish. If we wanted, Zeev and I could move to Tel Aviv and get work in factories or offices. We have complete freedom to do as we wish. But this is the life we have chosen and we are content." The two children tumbled into the room again, each carrying a piece of chocolate. Could they have it now or would they have to wait until after supper? Leah tried for a moment to be stern but she ended by laughing and saying, "You may have it now." And when four-year-old Gad asked his father to share his piece of candy, you knew by the smile on Zeev's face that he was indeed content.

Zeev and Leah are typical citizens of the community-operated settlements. There are a hundred and fifty such settlements and about twenty-five thousand men, women and children living and working in them. I had been to a dozen settlements on previous visits and every family seemed motivated by the spirit shown by Zeev and Leah. They have dedicated their lives to the land and their compensation is complete happiness and an inner satisfaction in knowing that they are helping to build a nation. Patriotism is not an idle word in Palestine; it is a living force in the hearts of the people. The citizens of the world's newest nation have shown that they are willing to die for their country; they are also willing to work for their country and to prepare it for the tens of thousands of immigrants who are expected within the next year.

CHAPTER FOUR

Haifa had been captured by the Haganah. Safad
had been wrested from a strong defending force of Iraquis and
Syrians. The Palmach had taken over the Katamon quarter in
Old Jerusalem, important because the Arabs had been sniping
with good effect from the tower of the Greek Orthodox Church
of St. Simeon's on Shahin's Hill. Katra, a town of 1,500 Arabs,
had fallen and a quantity of arms captured. The Arab town of
Acre had fallen and now the Haganah controlled the coast
from Tel Aviv to Ras el Nakura. The Haganah was amazing the
world by consistently beating superior forces of Arabs. There
was no military justification for the continued success of Jewish arms. They had virtually no tanks, no heavy guns, few
armored trucks or weapon carriers, no air force (beyond a few
Piper Cubs used for observation purposes). Sten guns, Bren guns
and mortars were the offensive weapons they were using, but they
were using them with magnificent effect. As May 15th neared,

the Jews intensified the fury of their fighting. They knew that the world would hardly recognize a beaten, broken country as a sovereign nation and they were bending every desperate effort to achieve clear military superiority by May 15th.

What had transformed a nation of peaceful farmers into a strong, skilled fighting army? Some strange metamorphosis had taken place here in Palestine. For centuries the Jew had meekly submitted to a tragic fate that had doomed him to be expelled from one country after another. The Jew of Palestine seemed to have no kinship with the submissive Wandering Jew of history. This Jew was thin but hard; soft-spoken but deadly with a gun or knife; sensitive, but completely without fear. This Jew took suicidal risks which no Allied commander during the war would ask men to take; he took military success calmly, and the pain of wounds with stoical, almost contemptuous indifference. Practically every correspondent in Tel Aviv (most of whom had World War II experience) said that the Palestinian was the greatest fighter he had ever seen, and when you mentioned the Commandos or American Marines they shrugged their shoulders and let their statement stand. But what made them into such amazing fighters? No one knew the answer to that. The only way to find out was to talk to the fighters themselves and to those who led them in battle. I told Moshe Brilliant that I wanted to meet the commander of the Palmach, the head of the Irgun Zvai Leumi, the leader of the Stern Group and some of the Haganah commanders.

"It is impossible, of course, to interview either the Irgun or Stern leaders," he said, and then he added, "however, I'll try to contact them and perhaps they'll see you. I know a few men who might be connected with one organization or the other. They've never admitted it, but I'll forward your request to them. I'll arrange for you to meet some of the Haganah commanders and I'll try to get Big Isaac for you. He's the Palmach boss and quite a man."

About thirty thousand Palestinians had seen World War service. Most of them, like Big Isaac, had served under the

British and there had, of course, been the Jewish Brigade, the unit which served with marked success in North Africa and Italy. These war veterans had learned their lessons well. Now they were using the tactics which, in the course of a dozen wars, had, through trial and error, been proven sound by the British. These tactics were modified to suit the peculiar topography of the country. Although officers wore no insignia, this was a well-trained, well-disciplined army, and it was led by men who knew the terrain well.

There were really three divisions of the Palestine defense forces. All were under the initial authority of Haganah (which means defense) and the eventual authority of David Ben-Gurion, who was Commander-in-Chief of the Army. First was the elite force, the Palmach. The youngsters of Palestine looked upon the Palmach with the same hero-worshiping eyes of American kids watching our Marines parade. Every young man of military age in Palestine wanted to belong to the Palmach, but its standards were strict and its training as arduous and back-breaking as that given to the Commandos or our Marines during the war, and only the best-conditioned men made the grade. The Palmach had grown to such an extent that it was now organized into brigades.

Second was the Hish—the infantry field force. Usually the Palmach spearheaded an attack; once the position was secured, the Hish would move in, consolidate, and hold the position. The Hish also fought in brigade units and it had supporting artillery (theoretically) and air cover (again theoretically).

The Mishmar, or Home Guard, was composed of middle-aged men who served part time unless an emergency made it necessary for them to be used twenty-four hours a day. Your waiter, your barber, your secretary, your cab driver were all members of the Mishmar. In cities and agricultural settlements they took over all guard duties, which released thousands of combat men for front-line action. Sometimes, as in the case of Jerusalem, Home Guard units had to be used as front-line troops.

In addition to the Haganah, there was the Irgun Zvai Leumi and the Stern Group. They operated independently of the government and the Haganah. No one knew the strength of either organization; few had ever seen their leaders or knew their identities. There was some support for the Irgun in Tel Aviv but none at all (that I could discover) for the Stern Group. Most people thought of this rebel outfit as we think of the Ku Klux Klan in America. The use of murder as a political weapon was distasteful to perhaps 98 percent of Palestinians, and the refusal of the Stern Group to follow the domestic and foreign policies of the duly elected provisional government completely alienated the populace.

The British foreign office had always underestimated the strength and fighting ability of the Jews. Back in New York I had talked to British correspondents and embassy officials who absolutely believed that one day the Arabs would get really annoyed and sweep the Jews right into the Mediterranean. One of them had told me that he expected to see the most horrible pogrom of all time in Palestine as soon as British troops began to evacuate.

Most of the correspondents in Tel Aviv knew Lieutenant General Gordon H. A. MacMillan, Commander of all British troops in Palestine. They all said that he had a great deal of respect for the fighting ability of the Jew, and he had expressed himself more than once as being convinced that the whole strength of Arab arms was not strong enough to crush the Haganah. But Mr. Bevin and the Foreign Office laddies back in London thought of the Jews as completely inferior, and to them it was unthinkable that they could put up any kind of a fight against, say, the Arab Legion, which was trained by British officers and equipped with British arms. In this war the Foreign Office was the boss, not the military, and it seemed evident that MacMillan's sober estimate of the ability and strength of the Haganah was not being taken at its face value by the Whitehall Warriors. This was the sentiment of two British correspondents who were in Tel Aviv, as well as the belief of experienced military observers such as George Fielding Eliot, one of the few men who had managed to spend some time with both the Arab and the Jewish forces. But the showdown was coming and the result would prove which estimate of the Jewish army was correct.

One morning I was awakened by the sound of booming explosions. These were not rifle shots nor were they heavy artillery. I dressed and hurried out to the terrace. Paul, the waiter, was there, eyes glued to his glasses and his glasses were directed toward Jaffa.

"The Irgun have attacked Jaffa," he said excitedly.

From the terrace you could see puffs of white smoke and dust rising out of the city. It was five o'clock, but there were hundreds down on the beach watching intently. The firing kept up all morning, and now it was being returned. Now and then the dull boom of mortar explosions would be interspaced by the quick nervous rattle of Sten guns or automatic rifles. Tel Aviv and Jaffa are separated only by a street. Watching the gunflashes, the smoke and dust of the explosions, and listening to the noise of the guns was an eerie experience. It was as though you were standing on the Queensboro Bridge in New York watching Long Island City being attacked.

The Irgun spokesman told us on the radio that the operation in Jaffa was not an offensive operation; it was launched to prevent the Arabs in Jaffa from continuing the sniping which had cost the lives of so many citizens of Tel Aviv. Walking along Hayarkon Street that morning you saw nothing but guarded smiles. It was not fashionable to enthuse over any activity of the Irgun, but how could one help it today? They had done something that the regular army had hesitated to do. Technically (but not geographically) Jaffa was outside the limit of the boundary set by the U.N. Technically, invading Jaffa was the same as invading Cairo. Jaffa was a complete Arab city and both the Cairo radio and the British-controlled radio from Jerusalem were severe in denouncing the Irgun for the

64

"inexcusable" invasion of sovereign Arab territory. Then came a radio communiqué from British Army Headquarters. The communiqué read:

"Owing to unwarranted aggression on the part of the Irgun Zvai Leumi in Jaffa, the situation in Palestine has seriously deteriorated and this theatre has now assumed operational priority over other commitments in the Middle East. As a consequence, considerable reinforcements of infantry, guns, tanks and Marine Commandos have had to be dispatched to Palestine in the course of general security."

This was repeated several times during the day. The Haganah radio presented it without comment, but there was plenty of comment from practically everyone in Tel Aviv. And a great deal of raucous laughter. Spokesmen for the British Foreign Office and the British Army seem to make a habit of making themselves ridiculous, and indirectly, of course, making the people of England ridiculous, which is tragic because there is nothing ridiculous about the people of England. The pretentious wording of the statement was enough to raise a roar of laughter from the people of Palestine. The statement bore all of the solemn, majestic formality of a war communiqué that might have announced the invasion of Normandy or some other huge military operation.

The British Army, which had been looking the other way when Syrians and Iraquis stormed across the border to attack Jewish settlements in Galilee, was now for the first time considering Palestine as a "theatre of war" which had "operational priority." For weeks, Arab invaders (not Palestine Arabs) had been pouring shot and shell into crowded civilian quarters in Jerusalem, and even now the city faced starvation and plague, but this condition had not prompted the British Army to announce that troops had been dispatched to Palestine "in the course of general security." Already more than three thousand Jews had died fighting, but until now the attitude of the British Army (acting as Charley McCarthy to Ernest Bevin's Edgar Bergen) was such that one might have thought these three thousand had died in traffic accidents.

The absurd communiqué telling of the reinforcements which had been summoned was obviously prompted by the fact that a relative handful of dissident troops under the aegis of the Irgun Zvai Leumi had finally become sick and tired of watching civilians being murdered in Tel Aviv. As long as the Jews merely stood their ground repelling attacks made by invading Arab forces, the British Army considered the situation normal. But now the Jews were answering back and the communiqué was undoubtedly issued to create an impression that all the trouble in Palestine was being caused not by invading Arabs but by Jews who had the temerity to do a little offensive fighting on their own. It was the last sentence in the communiqué that raised the most laughter. It was necessary to order reinforcements "in the course of general security." Whose security? The security of no British subject was threatened. The lives of thousands of Jews in Jerusalem were threatened, but it was hardly likely that at this late date the British were worrying about their security. At the moment the only security endangered was the security of British prestige and the security of Arab invaders.

I was finding it absolutely impossible to maintain any sort of objectivity during these frenzied days preceding the birth of the new state. There had been a time when I found it easy to be neutral and objective on the Palestine question. When I first visited Palestine, I had written a piece and had said, "This is a conflict between two rights." But that was a hasty judgment based on talks with British, Jewish and Arab leaders. Each side had pat, well-rehearsed arguments against the claims of the other. It is the nature of some men to remain neutral and objective all their lives. Such men undoubtedly make the best reporters and editors. I've never been able to achieve the detached viewpoint.

I was with the British during some of their darkest hours in 1940 and 1941, and the way they reacted to tragic adversity, whether they were civilians in London or Plymouth during bombings, or soldiers in the Western Desert during the retreat from Tobruk, made me their complete, uninhibited admirer. Before we entered the war I made two brief trips home, and I made no secret of my admiration and love for the people of England. When I had added that I felt that England was fighting our war for us, I was accused of everything from ordinary warmongering to being a British agent in their pay. It was true that the British had given me something very valuable; hundreds of them had given me their friendship.

All of my feelings and instincts are invariably in sympathy with the people of England, but now in Tel Aviv I could feel nothing but contempt for the British policy which had resulted in this war. Since my first visit to Palestine, I had spent a lot of time studying the whole problem. I didn't start with the mandate of the League of Nations; I went back to the founding of Petah Tikva in 1878, during the days of the Turkish administration, and followed the story of Palestine through to the latest speech of Ernest Bevin. I had read the books of anti-Zionists like Lessing Rosenwald of Philadelphia as well as books presenting the Jewish case. I had listened to the arguments of American oil men and State Department men, and the more I studied the more evident it became that the primary responsibility for the tragic turmoil in Palestine lay directly on the doorstep of Great Britain. Of course American foreign policy must be credited with an assist. I became convinced that every legal, ethical and moral precept involved, gave complete support to the Jewish position in Palestine. To me the issue was no longer a "conflict of two rights." It was black and white. It was as clear-cut as the issue between the British and Hitler had been in 1940, and I realized now that the people of Palestine were fighting for the same things that the British had been fighting for during the war.

I had been shocked and saddened by letters and stories in London newspapers attacking me for this attitude. And I was puzzled by it. I couldn't understand how the same warm, sympathetic, freedom-loving people I had known in London could for a moment support the sinister, economically inspired policy of the British Government (always echoed, sheeplike, by our own State Department). British blood had been shed in Palestine and that, understandably, aroused great indignation in England, but why hadn't the roar of indignation been directed at the British Foreign Office which was primarily responsible for the shedding of this blood? But, much as I despised the policy of Ernest Bevin, it could not lessen my deeply rooted affection for the people of England. They had survived a Baldwin, a Chamberlain, and they had fought and won a war, in spite of having a cabinet that included some of the most miserable, incompetent fools ever to hold public office, and the people would undoubtedly survive an Ernest Bevin and a policy that was a sickening contradiction of everything that was fine and decent in the British character.

On the third day of fighting in Jaffa the Irgun invited the press to take a look. It was a relief to get away from the voices that oozed through the radio loudspeakers, to the ugly but nonetheless honest reality of Jaffa. You got to the fighting area by getting into a cab and saying, "Take me to Herzl Street." It was a forty-cent cab drive. And it brought you within two short city blocks of Jaffa. Today uniformed Irgun men wearing white-and-blue armbands were directing traffic in the streets leading to Jaffa. Groups of people watched curiously from every corner. It was the first time they had seen the faces of Irgun members. Motorcycles ridden by Irgun men roared by, and trucks filled with troops followed them. Here the roar of the mortars was loud and occasionally a shell lobbed by the Arabs would overshoot its mark, whistle overhead, and the crowds would sway toward the shelter of the buildings.

I followed Moshe Brilliant down the street toward Irgun headquarters. Two blocks from busy, crowded Herzl Street and only a quarter of a mile from Allenby Street, where business was going on as usual, we arrived at a schoolhouse which had been turned into a hospital. Ambulances arrived from the "front" (some three hundred yards away) and women stretcher bearers in khaki and with blue-and-white armbands hurried the wounded inside. This was an advance hospital unit. There was an operating room with two white, gleaming tables, and shining instruments lay in neat rows ready for the surgeons. There were sutures and needles and sterilizers and penicillin and sulfa drugs. This was a complete portable hospital unit which had been set up only three days before. There was a ward holding a dozen beds, all of which were occupied. The wounded looked cheerful and clean. Nurses were giving intravenous glucose injections to several who were suffering from loss of blood or shock. The doctor in charge explained that they only did emergency operations here; for the most part, the wounded were sent back to Tel Aviv hospitals. This hospital was too exposed to be used for anything but first aid and emergency treatment.

Finally a conducting officer arrived to take us up farther. We walked two blocks toward the sound of mortar firing, and now we could see the result of the fighting. Virtually every building here had been damaged, some completely demolished by fire from both sides. Our conducting officer, a young, thin-faced soldier with a three days' growth of beard, made us walk in single file close to the buildings.

"From here on we will be under enemy observation," he said in a bored voice.

We arrived at what seemed to be a walled compound. This was G.H.Q., and tired-looking men with carbines, Lee Enfield rifles and Sten guns counted us as we filed through a break in the wall. An enormous woman had somehow penetrated this far and she was arguing heatedly with the guards.

"Her three kids slipped by the guards and are up there watching the fighting," Moshe interpreted for me. "She wants to go after them. The guards won't let her go."

One of the men patted her on the shoulder and said surprisingly in English, "Let the kids enjoy themselves, Mother. They're as safe up there as anywhere around here."

The mother was still arguing as we entered the compound.

A large stucco building, scarred in half a dozen places by shells, stood in the center of the walled area. This too had been a school. Surrounding the building was a playground for the children, and there were swings and other equipment which had been used by schoolchildren only three days before. Now there were mortars there instead of children. There were a dozen mortars, all being fired at regular intervals. They were two-inch and three-inch, and they made an unholy noise. They were firing at Arab positions only three hundred yards away. We were led into a schoolroom and asked to sit down. We sat at the tiny desks exactly like the desks in New York City schools. A smiling, rather plump girl in uniform told us that the press conference would be conducted in Hebrew but she would translate questions and answers into English. A representative of the Irgun would answer any questions. A slender man in civilian clothes stepped forward. He wore glasses and his hair was thin. He talked in Hebrew and the girl translated rapidly. He explained the military operation, referring occasionally to a map of Jaffa which hung on a blackboard.

"This operation was not intended to be a conquest of the city," he said. "It is a defense operation to stop the attacks made from Jaffa and the neighboring villages on Tel Aviv. It was also designed to open the road to Jewish communications between Tel Aviv and Jerusalem. Our present objective is to destroy the police station. Arabs are firing from there. The military operation is being led by 'Gideon.' He is here and will answer any questions."

"Gideon" was tall, and bright black eyes blazed in his gaunt, unshaved face. For all we knew he might be the fabled leader of the Irgun. It was generally agreed that his name was Menachem Beigin, and the British had put a price of 8,000 dollars on his head. The boys directed a barrage of questions at Gideon. He explained the tactics.

"The Arabs were expecting us sooner or later," he said, "and they had their guns covering all streets leading toward the center of Jaffa. But we didn't use the streets much. We went

70

from house to house, using explosives to gain entrance. This morning the enemy moved its guns. We wanted to locate the guns so we sent decoys out to draw fire."

"That sounds like a suicidal maneuver," someone suggested.

Gideon's thin lips curved into a smile. "You're fairly safe as long as they aim at you," he said dryly. "They don't shoot very well. We sent several groups along and across the streets and did draw their fire. These mortars outside," he motioned toward the window, "are taking care of their guns right now."

The first man took over again. He spoke with a strong sense of authority. He severely criticized some of the Tel Aviv papers which had described this as a terrorist operation that would embarrass the government and the Irgun. While he was talking, one explosion louder than the others shook the building. I was near the window. I looked out and saw four girls with a stretcher hurrying toward a man who lay on the ground. They carried him away. Evidently the Irgun was not doing all the firing. I'd attended press conferences all my life, but never one like this where your questions could be heard only if you shouted.

Finally our interview was over and our conducting officers led us up farther. When we came to street intersections we had to double over and scurry across. We were led into a half-ruined house and then through a neat round hole blown in the wall of the house. So we went from house to house, following the trail blazed with explosives by the advance troops.

"This is the kind of thing we are trained for," a conducting officer said. "We usually attack at night, and we are taught how to use grenades and explosives to advance from one house to another."

Finally we reached the advance command post. This too was a half-ruined building. Two men kept barking orders into telephones; others kept marking maps. You got a strong impression of calculated efficiency watching the Irgun operate. The noise wasn't so bad here. We were ahead of the Irgun mortars, but there was a constant crackle of rifle fire and occasionally a burst from a Bren gun, which is really a heavy automatic rifle. The destruction here was complete. Through slips in the wooden barricade thrown across a huge gaping hole in the side of the building, we could see the flashes of Arab guns. They were firing furiously, and occasionally we'd hear a dull plop as a bullet hit the outside of the building.

"Two weeks ago there were seventy thousand Arabs in Jaffa," one of the officers told us. "There are only about thirty thousand left. The others have fled."

"How many men have you?" I asked.

"Oh, around a thousand," he said casually.

We left finally, walking back over the rubble and debris of this devastated area which comprised about six square city blocks. Walking away from an advance command post is always an uncomfortable operation. Your back itches. Our guide stopped us at one street intersection while he reconnoitered. Standing there waiting, I heard an incongruous sound and, looking around, saw that it was coming from a huge black cat lying in the road sunning herself and making noises of protest because we had awakened her. You seldom see a well-fed child or woman in an Arab community, but you often see well-fed cats. Some Arabs still remember that Mohammed was fond of cats. They remember the story of his cat Muezza, who once curled up on his master's flowing sleeve. The Prophet, rather than disturb his pet, cut the sleeve from his robe and went about his business. No one here in Jaffa ordered the firing to stop, but everyone did walk carefully over the cat as our group crossed the street. I looked back. The cat had gone back to sleep.

Back at the compound we found that something new had been added. A group of Irgun boys had just brought in a group of prisoners. Prisoners always look dirty, bedraggled, worried, but these looked worse than the usual run of prisoners. They were all small and hungry-looking. One of the correspondents who spoke Arabic questioned them. Not one of these twelve prisoners was Palestinian. They were all Iraquis, which, to some degree, bore out the official assertion that very few Palestinian Arabs were doing any fighting.

One of the Irgun men guarding the prisoners looked strange with a rifle in his hand. His sideburns curled almost down to his chin. I asked Brilliant to explain this strange, dark-looking creature to me. Moshe laughed and talked to the man at some length in Hebrew.

"He is a rabbinical student," Moshe said.

A soldier who was in charge of the prisoners said, in English, "He's a very tough lad. He's convinced that we are fighting for a holy cause and he really doesn't give a damn if he's killed or not. In fact, he expects to die and accepts it very calmly. Every morning he strips and bathes himself from head to foot. The orthodox Jews always bathe the dead before burial. I suppose it's a symbol that your sins are washed away. Well, this joker figures he's a corpse already, so every morning he washes himself and then goes out and fights like hell."

I never heard anyone but an American G.I. use the phrase, "this joker," so I asked the Irgun man where he came from.

"I was born four blocks from the Yankee Stadium," he said, "and I was with the Ninth Air Force during the war. When we'd get a little flak-happy from too many missions they'd send us to a rest camp only a few miles from here. I liked the place, liked the people, and when I got out of the Air Force I came back."

"To fight?" I asked.

"Not especially," he said. "I was a foreman on construction jobs back home. I had no family and I'd saved most of my army pay. I knew there'd be a lot of building going on here so I figured I might do all right. I have, too. I got myself two partners, two kind old guys, and we bought a little property and now we're building. But I liked these Irgun boys and managed to get in with them. So the two old gents are carrying on our business while I serve with them. This is going to be a hell of a fine country once we get rid of these Ay-rabs. Funny thing," he laughed, "I don't know a word of Hebrew, but for God's sake, they talk better English here than they do in my neighborhood at home. Well, I got to wheel these characters to the clink. So long."

He led the prisoners away and Moshe and I walked three blocks and hailed a cab.

"You don't realize how amazing it is to actually see members of the Irgun," Moshe Brilliant said thoughtfully. "It is like a masquerade. At midnight the masks come off. Today in Jaffa they took off their masks. I recognized a banker, a lawyer, half a dozen students, three or four writers and, so help me, I recognized three men who for years have been on the British payroll as customs officials and two others who have been and still are British police officials."

I dropped him at his office and went back to the Kaete Dan. There were tables and chairs on the upper terrace now and an awning to shade you from the sun. Paul and Joshua Stern, the bartender at the Kaete Dan, were both there, looking very cheerful.

"Look," Joshua said, pointing toward Jaffa. "Look at those boats."

A dozen small boats were headed toward a large two-masted schooner anchored about a quarter of a mile off shore. Each boat was low in the water. Through Paul's glasses I could see that they were packed to the gunwales with Arabs fleeing Jaffa. The decks of the schooner, too, were thick with people.

"The man who owns that schooner will get very rich today," Joshua laughed. "He is charging each passenger a hundred pounds. That is what we hear."

"Why are they running?" Paul repeated my question. "They are running because they have nothing to fight for. Do you know that not one Jew has tried to leave Tel Aviv since the fighting began? We Jews no longer run. At last we have something to fight for. This is our last stand. With us it is either here," he paused and then pointed out toward the Mediterranean, "or there."

What made the Jews such great fighters? Perhaps Paul

74

was giving me the answer. It was Palestine "or there." It was life or death. It was slavery or freedom. Yes, it was London, 1941, all over again. The next day the Irgun broke through in Jaffa to the sea and a historic announcement was made by both the Irgun and Haganah radio. The Haganah had come to an agreement with the Irgun and would move in and hold the positions gained by the Irgun. The Haganah, too, would attack from the south. For the first time the two fighting organizations had come to terms to present a united front. There was joy in Tel Aviv that night, although a great many conservative diehard Palestinians still hated the idea of having the "terrorists" in the fold.

I spent the last phase of the Jaffa battle with the Haganah, and immediately saw the tremendous difference between it and the Irgun. The Irgun was a fine Commando unit capable of quick, fierce, improvised thrusts. It was like a football team which, under the spell of a coach who gives an inspired pep talk before the game, goes out and plays a superior team off its feet—for one quarter—before exhausting itself. The Haganah was like a great football team, with depth, a varied attack, an elastic defense and staying power. Its leaders were quiet men experienced in war, parsimonious of casualties, conservative in their use of ammunition. They gave orders almost casually, in the manner of an Omar Bradley.

They finished the battle the way Joe Louis at his best once finished his fights. A few tentative jabs, a feint to get the opponent off balance, and then the terrific right-hand punch that ended the battle. The way the Haganah handled the question of supply, liaison, and communications was highly reminiscent of the way Montgomery's Eighth Army handled the same problems (not surprising in view of the fact that so many Haganah leaders had served with Monty during the war). There was no hysteria, no emotional frenzy clouding sharp judgment. Every man (and woman) seemed to know his job thoroughly. Even men at advanced posts received hot meals; each man carried a first-aid kit similar to that carried by our G.I.'s during offensive actions; artillery spotters carried first-rate binoculars; weapons were polished and oiled; discipline was excellent. I watched the Haganah in action and all doubts vanished. This army, I felt, could not be beaten by anything but a major nation. May 15th was only a week or so away and then its real test would come, but it was impossible not to have confidence in this streamlined, capable army.

One morning I received a caller at the Kaete Dan. She was young and slim and wore a white sweater and a plaid skirt. She wore no hat and her brown hair tumbled over her eyes and she constantly brushed it back with her hand in a gesture that seemed almost automatic. She was just another very pretty girl until you noticed her eyes. They were dark blue and there was no laughter in them. They looked at you steadily, impersonally, as though they were seeing something beyond you.

"I represent the Irgun Zvai Leumi," she said in a firm, low voice. "It has been arranged for you to meet our commander tonight if it is convenient."

"It's convenient," I told her. She asked me to be outside the hotel at seven and also asked me not to tell anyone about it. Promptly at seven a car drove up. She was in the back. A driver and a young man wearing a khaki shirt were in front. We drove along Hayarkon Street. No one spoke.

"It's a nice night," I suggested brightly.

"Yes," she said shortly.

"Have we far to go?"

"Not far," she said. And that completed our brilliant dialogue. It wasn't far. In fact the apartment house we stopped in front of was only two minutes' drive from the Kaete Dan. The man who had been sitting alongside the driver got out of the car. His hand rested lightly on the revolver in a holster at his hip.

"Will you follow me?" he asked politely. The car drove off with the girl and driver, and the youngster and I went inside. We walked up a flight of stairs and the Irgun man rang the bell. It was opened by a big smiling man in shirt sleeves who said heartily, "Come in, we were expecting you." It was a nice apartment. Behind him I could see the kitchen and there was a woman singing quietly to herself as she watched a kettle on the stove, while a child sat at a table looking at a picture book. This was hardly the kind of setting in which you expected to find Menachem Beigin. The big smiling man ushered us into the living room, told us to make ourselves at home and left. The young soldier and I sat down.

"Is he the commander?" I asked, nodding toward the door.

"I don't know," the young man said. "I've never seen our leader. Very few of us have seen him. He issues orders through Gideon."

A moment later the door was opened and a man walked into the room with outstretched hand. It was the same man who had held the press conference in Jaffa; the man in civilian clothes who had so severely criticized the Tel Aviv newspapers. The young soldier snapped to attention and his eyes were shining. I'd heard that members of the Irgun had a fanatical devotion to their leader. This youngster certainly had the look of one who has suddenly found the Holy Grail. Beigin asked him a few questions and then dismissed him. Beigin was the antithesis of everything I had expected. The people of Palestine have held conflicting views on Beigin and until the Jaffa operation the majority of them were definitely against the militant form his Zionism took. To many he was an irresponsible terrorist intent upon bathing the country in blood; to others he was a glamorous twentieth-century Robin Hood and there were those who whispered that Beigin was the greatest patriot in the land, for he gave everything and asked for nothing—except freedom for his country.

Beigin had become a legend in his own lifetime, and you heard fantastic stories of his many miraculous escapes. He had a dozen aliases and you heard that both British and Arabs had dealt with him more than once in the mistaken belief that he was a harmless merchant, a grower of oranges or a mild-mannered schoolteacher. He seemed to have the capacity of inspiring tremendous loyalty among his followers and vicious hatred among those who opposed him. The British had long ago made it plain that it was a matter of complete indifference whether or not the head of Beigin was delivered with or without a body. What was he like? Was he an irresponsible fanatic? Was he a military genius? I'd asked Haganah and government officials and ordinary citizens, but Beigin meant something different to each man, so that it was impossible to get any clear picture of him.

He and the Irgun had always looked upon the British as foreign invaders who had no legal or moral right to be in Palestine exercising police authority. They believed that it was completely criminal for the British to exercise the sovereign power of collecting taxes and dictating the type of imports which could come into the country. Once you accepted this premise the activities of the Irgun became those of an army defending the rights of a country it represented. If, on the other hand, you believed that the British Army had the right to wield the power of life and death over 750,000 Jews in Palestine, the Irgun, of course, was an illegal terrorist organization.

Beigin explained that this was the apartment of a friend, a Tel Aviv businessman. Now that the young Irgun G.I. had left, there wasn't a sign of any protection for Beigin. This might have been a living room in Westchester County or Beverly Hills. There was a bright desert landscape on the wall by Rubin and an etching by Herman Struck—considered by many one of the truly great. There was a color photograph of the "friend," his wife and child. American and London magazines were piled on a small table and there was a portable bar in one corner on which there were bottles and glasses.

"You don't seem too well protected here," I suggested to Beigin. "There's still a price of 2,000 pounds on your head."

Beigin smiled and ran his hand through his thin hair. "It's not much of a head," he said ruefully, "but that isn't much of a price, either."

It was rather evident that Beigin had lived so long with

danger that it had become commonplace; a fact to be accepted casually, not a terror to shake the nerves or cause sleepless nights. He said that he would stay here tonight, and tomorrow move somewhere else. He had to keep moving, he said, but luckily he had a great many friends whom he could trust.

"No one has ever tried to betray me to the British," he said.

"It's lucky you have no family," I said. "It would be tough for them."

"But I have a family," he said, smiling. "A wife and child, and as you say, it is tough on them. I can't see them very often. They have to use another name. My boy keeps asking me the most awkward questions. He wonders why I don't wear a uniform. He wonders at my long absences. I have him believing that I'm a sort of traveling salesman."

Beigin's friend came in with a tray and glasses. There was Palestinian brandy, a bottle of Rishon wine and a large pot of tea on the tray. Beigin chose tea, and I followed his lead. He added milk to the tea. "I like tea the British fashion," he said, and added dryly, "I'm not sure the British would like to know that."

Our host opened the French windows, and sitting there we could look out over the Mediterranean. The sky was splashed with stars and a cool breeze was touching the slow waves of the sea with small white crests. The breeze brought the casual street noises into the room; a group of children playing a game a block away; the sound of men singing at Haganah headquarters down the street. We were alone now and Beigin talked of his early life. He had been born in Warsaw. His father had read Herzl's great book which really first presented the doctrine of Zionism to the world, and the younger Beigin too had read it and had become an enthusiast. He had become a lawyer and then a soldier in the Polish Army. He had been captured by the Russians in Lithuania and had been charged, ironically enough, with being a British agent. After two years in Siberia he had been released and allowed to join General Anders and his Middle East Polish Army. Since his childhood Beigin had lived for two things, he said: democracy and Zionism. He found neither in the anti-Semitic army of Anders and he had left to fight only for Palestine and his militant conception of Zionism. And he organized and led what became one of the most controversial underground movements in history. His followers, he said, were never well-armed.

"We made Sten guns in cellars and attics and in the desert," he said. "Sometimes we made them right under the noses of the British. We went underground in order to strike and liquidate the rule of the oppressors. Many quarreled with our methods but through those methods the State of Israel is about to arise. It was difficult to create this state; it will be just as difficult to maintain it. We established this state for the purpose of bringing homeless and stateless Jews here to live. We intend to bring in thousands and thousands; if there are not buildings enough we will use tents; if there are no tents we have the blue sky above us for cover."

"Once Israel becomes a state on May 15th will you emerge from the underground?"

"Of course we will," he said. "Then we will truly have Hebrew rule in this land, that is, in this liberated section of our homeland. In the new state we will be soldiers and builders. We will obey the laws, for they are our laws. We will respect the government, because it is our government. But if our provisional government or any government that succeeds it, enters on a policy of appeasement outside the country and tyranny within, we will again go underground. We insist that the government safeguard the principles of freedom and independence which have been won with the blood of heroes and martyrs."

"Even those who disagree with your methods admit that you have a great fighting force," I said. "What was it that changed the traditional peaceful Jew into a hard, tough, fighting man?"

"The world has had a completely wrong conception about Jews," Begin said earnestly. "They think of us as grubby shopkeepers or as ineffectual intellectuals. They forget that in most European countries it was forbidden us to own land. We could not become farmers or doctors or lawyers in many countries. We were put in ghettos and were forced to become shopkeepers to survive. Most European countries would not allow us to become officers in the army or hold public office. But one can learn anything, and we found that fighting was not hard to learn. Incidentally, this is the first time we really had something to fight for. We are fighting for our country; we are fighting to free it from foreign domination. We hate violence, but as your Thomas Jefferson once said, 'Sometimes it is necessary to shed the blood of tyrants.' We are fighting for a place where the remaining Jews of Europe can come and find peace and dignity. These things are worth fighting for and worth dying for. No," he added slowly, "fighting comes naturally to a man who has a country to fight for."

Beigin took a deep inhale of his cigarette and then coughed sharply. The years of being hunted and hiding in whatever refuge presented itself, whether it was a cellar, a viaduct, or an orange grove have left physical marks on his frail body, but when he speaks it is with the intensity of a man who is driven by some fierce inner compulsion. One may quarrel with the methods Beigin and his Irgun used in fighting the British, but it is difficult to quarrel with his motives. Even the Haganah leaders admit that he is a patriot who has never shirked danger and who always led the Irgun himself, no matter how suicidal the raid appeared to be.

"I know there are those who did not like our methods," Beigin said thoughtfully. "I do not like violence myself, but remember we were fighting tyrants who introduced violence into our country. People have forgotten that when my men were captured they were flogged and hung by the British. They were not treated as prisoners of war. They were treated as common criminals, except that they were not given the right of a trial by jury of their peers. In some ways the flogging was worse than the death penalty. You flog a beast, not a man, and that is how the British treated us. They captured Dov Gruner, who had been leading a military operation. They announced that they were going to hang him. I protested that this was against all rules of warfare and against all civilized procedure. I told them if they hung Dov Gruner I would be forced to take retaliatory methods. God knows I hated to do it, but if I didn't, the floggings and the hangings would continue. They hung Dov Gruner." Beigin put his cigarette out and I noticed that his hand was trembling. "Yes," he said slowly, "they hung Dov Gruner, one of the finest, cleanest, most decent boys who ever lived. Dov Gruner, whose only fault was that he loved his country and was willing to die to defend its principles. They murdered that boy."

Beigin was silent a moment. "If I had done nothing, other Dov Gruners would have been hung. The British condemned three other boys to death and then I ordered the execution of the two British sergeants; but I say that the responsibility was Ernest Bevin's. I wrote to the parents of both men explaining this. The father of one of the sergeants answered my letter. He agreed that the responsibility belonged to Bevin and the British Foreign Office. The world which sat by quietly when my men were flogged and hung suddenly became incensed at us. I have never bothered to defend my action. I will now. Not one citizen of Palestine has been flogged or hung since the execution of those two sergeants. I say that harsh as our methods were, they did stop the murder of perhaps hundreds of our citizens. Finally the British realized that we were not an outpost of their colonial empire nor were we slaves to their foreign and military policy.

"They called us terrorists," Beigin said slowly. "They called you Americans 'terrorists' when you were fighting for your freedom in 1776. You must remember this: as long as one British soldier (or any other foreign soldier) tramples the earth of our homeland, our sovereign independence is nothing but an aspiration, an aspiration for whose fulfillment we must be ready to fight. We have fought and will always be ready to fight for this principle."

"What kind of a country do you think Palestine will develop into?" I asked.

"A country something like Switzerland, perhaps," he said. "A small but strongly independent country with developed industries and foreign trade. We will foster and maintain friendly relations with the rest of the world—especially with the United States. True, the present American government—the Forrestal government—has forgotten what was preached by Washington, Jefferson and Tom Paine. However, I cannot think that this is the attitude of the ordinary American. I believe the forces of real democracy are strong in the United States. We will maintain friendly relations with every nation which is interested, as we are, in international justice and peace among nations."

"What form will the government take?" I asked.

"We will always have a democratic government," he said sharply. "Most of our people have suffered from the horror of totalitarianism. Freedom of thought and expression have been denied to them. It is this which they seek when they come here and it is this which we will provide for them. We shall always give due respect to the rights of minorities. I mean, of course, the Arabs of Palestine. They can live at peace with us. It might surprise you to know," he smiled, "that we of the Irgun have many friends among the Arabs. More than once they have hidden me and my men. It is the British who have been primarily our enemies, not the Arabs of Palestine."

"What is your chief disagreement with the present policies of Chaim Weizmann and the Jewish Agency?" I asked.

"It is entirely political," he said. "We believe that they have compromised too much, have appeased too much. Gradually the territory originally declared to be ours has shrunk. We insist that Trans-Jordan is a part of this country of ours. We will never stop fighting for our original boundaries, but after May 15th our fighting will be done under the law of the land—by ballot. Doctor Weizmann is a great scientist and a fine man, but we of the Irgun have always believed that inde-

83

pendence could never be gained by a constant retreating further and further from our original objectives."

We talked for three hours, and it is impossible not to be deeply impressed with the sincerity of this frail man, who had been risking his life for so many years for an ideal. His knowledge of Hebrew history was great, and his stories of previous attempts by Jews to found a homeland were fascinating. His admiration for Thomas Jefferson was obvious, and more than once he quoted from Jefferson and, surprisingly, from Robert E. Lee, whose military philosophy he had apparently studied thoroughly. He told of some of the Irgun raids and he gave full credit to Gideon for planning them. Apparently Gideon was his Chief of Staff.

"If it hadn't been for Gideon we never could have taken Jaffa," he said. "A couple of years ago Gideon and a small force stopped a British military train and captured considerable ammunition. We found it consisted almost entirely of mortar bombs. Well, we had no mortars to fit them so at the time we didn't value our prize too highly. But a few months ago another raid resulted in the capture of a lot of three-inch mortars. So we wedded the mortars and the mortar bombs and they spent their honeymoon in Jaffa. We fired several thousand of them.

"Sorry I can't give you his name," he said apologetically. "He is still on the British 'wanted' list. I really think he is a military genius. Some day his true value to the country will be revealed."

As I left he mentioned the press conference he had held in Jaffa the week before. He wanted to know if any of the correspondents had guessed who he was. I told him that as far as I knew none had.

"One of your American correspondents knew me," he laughed. "Richard Mowrer of the *New York Post*. He was hurt when British military headquarters in the King David Hotel was bombed. He and I met shortly after that. The other day at the press conference he looked me right in the eye and then turned his head. It was mighty decent of him not to reveal who I was."

Both Beigin and his apparently frank exposition of his political philosophy contradicted everything that Haganah and government officials had told me. Quite bluntly, they had said that Beigin wanted a "Leader State" along Fascist lines, with himself as the Hebrew *Fuehrer*. They said that his policy of intimidating those who opposed his views, and his gangster technique of window smashing, threats, robbery, all followed the familiar pattern set by the Nazis in the early 1930's. They said that part of his policy was to suppress the trade unions and eventually establish corporate unions on the Italian Fascist model.

"Beigin has preached a mixture of ultra-nationalism, religious mysticism and racial superiority," more than one man told me. "These are not compatible with our understanding of Zionism or democracy."

This appraisal of Beigin was made by level-headed, soberminded men, for whose judgment one had to have respect. Which was the real Beigin? The genial, charming man who had talked so frankly to me, or the Beigin so many thought to be a real source of danger to the democratic ideals of the country? I frankly don't know. Speculation would be fruitless and inconclusive; the real Beigin would only emerge when the fighting was over and the issue could be resolved on the political platform and settled by the ballot box.

The car which had brought me was waiting outside the apartment house. The driver, the armed G.I. and the girl were in the car.

"How did you like meeting the Boss?" I asked the Irgun G.I.

He turned around and his face was radiant. "I'll never forget that moment. He is a great man," the boy said.

They dropped me at the Kaete Dan. I was beginning to get a hint as to what had made the Jew a fighting man.

85

As *the last crucial week began,* a subdued air of excitement and anticipation made itself felt in Tel Aviv. Each night everyone in the hotel lobbies and bars became quiet as the radio told us the news in both English and Hebrew. Invariably the news announcer began with Jerusalem. The city was being shelled. The city was without water. But the Jerusalem Road had been cleared by the Haganah and there was hope that supplies could be rushed to the besieged city. Each night there would be a report of the activities of the Truce Commission in Jerusalem. The Jewish representatives had submitted the terms under which the government would accept a truce. They seemed reasonable enough. They were:

1. The Jerusalem-Tel Aviv Road remain open.
2. All foreign Arab armed forces be withdrawn from the Jerusalem area.

86

A truce was certainly needed, and the fact that the Palestinian Arabs had done virtually no fighting seemed an indication that they wanted to return to their farms and their bullocks and their narghiles. Everyone listened tensely each night, and when the radio voice told of things that had happened in New York or Paris or London or China, everyone paid serious attention. Then the news announcer would begin, "And now a report from Lake Success. . . ." and the tenseness and attention would dissolve. People would start chatting and laughing. Gradually the voice telling of the dawdling, the debating, the resolutions, the new policies decided that day by the United Nations for Palestine would grow less and less audible as conversation increased and people ordered drinks, and waiters who had stopped serving when the news broadcast began started to rattle plates and take orders. Loudspeakers had been installed at several crowded street corners in Tel Aviv, and if you happened to be near one of them when the news broadcasts began, you noticed the same tense, attentive air which immediately changed to indifference when news from Lake Success was announced. Long ago the Jews of Palestine had given up faith in the ability of the United Nations to settle their affairs. To 750,000 people Palestine was a nation and had been a nation for a long time. On May 15th it would be invested with the formal trappings of an accepted nation but this was merely a detail to the people of the country. Palestine was no longer a dream, a theory, an experiment; it was a fact, a reality, yet the representatives of the United Nations were discussing it as they might have discussed the proposed colonization of the moon. They were ignoring the reality that partition was an accomplished fact now and nothing said at the councils of the mighty could change that fact. This was the first real issue given the United Nations and its absurd temporizing and eternal long-winded speeches had resulted in nothing at all but the waste of thousands of columns in newspapers which could have used the space to much better advantage. In Tel Aviv the U.N. had lost all prestige. No one even gave it the compliment of anger or hatred; the council was simply regarded with indifference or contempt. It was obvious that the British representatives had, with horrible and almost unbelievable cynicism, merely been playing for time in the hope that a quick Arab military victory would solve the whole troublesome question. The policy of the American government reversing its stand once, and then stumbling witlessly from one lame expedient to another, had succeeded only in making the United Nations look ridiculous. The Soviet representatives had given lip service to the cause of Palestine but many in Tel Aviv felt that this gesture was about as sincere as the "Come in, my dear" of the wolf when Little Red Riding Hood came a-calling. Russia was supporting the claims of Palestine but her record at the U.N. was such that it was impossible to believe that this was for any other reason than to embarrass the United States and Great Britain.

The whole feeling of the people in Palestine during that last tense week was that they had won with their blood a just fight which the world had refused to concede them. Now they were on the point of becoming a nation and the world would have to acknowledge it. It didn't matter what the U.N. decided now; the blood had been shed and the cause was almost won. The Jew had done nothing but defend the boundaries which the U.N. had declared to be his own in November, 1947. The U.N. did nothing to defend those borders. Practically every delegate ever to arise to his feet at a U.N. conference has somewhere in the course of his speech said, "We decry and are against any act of aggression," and the other delegates have always nodded solemnly in agreement. We have heard delegates say, "We shall not submit to any act of unwarranted aggression," and have heard the others cheer in agreement. But where in hell was the United Nations organization when Arabs were sitting in the tower of a Jaffa mosque pouring lead into the undefended city of Tel Aviv, killing women who were shopping on Allenby Road, killing shoemakers bending over their lathes outside their shops in Herzl

Street, killing children in baby carriages on Hayarkon Street, killing girls who were bathing in the surf just south of Tel Aviv harbor? All this happened during March and April, 1948, and if this wanton, careless killing was not an invasion of the boundaries approved of by the U.N., I do not know what it was. Yet the U.N. did not even protest to the Arab League or to Ernest Bevin. The Jews themselves had to stop the killing without outside aid.

Even during that last tense week the people of Tel Aviv insisted on living their normal lives. The Rotary Club, for instance, held its usual weekly luncheon and Moshe Brilliant took me along as his guest. I have always had a soft spot for the Rotary Club. My first full-time newspaper job was in Newark and the thirty dollars a week I received didn't stretch too far. But I was given a pleasant assignment. Each Monday I had to cover the weekly luncheon of the Eagles, on Tuesday the Lions, and on Wednesday the Rotary Club. They met at the Robert Treat Hotel and the luncheons were very good, and, of course, strictly on the cuff. It was seldom that a speaker said anything significant enough to be used in a story, but who cared for a story if you could get a free lunch every day— and I always remembered that the Rotary Club luncheons were the best.

The speeches and the conversation at the Rotary Club luncheon in Tel Aviv that day were about the same as they had been in Newark twenty years ago. And the same spirit of fellowship and hospitality that you'd find in Glens Falls, or Jacksonville or Beverly Hills was evident on this occasion.

Attorney Charles B. Sassoon, president of the club, expressed his regrets that the Arab members of the club were unable to attend. Sassoon was not being ironic in his expression of regret; a quarter of the Tel Aviv Rotary Club members were Arab businessmen from Jaffa and on excellent terms with their Jewish colleagues. Incidentally, next year's president is an Arab textile merchant, Assad Effendi.

Wolf Cegla, an importer, chatted about finance to Herman

Ellern, president of a bank; Solomon Tolkowsky of the citrus control board discussed the export of oranges; we laughed at the quips of Ralph Kaplan, school principal and secretary of the club. Jacob Ben Sira, city engineer, talked of plans for enlarging the port and Alex Rubens talked wittily and intelligently of the problems of a businessman whose office had been partly destroyed in the Jaffa fighting. Brilliant Isaac Chizik, government expert on Arab affairs, discussed the difference between the Arab of Palestine and the Arab of Iraq or Trans-Jordan.

It was good conversation among the substantial citizens of a thriving, healthy community. A great many of these men had sons who were fighting, and some of them took out pictures which were passed around the table. Solomon Tolkowsky talked about his scn who had been a fighter pilot with the R.A.F. He had, he insisted, the easiest job in the Haganah. He was a pilot without a plane.

"I hope we'll have a few fighter planes here by May 15th," Tolkowsky said thoughtfully. "There is an ammunition ship out there trying to get in and there are a couple of Messerschmitts crated aboard."

"They only have four days to arrive. We'll be pretty defenseless without them," another said thoughtfully.

"I imagine the Egyptians will start work on us Saturday," Chizik said, and there were nods around the table.

"Well, we'll just have to take it until your son gets up there in a Messerschmitt," Alex Rubens said. "By now I guess we've learned to take it."

This was so much like the attitude of the businessmen of London back in 1940 and '41. It was incredible to me that the British (officially, at least) were in effect waging war against these people who had so much in common with them. It was incredible that my own government, by its arms embargo, had aligned itself against these people. The one fact that stood out above everything else after three weeks here in Palestine was that these were our kind of people with the same hopes and aspirations, with the same love of liberty and freedom. They all knew that they were in for a bad time (each night the Cairo radio told of dire things in store for them) yet there wasn't the slightest sign of panic or even of nervousness.

That night I had dinner at the home of Alex Rubens. His charming wife Zipora had a fine meal ready for us. Afterwards she suggested that we drop in to see Reuben Rubin, Palestine's leading painter. He lived near the Jaffa border section in an imposing house. The first floor had been taken over by the Haganah, but his huge high-walled studio was on the second floor and the painter's booming laugh could be heard as we walked up the stairs. Rubin, a big man with a high forehead, was glad to see someone from New York. He'd had a one-man show there three years before and another show in Los Angeles. We chatted about friends in Hollywood and his young, pretty American wife served coffee and brandy. There were several friends of the Rubins' there, and then dark, lovely Raja Yaglom came in. There was a chorus of greeting.

"Thank God you're out of that damn uniform," Rubin shouted genially. "God never intended women to wear pants."

"I just got out of it," she said. "I've been driving around Jaffa the past few days. Lord, it was good to have a hot bath and feel some decent clothes on me."

She was a driver for the Haganah and she'd been on duty three days without much relief. "My children hardly knew me," she said. "Though I must say I get more respect from them when I come home tired and dirty and in my uniform than I ever did before. My oldest son, by the way, has run his collection of bullets up to eighteen."

"Mine," the wife of the painter said, "found three today right in our own garden. Then he dug two more out of the front of the house. You know, collecting those snipers' bullets has become a craze with the kids."

"When they start dropping bombs," the painter laughed, "I suppose the kids will try to catch them."

"Could we see some of your paintings?" Alex asked.

"You are a good friend, Alex," Rubin grinned. "I was afraid no one was going to ask me. Any time a painter tries to act modestly about showing his work you know he is a liar. Me, I love to show my paintings."

His wife smiled. "I have them all stacked in order, dear," she said serenely. "The oldest ones first."

Rubin showed us a dozen landscapes. We didn't say much. We were seeing more than landscapes; we were seeing what a small nation was fighting so desperately to hold. One was a desert scene giving an impression of desolate waste relieved only by a few desert plants, and Rubin said, "Painted that about five years ago. Went back a year ago and did the same scene."

The second painting showed fertile land blooming not only with produce but with homes and with people. Rubin showed us others and each scene was recognized by someone. Then he showed us the ones he had done during the past months. They were all of flowers: gay red, blue and white flowers of all kinds.

"That's all I've painted lately," Rubin said, and he added, as though trying to straighten something out in his own mind, "I don't feel like painting anything else. . . . Things aren't good and they're going to be worse. . . . You have to get your mind off things—so you paint flowers."

I left the home of the painter and went back to the Kaete Dan to find a man waiting for me who was not painting flowers. This was a man with a small golden beard and deep blue eyes and a quiet chuckle. He was the famed Big Isaac, leader of the Palmach. Somehow, Moshe Brilliant, learning that he was in Tel Aviv for the night, had persuaded him to spend an hour or so with me. Big Isaac wore no insignia. He was dressed in the usual khaki with his short-sleeved shirt open at the neck. At the moment Big Isaac was the greatest military hero in Palestine.

I took him over to the Armon and searched for a quiet spot where we could talk, but both the lobby and the bar were crowded. Gene Currivan of the *Times* saw us come in and he grabbed me by the arm. "Go up to my room. You keep forgetting there is a reward out for certain characters around here."

I introduced him to the Commander and we went upstairs. Gene came up a moment later with Richard, who had glasses and a bottle of French brandy. "I remember serving you this once," the bartender said courteously to Big Isaac. "I remember that you liked it."

He did like it. So Gene and I sat down and listened to the fantastic story of one of the most amazing men ever to become a military leader. He was born Isaac Sadeh, near Smolensk in Russia, and he first fired a gun when he was fifteen (he is fifty-three now). In those days the Russian Army was a highly organized caste and when they wanted some fun they took it where they found it and in a manner which the impulse of the moment dictated. One day the fifteen-year-old Sadeh saw a group of them mocking an old Jew. For the first time he realized that he, too, was a Jew. He discussed it with a friend, Vladimir Rivkind, and together they organized an army of two to stop such practices. Sadeh and Rivkind had older brothers and the older brothers did some hunting in the forests beyond Smolensk. So each of the two youngsters requisitioned a gun from an older brother and set out to protect Smolensk Jewry from annoyance by the soldiers of the Czar. One day they saw a group of them tormenting a Jewish woman and both unleashed their heavy artillery.

"We didn't hit any one," Sadeh laughed. "That wasn't the fault of my gun. It was a nice gun—a Belgian F.N. revolver. That was about forty years ago, but I have used the same model ever since. What happened to my friend Rivkind? Oh, he learned to shoot very well. Today he is a General in the Soviet Army."

Sadeh served in the Russian Army during World War I and was decorated with the highest order that a noncommissioned officer could obtain. Jews were not allowed to be officers in the Czarist army. The war over, he came to Palestine to enter the Yagur Communal settlement, and here he began the studies which eventually made him one of the best-known philologists in the Middle East. Even when he was made leader of the settlement he still pursued research into the culture of ancient civilizations as revealed by their languages. He knows Hebrew, Arabic, Yiddish, German, Russian, Polish and English perfectly. There is no Slavic tongue that is a mystery to Sadeh. In normal times he would be a professor of languages or devoting all of his time to research in etymology or semantics or morphology. Instead, he lived with a gun.

In 1936 Orde Wingate (then Captain) organized the men of the settlements to defend the country against the Arab uprising of that year and Sadeh became a fighter. The transition from the study of languages to the study of military tactics was an easy one for Sadeh. He became the best-known of all Palestinian commanders. When France fell, Sadeh and four Haganah commanders organized the Palmach on the same lines that Wingate had organized his small, compact, highly mobile units that had been so successful in 1936 and 1937. The name Palmach came from a combination of two Hebrew words: *mahatz* (striking) and *plugoth* (force). Haganah had always been trained as a defensive army; the word itself means "defense," but Sadeh believed that the best defense was attack. The Palmach would be the group dedicated to a last-ditch fight should the Germans enter Palestine, but they would fight by attacking German bases outside the country. The British were grateful, for by now they were sorely pressed in Egypt, and they knew that once Alexandria was in the hands of Rommel (which seemed a highly likely contingency) Palestine would be next. The British helped train the Palmach in Commando tactics with special stress given to methods of sabotage.

"This came in handy later," Sadeh said dryly, looking at his glass reflectively. "Very handy when fate made the British our enemies."

Members of the Palmach (like members of the Commandos)

did not have a very long life expectancy. Its first operation was a failure. The British asked Sadeh to blow up the oil refineries in Tripoli. Sadeh sent forty-eight men on an amphibious raid but somewhere along the line they were intercepted and not a word has been heard of them since. It is assumed that German aircraft spotted them and sunk the small boat and all on board. Operations in Syria were far more successful. Sadeh led these himself.

"Then the war ended and of course we of the Palmach kept on fighting for our country," Sadeh said grimly. "Now the British with whom we had fought began to hunt us. It was sad to be forced into combat against men who had been our brothers in arms."

Sadeh's picture was now on the wall in every police station and military headquarters in Palestine. Moshe Sneh (Haganah commander) was No. 1 on the list of undesirables; Sadeh was No. 2; Menachem Beigin was No. 3 and Friedman Yellen, head of the Stern Group, was No. 4. Not one of them was ever apprehended, although Sadeh confesses to some very narrow escapes.

"They raided and searched my village of Yagur a dozen times looking for me," he said, adding, as he poured a drink, "Only the French can make cognac. I suppose it's something in the soil on the banks of the Charente River near the old city of Cognac. Perhaps the proportion of lime . . . I'm sorry," he apologized. "I've been out in the desert some time and we have no brandy there. It is pleasant to sit in a room again and sip a fine drink."

"You had many close escapes?" I prompted.

"I suppose so," he shrugged his shoulders indifferently, and then told us of some of them. And he told us things about the Palmach I did not know. It was a self-supporting army; perhaps the only such in the history of modern warfare. Each man in the Palmach had two years of training before he was a full-fledged member. However, during this training period he spent half of his time working for his settlement and half in actual training. As he trained he produced; he never became a drag upon the economy of the country. Virtually all Palmach members came out of the settlements. Now of course they spent all their time fighting.

Up to now perhaps Sadeh's most sensational victory had been his relief of Mishmar Haemek in April. Mishmar Haemek was attacked by 4,000 well-armed members of the so-called Arab Army of Liberation under Fawzi el-Kawukji. Sadeh flew over the hills where they were entrenched in a light observation plane. The photographic memory which enables him to master languages so easily came in handy. He mentally photographed every weakness of the Arab positions. And early one morning he led four hundred men against them. Mobility, quick sharp thrusts, close accurate work with grenade and machine gun; these form the military philosophy of Sadeh, and they were well employed that morning. His attack was so fierce that the Arab defenders were tricked into thinking that the Palmach forces equaled or exceeded their own number. They never realized that their own fire power accurately estimated by Sadeh beforehand surpassed that of the Palmach by a ten-to-one margin. This victory made the Arab Army of Liberation a subject for jest among Palestinian Arabs and Fawzi el-Kawukji never recovered his prestige.

"No one thought that the Hebrew fighter could cope with the Syrian or Iraqui fighters," I said. "What has made him into the fighter he has become, and what made your group in particular into such fighters?"

"That's easy," Sadeh laughed. "To begin with, I allow no one in my Palmach who is over thirty. That is," he added, "except myself. They are young and capable of great physical exertion. Nearly all of my boys were born here on the land. With their own hands they transformed huge stretches of worthless sand into acres of orange groves, into acres of fertile soil producing the food for the country. Fundamentally, this is not a political or religious war to them; it is a war to retain the land which they brought to life. In a sense, they gave birth to this land and they fight for it as any parent fights for a child.

"Something which amazes the Arabs and the British is the ability of my boys to engage in long night marches, to strike somewhere unexpectedly. That is training," he said, "training and more training. And they know the terrain and they know their weapons, yes, even in the darkest nights they can handle them with ease. Yes," he added thoughtfully, "they are good fighters."

"You have a great many women fighting in the front lines?" I asked.

"Not as many as we had six months ago," he said grimly. "The Arabs captured some of them. We found their bodies later. They died very slowly and very horribly. The Arabs can keep prisoners alive for a long time. They understand torture very well. So I ordered women away from the front. Some had great combat records and on the strength of those records they demanded the right to remain as fighters. I had to allow them to stay."

"What will this country be like twenty-five years from now?" I asked Sadeh.

His eyes lit up. He was glad to get away from the memories of the dead Palmach girls. "It will be the Belgium of the Middle East," he said enthusiastically. "By then we will have a Hebrew nation of five million people. They say our land cannot absorb that many. Nonsense! Your little city of New York manages to absorb more than that. We will be a highly developed country. Don't forget that here our farmers constitute only about one-third of the population; the same is true of your country. We have plans to develop industry, plans to expand our citrus crop, plans to enlarge and deepen our port of Tel Aviv. Even now while we fight for our life as a nation these plans are going forward. During the next few weeks we will lose some battles and we will lose hundreds of our best men, but we will beat off the invasion. This I promise you. And we will emerge as a small but important democratic nation, important not only in the Middle East but important in the whole world."

"Do the Communists present any threat within the country to your idea of a democratic nation?" I asked.

Sadeh looked at me with honest bewilderment on his ruddy face. "Communism? Good heavens, man, we are Zionists! How can a man be a Zionist and a Communist? There is not one Communist in my organization, as far as I know, and," he added, "I would know. But we are certainly not anti-Russian. The British and Americans have given us no support. Only the Russian bloc has supported a Hebrew nation and we would be guilty of ingratitude if we did not acknowledge this. That does not make us Communists."

Tel Aviv was asleep now, but Currivan and I stayed, fascinated by the talk of this man of the desert. He talked freely on every subject and the range of his knowledge was amazing.

He talked rather bitterly of the U.N. and how it had made Palestine a political football to be kicked around. He talked frankly of internal politics, and said that he did not in all things agree with Ben-Gurion but that these differences were matters to be decided by the ballot. He spoke with anger of Friedman Yellen and the Stern Group, and he talked of Menachem Beigin as a sincere and honest patriot, adding that he did not hold this opinion of all the Irgun leaders. The Irgun was all right "as street fighters, as exponents of gangster warfare," but he didn't think much of them as soldiers capable of a sustained operation under military discipline. It was quite late when we finished talking and I walked out with him into the street. He was driving directly to the Jerusalem front. His car was waiting, a khaki-painted Oldsmobile. I noticed that there was a jagged hole in the rear fender.

"This was Fawzi el-Kawukji's car," he laughed. "Captured it a little while ago and almost caught him with it." He shook hands and said *"Shalom,"* and then climbed into the car. The driver, like Sadeh, bearded and in khaki, slipped it into gear and it disappeared down the street.

The next night I met a leader of the Fighters for the Freedom of Israel (the Stern Group or, as it is invariably known in London newspapers, the Stern Gang). The mechanics of being led to him were the same as followed by the Irgun. Again an attractive girl came to the Kaete Dan to tell me to be ready at seven that evening. Again I climbed into a car with a driver who had a gun strapped to his side and again there was no conversation.

"What is the leader's name?" I asked the tight-lipped girl as we drove off.

"Names? What do names matter?" she said.

"Besides, I suppose your leader has many names?"

"Our leader has many names," she said without expression.

I gave up. We drove to the outskirts of the city and stopped in front of what appeared to be a new apartment house. I followed the girl and the armed driver inside and we walked up two flights. Again it was a comfortable, well-furnished apartment. A big burly man was sitting at a table. He nodded affably and the girl introduced me. He talked Hebrew and she explained that she would interpret. I told her I didn't like to talk to a man without a name; it was like talking to a ghost. Couldn't he tell me who he was? A smile flitted across his face; he knew English all right, but the girl didn't smile.

"Call him Commander, if you wish," she said indifferently, and he motioned to me to sit down. He had none of the magnetic personality or warmth of Beigin. But he was frank enough. There was no question that he would not answer. In fact, he answered questions almost too quickly and too patly. It reminded me a little of men I had interviewed when I was in Moscow. They always had a quick answer. They didn't have to weigh the issues; they had long been weighed by party leaders and the answers prepared and given to the indoctrinated. The "Commander" was like that. It wasn't that he was repeating doctrine parrotlike; it seemed obvious that he believed these answers. They were part of his political faith and so ingrained in him that he didn't have to think twice before answering.

Occasionally he asked me questions. When he learned I had worked in Moscow he asked me how I had liked it. I told him how impossible conditions were for a correspondent there and how I sympathized with Russian colleagues on *Pravda* and *Izvestia* who had to write what they were told.

"But," he interrupted earnestly, "by doing this they are serving their country, are they not?"

"Even Shostakovich has to write his music according to the party line," I protested.

"But music too," he said, "can serve the country, and an artist must have the same responsibility toward his country that a soldier has."

This made me blink a little. I had heard the same line of talk so often in Moscow that I could have repeated it myself without a deviation from the party line. I decided to bring the issue into the open.

"Is the Stern Group a Communist organization?" I asked.

He wasn't startled by the question. "No," he said seriously, "but we do not intend to let our country become an outpost of Western imperialism. It is obvious to us that American and British policy is directed toward war. I am sure the people of those two countries do not want war, but the foreign policy of both countries seems designed on forcing the world into war. Russia is most certainly for peace."

I asked him dozens of questions and he answered them all. I took careful notes and as soon as I returned to the Kaete Dan I typed them. His viewpoint and the policy of the Stern Group are pretty much summed up in the following verbatim quotations from him:

"We are primarily a political organization; during wartime, however, we must use the tools of war; during peacetime we will use the tools of peace. We have but one purpose: to build a free and independent state, free from domination or influence of any foreign power. The British dominate most of the

Middle East. Economically, things are going badly for Britain. Her industrial output is low; she has become a borrower instead of a lender. She has lost India; she can't support a large army. She is desperately afraid of losing her influence over the colonies she has and of losing her hold on the Middle East. She does not want war but she stirs others into thinking that there may be a war. This helps her keep her present hold on what she now has. She also stirs people up in the U.S. with fear of Communism, hoping to frighten America into following her lead.

"The United States certainly doesn't want war. Economically she is strong and her industrial genius can help the world. But a small group drunk with power is leading America further and further away from the Atlantic Charter. She can raise her standard of living and find world markets easily. America can get along with Russia, all right. England never can.

"What we have tried to do here is to demonstrate that Britain was not capable of maintaining law and order in our country. This we have done. The whole Middle East can be free of British domination and influence if others act as we did. Our methods (direct methods) have been criticized. We do not apologize for them. They say we have used terrorist tactics and have stabbed the British in the back. That is true. This is no time for knights in shining armor. We had to show the world that the British were interlopers.

"Once the British are out and their influence is gone we will use political weapons, in the democratic manner. We look forward to a state that will be politically free; a state that will own and guard its natural resources and transportation system. These should be nationalized. We believe in free enterprise as long as it does not interfere or hurt the country. We realize, too, that we need foreign capital to develop some industries.

"Do we favor a communistic state? No. There are peculiar problems existing here in Palestine brought about partly by climate, soil, lack of certain natural resources and the intended yearly repatriation of thousands of Jews. All of these factors peculiar to Palestine alone will determine the political set-up of our government. We cannot model it after that of any other country (including Russia) because our problems are different.

"We favor one economic scheme for Jews, Arabs and other non-Jews here. They should have equal rights, opportunity and wages and standing in trade unions. Persians, Romans and Turks all occupied Palestine at one time, but no one ever thought of it as a homeland but the Jews. For instance, the Arab national problem is outside of Palestine, but those who live here should have full rights of citizenship and, incidentally, full responsibility of citizenship. There shall be no discrimination here against non-Jews.

"What has our fight accomplished? It has changed a community fighting for its rights into a nation fighting for its freedom. The 'rights' were always ours. We take our political belief from the Old Testament: 'The voice of the people is the voice of God.' We will not disband. We will continue as a political group even after the British and the British influence have left Palestine. Later we will run candidates for office. After May 15th, if the Arabs continue to invade Palestine, we will join with the Haganah and the Irgun in repelling them. Of course we will. Our differences with them are political, but first of all we are Palestinians."

As he talked I studied him. I noticed that although his hair was black, the hair on the back of his hands was light. They were strong hands, too. Everything about the man was strong, assured. He knew where he was going, all right. His voice was calm, dispassionate even, when he discussed the murder of Lord Moyne. To him murder was a political weapon. He was no Beigin, no Sadeh, torn at the death of a Dov Gruner or anguished by the torture of women fighters. He was the real fanatic who long since had subjugated emotion to reason. He seemed out of place in Palestine—the only country in the world whose chief import was people. In many ways he was the greatest enemy Palestine had. He and his followers (there were never more than five hundred of them) had, by their tactics, alienated thousands and thousands of Jews outside of the country. Everyone in Tel Aviv admitted that the Stern Group was actuated by sincerity and by its own type of idealism, but their refusal to follow the will of the people as expressed by Ben-Gurion had earned them nothing but hatred among the people of the new nation. Had they and the Irgun bowed to the authority of the people and become incorporated in the Haganah, Palestine could have presented a united front to the world as well as a more compact military organization. Everyone was worried as to what the Stern Group and the Irgun would do after May 15th. If they continued to exist as military organizations it would mean civil war, for once the state was declared it was inconceivable that three independent military groups represent it.

But this was three days away.

CHAPTER SIX

On *May 14th* there was a feeling in the air that I'd only known as a kid on the day before Christmas. Paul had been on duty all night but he was there bright and early to serve breakfast. He asked me to step out on the terrace. He pointed toward Jaffa. There was just one good-sized ship, low in the water, anchored there.

"That is the ammunition ship we have been waiting for," he said. "The British stopped it last night. We will be in trouble without it. There are two fighters crated on its decks; there are anti-aircraft weapons and plenty of ammunition in the hold."

"That's a tough break," I sympathized.

"Yes," he said slowly, "but negotiations are going on. It will cost us a great deal but we hope to get it in during the night."

The bribery of British military and civil officials was an

104

established practice, and had been for some years in Palestine. Any time you were with the Haganah you saw British rifles, mortars, stores of all kinds. The Haganah "bought" them, and now "negotiations" were going on to release this ammunition ship.

Through the magic of Moshe Brilliant's backstage manipulation, I had received an invitation to attend the National Council that day; it was the meeting that would officially proclaim Palestine a sovereign nation, that would baptize it with a name and would present the country with a formal declaration of independence. Moshe Shertok had arrived from Lake Success the day before. He had spent the whole night writing and rewriting the Declaration of Independence. I met his secretary at the Haganah P.I.O. (Press Information Office) and she had confided that twice during the night she had been sent to the library to get books written by Thomas Jefferson. I heard other more disquieting rumors coming from men too highly placed in the government to be dismissed as rumors. One story (which I afterwards ran down and confirmed) was that President Truman had urged David Ben-Gurion to postpone the proclamation of a Hebrew state and to accept a trusteeship by the United Nations to last two years. He had called Moshe Shertok from Lake Success to Washington to present his plan. Shertok (knowing that Palestine was virtually defenseless against the air attacks which seemed inevitable) brought Truman's plan to the Jewish Agency in New York.

The Jewish Agency had always been the parent organization which had supported and helped arm Palestine. It formulated Palestine policies and now Shertok brought the Truman proposition to the Agency. The American members held an emergency meeting to vote on the new plan. They rejected it, subject to Ben-Gurion's approval.

Ben-Gurion flatly rejected the Truman proposition which had really come from Forrestal, Loy Henderson and the same old pro-British State Department bloc.

"Ben-Gurion is either a reckless lunatic or a genius," my informant said. "Reason dictates that we accept Truman's proposition. Despite the attitude of his State Department, we feel he is, well, at least neutral. And we know we haven't a thing to combat an air attack. But Ben-Gurion turned the proposition down flatly. It is now or never, he said, and that's that. Perhaps you've noticed the Haganah communiqués these past two weeks. Every time they talk of a fight with the Arabs they say, 'We allowed the Arabs to come to close quarters before opening fire.' Think that over. Why does the Haganah allow the Arabs to come to close quarters? It's because we have no ammunition left for anything but Sten guns which are only good up to fifty yards. If the Arabs knew how badly off we are they'd walk into Tel Aviv. Well, we've decided—all of us —to sink or swim with Ben-Gurion, and it may damn well come to swimming." He nodded toward the Mediterranean.

Had Ben-Gurion accepted Truman's proposition and postponed the proclamation of the new state, there is no doubt that an immediate revolution would have taken place. And, quite likely, Israel would have destroyed herself. Perhaps this was the intent of the plan. The Haganah might possibly have supported Ben-Gurion, but there is little doubt that the Palmach would have rejected the plan and thousands would have flocked to the banner of the Irgun and the Stern Group.

The people of Tel Aviv did not know how precarious the situation was. The cabinet meeting was held at the National Fund Building. It had not been announced, but when a dozen big Chryslers roared through the streets, each bearing small blue-and-white flags, the crowds began to gather. Haganah soldiers in khaki shorts stood at attention, flanking the doors of the big white building. I watched the cabinet ministers walk up the eight steps. Ben-Gurion arrived with his wife, Paula. Perhaps the bright sunlight blinded her for a moment; she stumbled on the first step and fell heavily. She put her hand to her left eye; it was obvious that she was in great pain but her husband held her arm and helped her up the steps. I followed. The thirteen cabinet members sat at a circular table with Ben-Gurion in the center. In front of the large table which was on a raised dais twenty members of the Council sat. (Four were trapped in besieged Jerusalem.) Behind them were a dozen chairs for other officials. I sat next to Mrs. David Ben-Gurion. Her eye was badly swollen and an attendant brought her a glass of ice water and she kept dipping her handkerchief in the water and applying it to the eye. She was Russian-born, but she had met Ben-Gurion in Brooklyn and it was there they had married. I chatted with Paula Ben-Gurion awhile and she said she would translate for me. The proceedings would be in Hebrew.

Ben-Gurion opened the historic meeting by reading the Declaration of Independence. As she translated, I realized why Shertok had sent out for copies of Thomas Jefferson's works. The language of the Declaration was very similar to the language of our own Declaration of Independence. Ben-Gurion announced that the name of the state would be Israel.

A cheer went up from the thirty-three Council members. There had been much speculation as to what name the cabinet might choose. Many wanted the name Zion. They knew that the country would eventually be a full-fledged member of the United Nations. When the roll call is made at U.N. meetings it is done in alphabetical order. If the new nation was named Zion it would always be the last nation called upon to vote. This would give it a tremendous advantage. If the vote was tied, the last nation voting would decide the issue. She could make deals with other nations based on her advantageous voting position. But other cabinet members objected that Zion was a hill in Jerusalem and had been for a few thousand years—and Zion was voted down. So the nation became Israel.

When the cabinet had ratified the Declaration of Independence and the name of the state, one of the members made a motion that the site of the capital be discussed. Should it be Tel Aviv? Should it be in the Negeb? Ben-Gurion stopped him.

"My best information is that Tel Aviv will be bombed by

the Egyptian air force at one minute after midnight," he said gravely. "They may come over in great force and as yet we are not equipped to meet such an attack. There is a strong chance that they will destroy the city and us with it. If that happens, any discussion as to where our capital shall be will have been merely academic."

I watched Ben-Gurion intently. Genius or reckless lunatic? A halo of electric white hair surrounded his head. He was clean-shaven and his face had deep lines in it. It was a strong, obstinate face, and Ben-Gurion was a strong, obstinate man. He wasn't loved in the country—but he was highly respected. He was a rather strange combination of labor leader, military commander and philosopher whose only interest outside of fighting for his country was the study of Greek philosophers and Buddhism. His hands were gnarled as though they had spent years gripping plow handles. As a boy, he (like so many others who had achieved prominence in Israel) had been converted to Zionism by the writing of Theodor Herzl. Zionism had been his life ever since. Weizmann was a great scientist, a great dreamer, a great humanitarian and, in his idealism, almost a saint. Weizmann was the conscience of Zionism— Ben-Gurion the arm of Zionism. Ben-Gurion was the practical dreamer. It was he who authored the policy that all immigrants arriving in the new land should become either farmers or factory workers. The new land did not need lawyers or doctors or merchants. And so the country grew on a firm basis. It was Ben-Gurion who developed the Haganah and who organized the Histadrut (General Federation of Jewish Labor) which today controls nearly thirty percent of the nation's economy. But for these and other policies, all either conceived or put forth by Ben-Gurion, the new nation would never have been anything but a burden on world Jewry. He is impulsive, impatient, uncompromising and tough. When he sets his eyes on a goal he plows toward it, not caring whose toes he treads on. He has none of the charm of a Weizmann. It was Weizmann who represented Palestine to the world—it was Ben-

Gurion who stayed at home building the state. Each was essential. Each complemented the other. Neither was capable of doing the job of the other.

When Ben-Gurion told his fellow cabinet ministers and council members of the impending bombing he was calm. So were the others. He was flanked on one side of the table by well-groomed Felix Rosenblueth, Minister of Justice, looking like an American business executive. He merely raised his eyebrows when he heard Ben-Gurion. On the other side was Rabbi Juda Fishman, who had been given the portfolio of Minister of Religions as a recognition for past services. Fishman is seventy-four. He looked tired but he smiled a little at what Ben-Gurion said and pushed his sparse hair back with an automatic gesture. Moshe Shertok had been up all night but he looked well rested and urbane as usual. He heard Ben-Gurion's announcement with no change of expression and then turned to whisper something to David Remez, easygoing, genial Minister of Communications, who smiled. When Shertok was a youngster he graduated from the Tel Aviv equivalent of high school with such amazing marks that it was decided to send him abroad to study. He became a linguist at Istanbul (he speaks fourteen languages) and learned law and economics at Oxford. He is perfectly equipped for the role of Foreign Minister. He has an easy, charming manner and quick responsive smile.

I looked at the other faces. Eliazer Kaplan, Minister of Finance, considered by many to be the soundest man in the cabinet, was looking thoughtful. He looks and acts like the late Jan Masaryk. He came up through the ranks of the Labor Party. There is nothing spectacular about Kaplan and on the two occasions I heard him speak his audience was restless. But when you read his speech afterwards you realized that this was a real intelligence speaking; the kind of man needed as a solid balance wheel to the right and left extremists in the cabinet.

There was absolute quiet in the room for a few seconds

after Ben-Gurion had exploded his bombshell, but there wasn't a sign of fear on the faces of anyone there. In fact, there was quiet amusement on most faces. They believed Ben-Gurion, but there was no use submitting to fear at this late date. Anger —righteous anger—seemed to be the dominating force everywhere in the country, and sitting there I realized that a psychologist I once knew had been right when he was discussing fear way back in the days of the London bombings. Anger, he had told me (I hadn't believed him then) was, in its raw state, a force designed to help us survive. It had its origins in the primitive animal impulse which enabled early man to fight against the forces which were trying to destroy him. Anger was like a jolt of adrenalin which gave a person renewed strength, and it was such a dominating impulse that it precluded the possibility of any other emotion taking hold. It was strong enough to completely banish fear. I believed this while looking at the faces in that room. There was no place for fear in their hearts or minds.

Finally Ben-Gurion adjourned the meeting. The first public proclamation would take place in the museum on Rothschild Boulevard. This meeting had long since been planned. There were cars waiting below. I slipped into a car with Minister Rosenblueth and swarthy Behor Shitreet, Minister of Minorities. Shitreet has spent most of his life in the desert with the Arabs and, by virtue of his appointment by the British as Chief Magistrate, holds great power over them. His headquarters were in Southern Judea and there he administered justice over a large group of Arab villages. A few years ago the British Chief Justice announced that Shitreet was to be transferred but the Arab lawyers and villagers raised such a howl that Shitreet's transfer was forgotten. His job in the cabinet was that of safeguarding the rights of minorities and seeing that even the Arabs received all benefits of citizenship.

I offered Shitreet a cigarette but he choked on my American brand. He was accustomed to the milder Arab tobacco, he explained. Our caravan moved on toward the museum. The route of the procession had been given out and the streets were jammed with people. We drove slowly, hearing the roar that greeted the first car which carried Ben-Gurion. Waves of roaring seemed to break over us. I noticed that Shitreet was very solemn.

"Look at the joy on those faces," I said to him.

"Yes," he said slowly. "How horrible it is to think that so many of them will have to die before our nation is secure."

I couldn't take my eyes off the people who lined the sidewalks. I have never seen that kind of deep, fierce happiness on faces before. Thousands were crying openly, as though their joy was too great to be contained. Today their dream had come true, not because a kindly fate had willed it so, but because they had worked and fought to make it come true.

The crowd in front of the museum was huge. Haganah men stood guard with rifles as the cabinet ministers stepped from their cars. Most Israelis refer to the Prime Minister as B.G., and there were roars of approval for B.G. and then for Shertok, who seemed startled, amazed, perhaps, at his enormous popularity.

The proceedings inside have been described often enough. The thirteen cabinet ministers sat down at a long table and in back of them was a huge picture of Theodor Herzl. The Council members sat on chairs in front of them and Robert Capa took over. Capa had arrived only a few days before. I have seen Capa operate in a dozen countries and he always takes over. He is not only a great photographer but he has the kind of personality that commands attention. He was all over the place with his camera. When he cried, "Hey, B.G., please —a little smile," the Prime Minister smiled. There were half a dozen other still and newsreel cameramen there, but as usual it was Capa who ran things.

Finally Capa had enough and he nodded to Ben-Gurion to go ahead. The meeting proceeded. There were six hundred people crowded into the chamber and they were all gripped by the same intense joy that I had seen on the faces outside.

It was soon over and then an orchestra (the Palestine Philharmonic) upstairs began to play "Hatikvah," the national anthem. Loudspeakers piped it into the room and some began to hum the tune; others took up the words and then even Ben-Gurion and Shertok and the rest joined in and the room trembled with their voices. The words and the music of "Hatikvah" are overwhelming and majestic. It is a prayer set to music; a prayer that has real significance today.

> "As long as a Jewish heart beats
> As long as a Jewish eye turns eastward
> Then our two-thousand-year-old hope
> To be a free nation in Zion and Jerusalem
> Is not dead."

The words no longer constituted a prophecy or a hope (Hatikvah means hope). For the first time they described a fact. Israel was now a nation, no matter what the U.N. said tonight, no matter what the Arabs did tomorrow. Tears streamed down the faces of men who had worked for this moment all their lives. Capa stood beside me, his camera forgotten. "Jesus," he was breathing, "Jesus—never saw anything like it—what people—my God, what people!"

All of us who were there were shaken. Even those of us who hadn't shared the dream and hadn't shared the suffering and sacrifice which made the dream come true felt as though we had lived through a very great moment. We all filed out, quiet now, drained of emotion. I walked back to the Kaete Dan. Sam Federman came from behind the desk, his eyes shining. We went downstairs to the bar. He didn't say anything—just walked behind the bar and picked a bottle out of an ice bucket. There was no one else there. The bottle was Veuve Cliquot, 1937. He pulled the cork and the champagne bubbled merrily over the neck of the bottle and then he filled two glasses wordlessly.

The ordinary toast, *"L'ach chaim,"* which means, "Here's to life," didn't seem important enough for this occasion. I remembered another Hebrew phrase, *"Am Yisrael Chai,"* ("Israel lives!") and Samuel repeated it with shining eyes, sipped his drink and added a second toast, "To the baby."

"You mean the baby nation?" I asked.

He shook his head. "They took Ruth to the hospital this morning. The baby should arrive tonight. Perhaps tomorrow."

For two weeks all of us had been speculating as to when the Federman baby would arrive.

"If it arrives tomorrow you've got to name him Israel," I said.

"But both Ruth and I want a girl," he protested.

"You're a liar, Sam. Save that story for Ruth."

"Well, I'll be happy, no matter what it is. But if the baby is born tomorrow, think what that will mean. To be born on the same day that your nation is born is not something that happens to many."

"I hope it is either a boy or a girl," I told him.

"I will settle for either," he said seriously.

Others came into the bar now and all drank to the new nation (that technically would not be born until midnight) and to the new baby (which might be born any minute). No one in Tel Aviv that day had grown an armor of sophistication heavy enough to ward off the attack of emotionalism or sentimentalism that had struck us all so hard. It was a memorable day and it developed into a memorable night. Gene Currivan, Capa and some of the others finished work a little before midnight and we gathered at the Armon to hear the radio news. The B.B.C. was icily cold in describing the events of the day. We couldn't get American stations, but a little after midnight the Haganah announced the startling news that Truman had recognized Israel. America had been the first to recognize the new state. The news spread quickly. I left the Armon and ran right into total darkness, only slightly relieved by a waning moon. I had forgotten that a blackout had been announced for midnight. Back at the Kaete Dan I looked out of my window. There were thirty ships lying off the port, each ablaze with lights. The Tel Aviv blackout wouldn't do much good if Egyptian planes came over.

It was hard to get to sleep that night but it was easy to wake up the next morning. It wasn't a pleasant awakening but it was an effective one. Once you've heard the horrible sound of bombs exploding you recognize it even in your sleep. As soon as I awoke I knew what had awakened me. I ran out on the terrace. It was five-thirty, a beautiful day with the sun already beginning to climb the horizon. Paul the waiter was there, and my banker friend Franz Winkler and Sam Federman. Paul pointed wordlessly to the right. For a moment I saw nothing but white clouds hanging from a blue sky and then, the sun having washed the sleep out of my eyes, I saw the Spitfires. There were four of them circling above the port; circling confidently at about 5,000 feet. Ack-ack began to bark shrilly and small black and white puffs blossomed far below the four planes. The ack-ack consisted only of machine guns and Brens. Then the lead Spit peeled off in a steep glide. It came down to within five hundred feet of the ground and then we saw tiny dark objects detach themselves and we watched them fall and then a great splash erupted from the water a hundred yards from the docks, and then—only then—did we hear the explosions of the bombs. The second, third and fourth Spits followed. Ben-Gurion's timetable had been off; they hadn't bombed Tel Aviv at one minute after midnight but they hadn't wasted too much time.

When the Spitfires had finished they turned south. They flew low, indicating their contempt for the inadequate anti-aircraft defenses. They flew over the beach past the Kaete Dan and we (and the whole city) could only watch impotently. They returned four hours later, with bombs attached to their undercarriages, and again they hit and ran away. Even their attacks couldn't entirely dispel the new feeling of confidence and joy you met everywhere that day in Tel Aviv. This had been expected. Fighter planes were on the way to help. When would they arrive? No one knew. But there were pilots waiting to fly them. Meanwhile, the bombs had done little damage and the unloading of the ships continued. Some thirty men had been killed by the bombs—that was all.

Blue-and-white flags had blossomed during the night. They were everywhere. And no one seemed perturbed about the bombing. Moshe Brilliant phoned to say that the Israel broadcasting station would begin operations that evening at seven o'clock. Would I broadcast? Of course I would. A car picked me up about six-thirty and took me to the government station. Everywhere there was evidence that a lot of planning had been done. The station was all set to operate. Twice a day there would be broadcasts in English, I was told, and it was this part of the program I was to inaugurate. I had written a fifteen-minute piece and I delivered it. As I talked, I happened to glance through the glass that separated the studio proper from the office outside and there was the unmistakable leonine head of Ben-Gurion. He was to follow me. As I finished he walked in and said, "If you wait for me, I'll drive you home." I sat with Mrs. Ben-Gurion while the Prime Minister broadcast. Her eye was now purple and black and badly swollen.

"If you need a witness as to how you got that eye, remember I was there," I reminded her.

She smiled, but it was obvious that she was in pain. "A good night's sleep will take care of it," she said. "But God knows when we will get it. My husband was up all night. They wanted him to broadcast to America at 4 A.M. our time and he was busy with his ministers until then so he got no sleep. He came home after the broadcast and just as he got to bed the bombing began and he hurried to the port. He was there most of the day."

"That's no place for the Prime Minister to be," I said, shocked. The death of Ben-Gurion at this time would have been tragic.

"I wish you could convince him of that," she said dryly. "I can't."

When Ben-Gurion finished we went down to the street. The

darkness was intense. We climbed into his car, not one of the big black Chryslers of the day before but a five-passenger car —either a Ford or Chevrolet. A driver and a Haganah man sat up front. Two motorcycles preceded us; that was the only concession Ben-Gurion made to his position as Prime Minister.

"How long will Tel Aviv have to take this bombing?" I asked.

"God knows," he said wearily. "We have some fighter aircraft on the way but it is impossible to hurry them. They are on slow ships. Meanwhile our people will have to suffer. There is something horrible about watching planes bomb a defenseless city, knowing there is absolutely nothing one can do about it."

"There is a report that in retaliation you are going to order the bombing of Cairo," I said. "Is that true?"

"Bomb Cairo?" A rueful smile flitted over his tired face. "With what? A week from now we could make such a threat because I hope by then we will have planes here, but tonight we can make no threats because we could not carry them out."

He rested his head against the back of the seat and closed his eyes. The car was traveling slowly; the driver was not accustomed yet to driving in total darkness. Then I heard Ben-Gurion say, and it was as though he were thinking aloud, "They can bomb us and murder our civilians. They can kill us, but they will never kill this nation of ours. . . . They can come over every day and every night . . ." His voice trailed off and I saw that he was indeed asleep. He was sitting between his wife and myself. She leaned over and put a warning finger to her lips. We drove in silence for five minutes. Then we turned a corner sharply and Ben-Gurion was thrown against me and his eyes opened and he smiled apologetically. "I think I dozed off. We were talking about—about—I think you asked me how we could win with no defense against their attacks by air. Is that it?"

It wasn't, but I nodded, and he said, "You see we have a

very large army—a tremendous army. And our enemies will have to kill every member of that army in order to beat us."

"A very large army?" I repeated, completely puzzled.

"Yes," he said, and the weariness had left his voice. "We have an army of 750,000."

"But," I began, "that's the entire population. . . ."

"That's right," he said calmly, smiling a little. "That's right."

Just then the car stopped in front of the Kaete Dan. I blinked when I met the bright light inside. Sam Federman was there, beaming. "It was a boy," he said happily. "And we will name him Israel."

That meant that Ben-Gurion now had an army of 750,001.

CHAPTER SEVEN

May 15th was now in the history books. Three days later a ship anchored off Tel Aviv. It was the same ship I had seen lying off Jaffa on May 14th—the ammunition ship. It came in at dusk and it seemed as though everyone knew that it had arrived. The Egyptian planes never came at night. A half dozen lighters hurried out to meet the ship. Men worked all night unloading it, and the precious ammo, guns and crated aircraft were brought ashore, put on trucks and hurriedly sent to some spot less vulnerable than the port of Tel Aviv. The Spitfires kept coming over three and four times a day. One was hit but the pilot managed to land it on the beach north of the harbor. Before he could destroy it and himself, Haganah men had grabbed the plane and the pilot.

Several of the correspondents had received queries from their home offices asking if it were true that there were a

118

number of high-ranking American officers fighting for Israel. I tried to run down the report but got nowhere. We often heard of a "Mickey Stone," an American who was a Haganah commander with rank of colonel. He was a genius on planning, we heard, and he had actually revised the field training manual. He had led a dozen operations himself but as to who he was beyond "Mickey Stone" no one knew. But one night Moshe Brilliant phoned me in high excitement. He had located "Mickey Stone" at the Park Hotel. I hurried over, went into the restaurant and at a table saw a familiar face; it was "Mickey Stone," but when I knew him he had been Colonel David Marcus, West Point, 1924, and Commissioner of Corrections in New York City.

"I'm Mickey Stone around here," he grinned. "Stick to it, will you?"

There were three men with him. One of them grinned at me and said, "Has your left hand improved any?" He was Harold Jaffer, of Brooklyn. The last time I'd seen him was in George Brown's gymnasium on West 57th street, New York. We were old handball opponents. The second man had graying hair, a mustache, and that unmistakable carriage that distinguishes the professional army man. He was Captain Fred Martin of Arlington, Virginia, and he had fought the war with the 79th Division. The third was Lt. Colonel Tom Forrester of Plainfield, New Jersey, who had served with H.Q. Fleet Marine Force in the Pacific.

"I'm just here as an observer," Forrester said, grinning. "These other fellows are doing the fighting."

"This war is getting to be a sort of neighborhood fight," I said. "Every time you turn around you meet someone from home."

"There are a lot more American and British fighting here than anyone realizes," Captain Martin said.

Mickey had been with the Haganah for some months now and tonight he was off on a new operation. He had come to Tel Aviv only to see how his ack-ack boys were doing at the port.

Several of them had been killed but they had done a great job, he said.

"They've been shooting popguns at those Spits," he said, "but they got three so far. One was intact, the one they got this morning. I was talking to that Egyptian pilot tonight. You know, when he was forced down he expected to be torn to pieces," Mickey shook his head. "These Gyppos get funny ideas. Hell, we put him in a hotel and gave him a good meal and a lot of books and he's the happiest Gyppo you ever saw."

We talked of many things sitting there; we talked of teams that Mickey had played with at West Point. We talked of the Notre Dame team of 1924 and I foolishly bet Mickey a bottle of wine that he couldn't name the whole team. He did—including half a dozen substitutes. We talked of Flanagan's run against Army and of Schwartz and Carideo and of Garbisch and Chris Cagle. We talked of Eisenhower and Patton, with whom Mickey had served for awhile in Sicily and, inevitably, we talked of the Haganah.

"They're the best," Mickey said, his small oval face wrinkling into a smile. "I don't know what it is, but, my God, they've got it. Look, first we have to go out and capture the weapons we need for fighting. What have we got? You know what we've got—small stuff. We have to go in and capture heavy machine guns before we can take on any major operation. We pulled one off last week out in the desert. We knew the Arabs had a dozen good machine guns on this hill. We needed those guns bad so my boys pleaded with me for a chance to go after them. Why, it was suicide with what we had. But damn it, they talked me into it. This was a hill— see?"

Mickey drew the position on the tablecloth. "Now I put a few of the kids with two-inch mortars at strategic spots covering three sides of the hill. We managed to get pretty close without being spotted. Then I had the mortars open up on three sides. They make a hell of a noise, you know. Well, they turned those machine guns on our mortars but, by golly, I had my main force run up the fourth side of that hill, and before the Arabs knew what in hell was going on we were on top of them. We got the twelve machine guns intact and four hundred prisoners. You don't know what those twelve machine guns mean to us."

"You lose many men?" I asked Mickey.

He shook his head. "Not one. Soon as we secured everything I asked about the wounded. Nobody wounded, they told me. I said this is a bloody miracle. An hour later I saw our medicos working on a dozen men and I asked, 'What gives around here?' Well, it seems that these kids who were wounded didn't want me to know about it. They thought I'd send them back to a base hospital, which I damn well did. My God, all they want to do is fight. Never seen anything like it."

"How did you get that ammo ship back from the British?" I asked Mickey.

His small eyes twinkled. "That's not my job. That comes under the Minister of Finance. But we got that stuff all away from the docks. Give us another two or three days and we'll have some fighters sitting up there. It's going to be a lot of fun to see what they do to those Spits. And we'll have that Spit we got intact up there too. All with combat pilots in them; good combat pilots out of the R.A.F. and the Canadian Air Force. Three or four more days and this nightmare here will be over."

"What kind of fighters are the Arabs?" I asked Mickey.

"Nobody is a good fighter if he hasn't anything to fight for," Mickey said. "What have they got to fight for? Abdullah? Farouk? Bevin? I imagine if you invaded their country they'd defend it well, but this isn't their country and they know it and they don't seem to give a damn. And they have no discipline worth anything. That goes for the Arab Legion, even with their British officers. The way I figure the Arab is this: he's a loner. If you corner him he'll fight back as well as anyone. But put him into a brigade and he's hopeless. And he is no offensive fighter. All my boys want to do is to attack. They think along those lines. They think like Commandos or our Marines. They don't give a damn for holding static defensive positions. They want to get in close and slug it out. They're the best, believe me, the best I've ever seen."

"Whatever made you come over here, Mickey?" I asked.

Mickey looked puzzled, as though trying to find words to explain something which to him was too obvious to need an explanation. "Well, I'll tell you. I guess I just liked these people." He looked at his watch. "Hell, I have to go. I got to be a hundred miles from here in three hours."

And Colonel David (Mickey) Marcus shook hands, grinned, and went out into the night.

Life wasn't too easy for the ordinary family in Tel Aviv during May, 1948. There was a shortage of everything, but neither courage nor humor was rationed. Even the bombings couldn't prevent the typical Tel Aviv family from living a near normal life. Meet the family of Mr. Wolf Cegla. One day I met him hurrying home from his office. He was lunching at home and he asked me to join him.

"How about phoning your wife first?" I suggested, but he laughed.

"I live a block from here. Come on along," he said, and I did.

Mr. and Mrs. Wolf Cegla and their thirteen-year-old son, Michael, are a typical Tel Aviv family. Wolf Cegla came from Germany in 1936. He had been a lawyer in Berlin but there were plenty of lawyers in Tel Aviv so he went to work for an importing firm. Like most businessmen in Tel Aviv, Wolf Cegla and his family speak English. I had first met him at the regular luncheon of the Tel Aviv Rotary Club.

Cegla is a big, smiling man who looks older than his thirty-nine years, but some of them have been hard years. His apartment is on Hayarkon Street, which overlooks the Mediterranean. His blonde wife, Elsa, blinked a bit when she saw that her husband had an unexpected luncheon guest with him, but beyond that she displayed neither dismay nor reproach. "It will take me only a minute to put an extra plate on the table," she said hospitably.

Young Michael, aged thirteen, blond like his mother, bounced in and threw his arms around his father. I was introduced and Michael said courteously, "I am very pleased to meet you," and then looked at his father questioningly.

"That's right," his father said approvingly. "They're teaching you excellent English at school."

The Cegla family lives in a four-room apartment and each room has a balcony. It is a sun-drenched, cheerful apartment and Cegla is proud of two paintings on the wall of his living room. They were done by Kahn and Reisser, two well-known Palestinian artists.

In Tel Aviv, the main meal is usually at noon. We had noodle soup with bits of chicken floating in it; broiled chicken with potatoes and peas and a dessert of apple sauce embellished with sliced bananas. During lunch we discussed the differences in the way the Cegla family lives and the way the Jones family in America lives. The similarities were more striking than the differences.

Wolf Cegla, for example, makes seven thousand dollars a year. His rent is sixty-six dollars a month and his electric-light bill about twenty dollars a month. In the kitchen a gleaming electric refrigerator and an electric stove for cooking explained the relatively high electric bill. Like most American families of his income bracket, Wolf Cegla owns a car. His is an American car and he is very proud of it.

"The British did their best to make us buy British cars," he explained, "but the British cars weren't powerful enough to use on the steep hills around Jerusalem. I was lucky enough to get an American car. It cost twenty-four hundred dollars but it was worth it. I don't use it much now because gasoline is so expensive. We pay seventy-five cents a gallon. I have never been able to understand why gasoline is so much higher here than in the United States. It comes from the refineries at

Haifa, only a few miles from here. But that is one of those mysteries of taxation an ordinary businessman cannot understand."

Elsa Cegla has no servants but twice a week she has a woman who comes in for three hours to clean house. And every morning, like Mrs. Jones of America, Elsa Cegla shops.

"I've been going to shop around on Ben Yehuda Street," she said. "Prices are rather high. Fish, even though it comes right out of the Mediterranean, is a dollar a pound. Like any housewife, I make a budget. I allow myself forty-eight dollars a week for food. That is high, but my husband and Michael have all their meals at home and they are two healthy, hungry men, both of them."

Michael laughed with pride at being bracketed with his father as a man. Michael attends a private high school called the Shalva Gymnasium. He is studying algebra and elementary geography, which he likes, and Hebrew and English, which he finds more difficult.

"We parents aren't much good helping our children with homework," Wolf Cegla said. "Neither my wife nor I know Hebrew. When the children want to have secrets from their parents they talk Hebrew among themselves. Few of us who came from Germany know the language well."

"I'm a Sea Scout," Michael interrupted shyly.

He explained that a Sea Scout was really a branch of the Boy Scouts, except that instead of going on hikes the Sea Scouts went on boat rides. They learn how to handle rowboats on the Yarkon River and sail boats out in the Mediterranean and they learn to swim.

Michael was also on his class soccer football team, he told me proudly.

"We don't know what Michael will be when he grows up," his father remarked. "Last month he had decided to be a children's doctor. The month before that he wanted to be a dog doctor. Now he wants to be a soldier."

At this point our conversation was stopped by the rat-tat-tat of anti-aircraft fire followed a moment later by the sound of bombs exploding. This was the third time during the day that Egyptian Spitfires fitted with bombs had come over. The port was only about a quarter of a mile from the Cegla apartment. Michael rushed to the balcony.

"They are coming again," he cried excitedly, pointing above. The Spitfires high above wheeled almost lazily and then dove. There was still very little effective defense in Tel Aviv against enemy aircraft.

They dove and the roar of their motors hurt your ears and puffs of white from the exploding anti-aircraft shells blossomed around them, but at four hundred feet they released their bombs. Neither Wolf nor Elsa nor I liked it. We knew that those bombs were killing men only a quarter of a mile away. Michael rushed out to join his pals who had, he said, found a fine place to watch the bombing.

"Kids have no sense of fear," Wolf Cegla said gravely. "Perhaps it's just as well."

The four planes, having discharged their obscene duty, turned south and we came in from the balcony and tried to make believe that it had never happened and that it would not happen again in a few hours. We talked of things that Mrs. Jones might talk of to a visiting Palestinian correspondent.

"I suppose by American standards we lead a very quiet life," Wolf Cegla said. "I work pretty hard. We begin at the office at eight and I seldom get home until seven. Except on Friday, when we quit before sundown."

"And then you bring me flowers," Elsa said softly.

Wolf looked embarrassed. "It's a sort of custom to bring flowers home on Friday."

"We go out sometimes," Elsa said. "About once in two weeks we go out to dinner at the Park Hotel and usually I manage to persuade him to take me to the Kaete Dan for tea on Saturday afternoon."

The Kaete Dan terrace is always crowded on Saturday afternoons. People come to have tea or coffee and to watch one of nature's best performances: sunset over the Mediterranean.

"And we do go to the movies," Elsa said. "Especially when there is an Ingrid Bergman picture in town. My husband is in love with Ingrid Bergman."

They smiled with easy companionship and understanding. So Mr. and Mrs. Jones of America might have smiled. And Elsa talked of the hairdresser on Allenby Road she went to every other week and how it cost her three dollars for a hairdo and a manicure. She told of a new dressmaker she had found. She had just had a lovely linen dress made. Expensive? Of course, she laughed. The dress cost sixty dollars, but it was worth it. She looked at her husband.

"Yes, my dear," he said tenderly. "It was well worth it."

It was time now for the two o'clock news, so Wolf turned on the radio. It was a radio made in Holland and it cost a hundred and twenty dollars. None of the news was good, so Wolf turned the radio off.

"Things are going to be difficult for a long time," he said. "But we will survive. We seem to have some pretty level-headed men in our government."

"What party do you belong to?" I asked.

"No party at all," he answered. "I suppose I am what you in America would call a middle-of-the-roader. In fact, I am a little to the right of the middle. But I am not interested in politics."

"Nor am I," Elsa said firmly. "And there's a concert of the Philharmonic next Wednesday. Don't forget we have tickets."

"I won't," Wolf said, "and now it is time I got back to the office."

And I left too. Just another ordinary, pleasant family—the Ceglas. But Israel, like most countries, is made up of ordinary, pleasant families with kids who like to follow fire engines—or watch Egyptian Spitfires dropping bombs.

When I returned to the Kaete Dan there was a message from the Czechoslovakian Airlines. They were bringing a plane in tomorrow and it would leave immediately for Rome. Would I

126

like passage on it? Would I? I had a date with one small blonde wife in Rome. No passenger plane had entered or left the country since my Air France plane had landed at Lydda in April. The man told me to be at the office on Ben Yehuda Street at seven the next morning. If the Egyptian planes followed their usual custom, they would bomb the port and airfield around six and not return until around nine. That would give the Czech plane time enough to land and take off.

That night I said good-bye to men I hadn't known a few weeks ago but who now seemed old and valued friends. I went to Piltz' to see kind and gentle Joseph Rosenblueth. We had a farewell drink and then I heard an unmistakable English accent asking for whisky and soda. The voice sounded familiar and when I turned I saw a lanky, grinning man in civilian clothes who let out a very un-English yell. The last time I'd seen him was in London and he was then in the uniform of an R.A.F. squadron leader. He had come to London to be given his D.S.O. and had stayed with me at the Savoy. He was one of the few Battle of Britain fighter pilots who had survived.

"You two know each other?" Joseph asked.

"But for years," the squadron leader smiled. "My God, Quent, do you remember the time . . . ?"

It would serve no purpose to mention the name of the squadron leader. It wouldn't do him any good in London. He was about thirty-four now and he had a plane of his own which he chartered. He had just arrived at Haifa that afternoon.

"I've made about fifteen trips here," he said gaily. "I bring supplies and personnel from London. What kind of supplies?" His voice was bland but his eyes were mocking. "Garden seeds, old boy, and Bovril, and now and then some sprouts. The personnel I bring? Tourists, my friend, just tourists. But they pay well. I am a businessman now with a charter to transport freight and personnel from London to Athens. But I am such a godawful navigator that I keep losing my way and always end up in Haifa."

"I never knew you were a Jew," I said.

"Let's have the other half," he said to the bartender, and then to me, "I'm not a Jew, far as I know. Good old Church of England since the Battle of Hastings. I'm a businessman, chum: that's why I deliver packages and people here every week."

"They would grab your license pretty quick back home if they knew about these trips," I said.

"They would take a very dim view of it," he said cheerfully. "But I'm a pilot, not a bloody politician. These are nice people here and why shouldn't I fly stuff in for them? I'm not the only one who does it, you know."

"Mr. Bevin wouldn't like it."

"Bloody fool, Mr. Bevin," he laughed. "Remember what we thought of the Arabs when we were in Cairo? Now all of a sudden they're our little brown brothers."

A dozen men came in and they all greeted the ex-squadron leader. "Lost your way again?" one Haganah officer asked.

The pilot shook his head sadly. "Must take some lessons in navigation. Or buy a new compass. Mine is two points off. Had a nice easy trip this time," he told me. "Amazing thing. I had three passengers—all tourists, mind you—but it developed that each one could pilot an aircraft. Imagine that? So I slept most of the time and they took turns piloting my crate."

"Maybe they'll be sitting there in a day or two taking care of the Gyppos," I suggested.

"How can you even suggest such a thing," he said mockingly. "They're just tourists out for a holiday."

Back at the Kaete Dan I asked Sam Federman to have me called at six. "Those Spitfires will probably take care of the call," he laughed. Franz Winkler was there, and the banker was in high spirits. At last a letter had come through from Jerusalem; his wife and child were safe.

"Let's have one last swim together in the morning," he said, and that seemed like a good idea. The Spitfires did awake us about five-thirty. Franz and I slipped into trunks and walked down to the beach. Even at this hour there were perhaps two or three hundred bathers in the cool water. Many were Home Guard men who had just finished the night's duty. Others were the usual Tel Aviv businessmen taking a dip before heading for their offices.

Back at the hotel, Paul had an amazing breakfast waiting: a small steak, a great rarity in Israel because all beef must be imported. Moshe Brilliant and his wife had sent a present for my wife, a lovely black leather handbag with gold clips made in Tel Aviv. And Franz Winkler gave me an etching by Herman Struck, a truly fine artist. There was a third present in a long white box. I thought it was a box of flowers. It wasn't—not quite. It was a Sten gun. On the wooden stock of the gun was an engraved plaque. Sam Federman translated the Hebrew. It read: "To Quentin Reynolds, a friend of Irgun Zvai Leumi." This was a little embarrassing because my admiration was all directed toward the Haganah, the Palmach and the people of the country. But it would be an interesting reminder of this stay in Israel. I put the wooden stock in my bag and distributed the more lethal-looking barrel, bullet clip and trigger in different pockets of my trench coat. Then I took off for the air terminal on Ben Yehuda Street.

At the office we were told that the Czech plane was en route from Athens but that Israel airport officials had wirelessed it not to land because the raid of that morning had done some damage to the runway. So we had to go to Haifa, some eighty miles north. We piled into cars for the trip. The road to Haifa was, technically, clear, but each of our drivers had a gun alongside him and we were preceded by a car in which there were a half dozen Haganah men. On the outskirts of Haifa we saw a rather amazing sight. This was a region of Arab farms and we saw hundreds of Arabs working peacefully in the fields. They didn't even look up as our caravan passed. Haifa itself was badly damaged. Here, early in April, the Haganah had scored perhaps its most amazing victory.

The fighting had been house-to-house and the center of the city looked like a miniature Stalingrad. From the looks of the rubble it was obvious that the Haganah had been clever with grenade and explosive; the destruction was the kind you associate with heavy shelling and heavy bombing from the air. But the Haganah had no heavy artillery and no bomber planes. This had all been accomplished by the Commando tactics of getting in close and blasting.

As we reached the big field a DC-3 circled and landed, and within a few moments we were off. The shoreline of Israel began to recede. It was impossible not to reflect upon the happenings of the past weeks and come to certain conclusions. There were tough times ahead for the new nation but you knew, somehow, that nothing could crush it. You couldn't rationalize this conviction any more than you could rationalize the conviction you had in 1941 that the British could not lose.

The people of Israel were completely on their own. But they weren't counting on any outside help—not even divine help. Not once during the weeks I had been in Israel had I heard anyone say, "We will win because God is with us." They were realists and they felt that God maintains a sort of brooding neutrality in war. It wasn't that the people of Israel were irreligious; they attended their temples about as often as people in America attend church. The percentage of the devout in Israel was proportionately about the same as the percentage of the devout in Chicago or London. This was not a "holy" war to the people of Israel. It was a war for their land, and there was no hypocrisy about invoking divine power in the fight. In Israel men did not wear their faith on their sleeves; they carried it in their hearts.

I recalled attending the fights at Madison Square Garden with Toots Shor, Bob Hannegan and a priest. Nearly all of the fighters, while waiting for the bell to ring, blessed themselves. Toots Shor, the restaurant philosopher, said, "I wonder if that helps a boy in the ring." The priest had smiled and said softly,

"Only if he can fight." It was like that in Israel. They were not depending upon divine intervention; they were depending upon their arms, their skill and their courage. This attitude sometimes shocked the members of the Mizrachi (the orthodox Jewish party) who thought of the war only in terms of a religious crusade. The Palmach and Haganah lads knew that war was nothing but organized murder and that victory went to the one more skilled in the science of murder. They had exactly the same spirit which had made our Marine Corps so great. Israel was not using the Talmud or the Torah as weapons; she was using her young strength and it was paying off.

Her military victory seemed assured and that in itself was a miracle. Once fifty-one nations had decided that this land should be a Jewish National Home and these nations had fixed the boundary. Years later, Great Britain, acting entirely on her own had severed Trans-Jordan (three-quarters of the land) from the mandated territory. Then in November, 1947, the United Nations had amputated again until now but a scant 2,500 square miles of arable land remained of the original 45,000 square miles mandated by the League of Nations. Yet she had fought and won against five sovereign nations who had the physical backing of Great Britain and the moral backing (if you'll forgive the expression) of our own State Department. Her population was 750,000 and she was surrounded by a Moslem (or Arab) population of forty million, yet she had survived. During the past year these incredible people who had to pay for the instruments of war which they needed had somehow managed to raise twelve million dollars as a contribution to the United Jewish Appeal; money earmarked to keep the displaced persons in Europe alive and to bring them to the new state.

Things would be difficult for a long while after peace came, but the internal difficulties were certainly not unsurmountable. Political differences were sharp but no sharper than those faced by England or America, and they would be settled in the democratic manner. Organizations like the Irgun and the Stern Group would have to disband and bow to the will of the people or be classed as outlaws. Israel had a Bill of Rights to protect free speech and honest political nonconformists, but it also had a Sedition Act (much like ours) and the punishment for treason was death. This would probably have to be invoked more than once by the young nation.

The struggle of Israel was, I thought, a tremendous tribute to the democratic spirit. The fight for existence had been conducted within a framework of democratic government which not even in the darkest hours had been allowed to degenerate into a police state. There were twelve daily newspapers in Tel Aviv, representing all shades of political opinion, and there had never been any political censorship imposed by the government. They could, and occasionally did, criticize the government and the Haganah to their heart's content.

The Czech DC-3 slid smoothly along and the stewardess (she too wore the inevitable lacquered smile on her broad face) asked in slow precise English if I'd like to see some London papers. England, judging by the newspapers, seemed to be in a state close to chaos.

The contrast between the England I was reading about and the country I had just left was sharp. The whole tone of the London newspapers was that of discouragement. The whole spirit of Israel, physically exhausted by the war, was that of hope. The young nation had great plans and optimism was in the air. The tremendous military and economic difficulties she still faced were accepted as a challenge. The difficulties England faced (to judge by the papers) were creating nothing but pessimism. However, the newspapers of a country are not always the best reflection of the people. If Great Britain would leave it to the people, their greatness would assert itself. Never had they refused to make even the most severe sacrifices when the life of the country was at stake. Fundamentally they were the same in spirit and in their love for their country as the people I had just left. Israel had just one advantage—her youth.

"We are passing over the ancient islands of Greece," the stewardess said. "Would you like lunch?"

There was bread and a version of Prague pastrami and cheese and a chocolate bar and an orange. The stewardess wanted to practice her English. She was an apple-cheeked girl who had worked in a munitions factory during the occupation of her country.

"We would work so slow," she said, smiling. "The Germans thought we were very stupid. Now and then they would take some of us out and shoot us, then the rest of us worked even slower. When the shells were finished they were always a little too fat or a little too thin and they would fit no gun ever made. It was very droll. Droll? Is that correct?"

Soon we were climbing up the boot of Italy and she gave me a map. We passed over Salerno and the beach gleamed whitely. There was no visible reminder of the wrecked L.C.T.'s and wrecked tanks and wrecked bodies that had littered this beach the last time I had seen it in September, 1943. We skirted Naples, flying low over ground that had been won foot by foot back in 1943, but now you saw nothing but soft green valleys and terraced hills blooming with vines and fruit. It hadn't taken nature long to hide the hideous scars of war. Finally the sturdy plane circled and came down to a nice landing at the airport called Ciampino.

I put on my trench coat and my knees buckled under the weight of it. The customs men were waiting with the usual anticipatory gleam in their eyes. They looked at my big bag and typewriter and one of them rubbed his hands happily as though he just knew the bag was filled with atomic bombs or nylon stockings.

"You are allowed two hundred cigarettes," he said.

"I've only got two packages left," I told him truthfully.

"What have you to declare?" he demanded sternly.

"Not a thing," I answered.

"In that case," he said, making a chalk mark on the bag and the typewriter, "there is no use opening these bags. Welcome to Italy," he added, and I immediately decided we should send an extra billion dollars to this country under ERP.

There were cabs waiting and I climbed into one. We drove through the outskirts of Rome and finally reached the city. The car stopped at a street intersection. The driver, who up to now had said nothing, turned a smiling face and said, "American cinema, hey?" and pointed to a huge sign. There was the scowling face of Paul Muni, tommy gun in hand, and in big red letters the word, *Scarface*.

CHAPTER EIGHT

There *was* a lot of mail for me at the Grand Hotel and I lay in a hot bath and read it leisurely. There was a cable from an old friend, Ulrich Calvosa, formerly picture editor of *Collier's* and now with Transatlantic Films, saying that he was en route, and, most important of all, was a cable from Ginny that she had arrived in Paris and would be in Rome the next morning.

The Grand Hotel in Rome is old but time has been kind to it. If the drapes on the windows are faded and if the carpet is worn, they still retain a kind of shabby elegance. Meerschaum pipes, brandy, violins and Bing Crosby are about the only things I know which improve with age and the Grand Hotel must be included in that list.

I assembled my Sten gun and then, suddenly realizing that it might not win me friends among the hotel servants, shoved it under the bed.

135

Now my job was to get acquainted with Rome. I walked around the city and that night sat and watched the fountains playing in the Piazza Colonna, a block from the hotel. The plane from Paris was due at the unearthly hour of 4:30 A.M. I ordered a car for three-thirty and it sped me through the dark streets to Ciampino. We were halfway there when a terrific lightning and thunder storm broke. The rain lashed the car and not even the windshield wiper could give the driver any visibility. I thought with horror of Ginny, who has an almost pathological fear of flying, up in that storm. When she had to fly she began her preparations about eight hours before the trip. She began with all kinds of capsules to ward off air sickness and just before the take-off she always took a sleeping pill. She would go through this routine even for a fifty-minute flight from New York to Boston. When she entered a plane she would sit down, grasp the arms of the seat with an iron grip, and look straight ahead. Then she would enter what appeared to be a cataleptic state.

There was a small restaurant at the airport and a day-old copy of the *Rome American,* an amazing little daily published by some former *Yank* men. It devoted a full page to baseball at home and I saw that John Mize was leading the league in home runs and that DiMag was hitting above .300. Everything at home was normal.

The thunder and lightning continued until the plane landed. I envisioned a gray-faced, miserable, sick girl alighting from the big American Overseas Airline Constellation. The passengers emerged one by one, but no blonde appeared. Finally the two pilots emerged from the cabin and with them was my wife. She was chatting gaily with the two good-looking pilots.

She introduced me to them. "They let me sit up in the pilot's compartment," she said excitedly. "I practically flew the plane."

"Didn't the storm bother you?" I asked anxiously.

"What storm?" She looked bewildered. "We never hit a bump the whole way."

136

Back at the Grand I told Ginny I had brought her a present from Israel and added that it was under the bed. She reached down and pulled out the Sten gun. I should have known that no girl is going to swoon ecstatically over a gun.

"Get rid of this thing," she said coldly. "Hide it somewhere."

I wrapped my old trench coat around it and shoved it into the back of the closet. I was beginning now to feel like the mariner who was stuck with the albatross.

The next morning we went to see His Excellency, James Dunn, American Ambassador to Italy, a handsome and amiable man. When I told him this was our first trip to Rome he shook his head, puzzled.

"That's odd," he smiled. "Rome has been here waiting for you for several thousand years."

During the following weeks we learned to know the city. There is nothing new that anyone can say about Rome. It lives up to all advance notices. Calvosa, who knew Rome thoroughly, had arrived, and he acted as our guide. To me, the most significant ruin in all Rome was the Arch of Titus. This was built in honor of Flavius Sabinus Vespasianus Titus, "divine" son of the Emperor Vespasian, to commemorate his victory over Jerusalem in 70 A.D. On top of the arch is the triumphant inscription: "Judea Is Dead." But down below, on the supporting columns, there is another inscription, repeated a hundred times and carved roughly, as though done with bayonet or knife: *"Am Yisrael Chai"* (Israel Lives). This was the contribution of the Jewish Brigade (incorporated in the British Eighth Army) which fought its way up the boot of Italy to enter Rome in 1944. Nothing in the city so mocked the transitory glory of the old Roman emperors as did these roughly hewn words.

The most impressive sight in all Rome, however, I thought to be the modern catacombs which are called the Ardeatine Caves. Today these Caves are a monument not to the forgotten glory of a mighty Roman city but to the beastliness of a modern Caesar.

In March, 1944, an Italian threw a bomb at a group of German soldiers, killing several of them. In retaliation, the Germans took 335 Italians to the Ardeatine Caves and slaughtered them. About a hundred of these were political prisoners, suspected saboteurs or resistance fighters, many of whom were Jews. The rest they plucked from the streets. After they had machine-gunned them they tossed grenades into the caves and the debris and rubble filled the openings, the Germans hoped forever. But when the Americans liberated Rome one of the things they did was to reopen the caves and clear them. Families and friends identified the bodies of most of the dead. They made rude wooden coffins and today the caves, lighted by candles, form a huge tomb for the 335. Each week relatives of the dead place fresh flowers on the coffins. On each coffin there is a picture of the victim and a brief sketch of his life. About one-third of the dead are Jews, and a Star of David adorns the coffins in which they lie.

The air in the caves was remarkably fresh and cool and heavily scented by the flowers. There was a story in the life and death of each of these 335 men. Here was the oddly named General Simone Simone, born in 1880, and on the top of his coffin were six medals he had won fighting for Italy. Here were twins, Umberto and Bruno Bucca, two handsome seventeen-year-old lads who were laughing merrily in the pictures which stood on their coffins. Here was twenty-two-year-old Armando Lucarelli, a medical student, and here, Adolfo Caviglia (Jewish), a pilot. Here, rather incongruously, was the picture of a grim-looking youngster in boxing trunks; this was Angelo Aldo, twenty-two, lightweight champion of Italy. Here was Gino Dulio, seventeen, and, next to him, Professor Paolo Petrucci, venerable and bearded. Here was Colonel Roberto Rendena, veteran of three wars, and here a very small coffin, with a sign on it, "Unidentified."

More than the bodies of 335 men lies in this tomb; here

fascism, too, lies buried, and if another totalitarian leader should ever arise in Italy the people would need no other eloquence than the mute story of the Ardeatine Caves to shout him down.

Rome is a golden city at its best at dawn and at sunset. But the most attractive thing about Rome is its people. As I came to know them better, I was pleasantly surprised to find that they actually liked Americans. This liking was too obviously sincere and widespread to be inspired merely by economic necessity. If you didn't have enough lire to tip a waiter or cabdriver adequately, he would shrug and say, "Next time." Decency and honesty had survived, despite the fact that for twenty-three years they had been crushed under fascist rule.

Prices were reasonable in Rome and there was no great gap between the prices in ordinary side-street bistros and those in well-known luxury restaurants like Alfredo's, which admits modestly that it makes the best *fettuccini* in the world, and Passetto's in Via Zanardelli which, as far as we were concerned, could have boasted that it served the best food in the world.

Nearly every afternoon about five, Ginny, Cal and I would join the crowd at Donay's, a sidewalk café next to the Excelsior Hotel on Via Veneto. Here the Italian equivalent of café society met each afternoon to see and be seen. Here well-dressed men and women sat and ate *gelati* or drank coffee and discussed the state of the world, the price of cigarettes and other subjects discussed at five in the afternoon by the idle rich the world over. We met an old friend of mine, Count Giovanni Perdicari, who had lived in New York during the thirties and who somehow had survived the war years in Rome without losing his sense of humor or his health. Even the youngsters diving under tables to reclaim cigarette butts tossed to the pavement knew "Johnny" Perdicari. And Johnny knew everyone.

A beautiful girl would emerge from the Excelsior and look

for a seat at one of the sidewalk tables. "She is a countess," Johnny would inform us. "Very lovely woman."

Another girl would emerge, squinting in the sunlight, and again Johnny would explain that she, too, was a countess. It seemed as though the Excelsior catered only to women with titles. Ginny finally asked him, "Just what is an Italian countess?"

It was obvious that he had been waiting for this question. "An Italian countess, my dear," he said cheerfully, "is a tart who lives at the Excelsior."

Johnny held court here at Donay's as he had once held court at "21" in New York, and, as always, when Johnny was around, no one else was permitted to pick up a check. Well-groomed, handsome men stopped to greet Johnny at our table.

"That Alfredo who just left is a fine man," Johnny would say. "He owns a textile factory in Milan and in the last election he did great work for the Christian Democrat Party. A real good man—what you would call in America a pillar of the church. He has a fine wife and six children."

"Is that his wife with him?" Ginny nodded toward a sleek, dark girl with a mink stole around her shoulders, who had come out of the Excelsior to join Alfredo at another table.

"Good God, no!" Johnny seemed shocked. "That is his mistress. She is very sweet, that girl. She has been his mistress for nearly eight years."

"He doesn't sound exactly like a pillar of the church to me," Ginny said.

"Here in Italy we never confuse morality and religion," Johnny said. "Some of our most religious citizens are completely immoral. And of course some of our most moral citizens are sadly lacking in religion."

"Sounds very confusing," I admitted.

"Not at all," Johnny said earnestly. "Our customs are hallowed by tradition. Always in Italy men made a distinction between morality and religion. Every man marries young and has children. This is his duty to his Church and his country.

140

Then, when he can afford it, he takes a mistress as a matter of course. But you cannot say," Johnny added sternly, "that such a man is irreligious."

A newsboy passed and Johnny bought a copy of *Il Tempo*. "There is a story here that explains what I meant to say about morality," he said. "The *Giro d'Italia* is being held now. The *Giro* is our biggest sport event—a bicycle race around Italy. Now these championship bicycle riders are great heroes in Italy, greater even than baseball or boxing heroes in America. For years the course of the *Giro* has been the same and the riders are accustomed to staying in the same hotels at each stop. They are accustomed to the same food they get each year and to the service given by these hotels.

"Now they threaten a strike," Johnny continued, pointing to the newspaper article. "Why? Because they find that the hotels en route have given the regular chambermaids and waitresses vacations and have replaced the usual attractive girls who hold these jobs with old harridans. The bicycle riders have made a formal protest against this. The riders say they are being discriminated against. For years the pretty maids and waitresses have—how shall I say it?—co-operated with the tired riders who arrive exhausted and who need the proper kind of relaxation. To make it worse, the riders claim that local swains, aware of the great attraction the athletes have for local girls, have been affecting the distinctive dress of the riders and are posing as champion bicyclists. By the time a rider has a hot bath, a bit of a rest, and is ready for relaxation he finds that the local girls are all out with these pseudo-athletes who are busy garnering the fruits of their fame.

"I am quoting literally from this article in an eminently respectable newspaper," Johnny said. "The riders insist that they either be put up at what they call 'non-rationed' hotels or that the pretty hotel employees be recalled from their vacations at hotels which are to be visited during the remaining week of the race. Today the management of the *Giro* is meeting to decide what to do. If the decision is unfavorable the riders say they will go on strike.

"Could this happen in any other country? I doubt it. I am sure most of these athletes are religious but, after all, if a man has been cycling over mountain roads for eight hours he does need relaxation, and not the kind of relaxation given by a seventy-year-old waitress."

The next day the management announced that the demands of the riders had been met and that henceforth there would be no further "rationing" of female hotel employees. It is an odd commentary that in Italy and France, where religion is so important, morality is relatively unimportant. But some-one else can write the sermon to explain that. I just don't understand it.

Ginny and I haunted the film studios and met the great Rossellini and other leading directors. One day we visited the Centro Sperimentale di Cinematografia (Moving Picture Experimental Center) at Cinecitta on the Frascati Road just a few miles outside of Rome. Director Luigi Chiarini was rehearsing a couple of talented students. The great Alida Valli, now a Hollywood star, had once listened to Chiarini on this set. Such established favorites in Italian films as Clara Calamai, Adriene Benetti, Mariella Lotti, Elena Zareschi, had once been students here at the Centro Sperimentale di Cinematografia. Andrea Checchi, one of Italy's foremost stars, had been only eighteen when he had studied here under Director Chiarini, and Massimo Serrato, too, had gone on to find screen fame after graduating from the school.

During the past three years the whole film world has been startled at the excellence of Italian pictures. When *Open City, Shoeshine, Paisan* and *To Live in Peace* and a dozen other superb films appeared in succession, American, British, French and South American critics began to realize that *Open City,* the first of the series, had been no accident. The Italian film industry had approached the point where it could successfully challenge the products of any film capital. But how had they

142

done it? Italy was economically bankrupt. Long ago the Germans had removed her film equipment out of the country. Most of her studios had been bombed, and the electric power needed to feed the powerful arc lights was weak, erratic and constantly going awry. Italy's directors had been working with obsolete, broken-down sound equipment.

The answer quite obviously can be given in one word—talent. What the film makers of Italy lack in equipment they make up in trained personnel. The Experimental Center at Cinecitta in itself is not, of course, responsible for the solid success of recent Italian films; it is merely an indication of the attitude of Italian film makers. The school was part of a grandiose scheme Mussolini had had of building a super Hollywood. He had also constructed large modern studios complete with sound stages, and named the whole plant "Cinecitta." Here there would be produced glossy, sugar-coated film packages which would sell his brand of Fascism to the world. It was beginning to produce at full blast when the war interrupted. The studios were all damaged by bombing, but the large white stucco building which housed the school was marked on every Allied air map with a red cross. It had been converted into a prisoner of war camp for British officers and it escaped destruction.

The war was hardly over when youngsters began applying for scholarships to the school. Each year some two thousand budding actors, directors, script writers and technicians beg to be admitted. Written and oral examinations are given the young hopefuls and the two hundred who seem most promising are selected. They are given an intensive two-year course, all at government expense. The standards of the school are so high that graduates are assured of jobs on graduation. During their final year they gain practical experience by working in the near-by studios as extras, assistant directors, or technical men.

An Italian director does not conform to any pattern. Unlike his Hollywood colleague, he is not rigidly bound by "front-office" policies nor is he plagued by having to hire relatives of the boss. In Italy the director is almost invariably the producer of his picture, and usually he is the writer as well. Just to make his job more difficult, he has to go out and raise the money to make it and then arrange for its distribution.

At the moment, Roberto Rossellini, maker of *Open City* and *Paisan,* and Vittorio de Sica, who gave *Shoeshine* to the world, are the leaders in the making of realistic Italian films. Under the Fascist regime Rossellini was a little-known producer of pictures which showed the habits and family life of fish. De Sica was a handsome, romantic stage actor who concealed his other talents lest they be regimented by Il Duce. Neither emerged until the liberation of Italy, and then both threw off the shackles which had bound Italian art for twenty-three years, to plunge boldly into making pictures which showed Italy as it was.

Roberto Rossellini is a kindly man who practically never loses his temper. Those who have worked with him for years will tell you that they only saw him blow his top once. He was directing a simple scene in which Anna Magnani was to cross a field. Magnani had gone through several rehearsals and everything was ready. Rossellini called "Action," but his cameraman cried out, "Just a moment, Boss." He left his camera, ran out on the field, picked up a large white rock and carried it out of camera range.

"Why do you do that?" Rossellini asked ominously.

"All the rocks in this field are dark gray or brown," the cameraman said cheerfully. "Looking through the lens I noticed that one white rock. It sort of stood out like a sore thumb so I wanted to get rid of it."

Rossellini exploded. This field had been there a hundred, maybe a thousand years, he told his cameraman. It had taken nature that long to fashion the field, to distribute and color the rocks. What right had he, the cameraman, to think he could improve on nature? Still hurling invectives at the open-mouthed cameraman, Rossellini replaced the white rock. Then he waved the offender away and took his place behind the camera. He shot the rest of the picture himself.

Rosselini's passion for realism is well known. It has also brought him the accolades of film critics wherever pictures are shown. Ever since his disturbing, tragic *Open City* startled the world's film centers, the Rossellini cult has grown, and today there are many thoughtful picturemakers in London, Paris and Hollywood who insist that Rossellini is the greatest living director.

A Rossellini picture is a complete one-man show. He does not work from a shooting script but from an outline. He concocts dialogue and additional scenes as he goes along. Occasionally he uses a script written by someone else, but he never sticks to it. Rossellini, a dark, handsome man of forty with troubled eyes, is a complete individualist who recently turned down a seven-year Hollywood offer that would have earned him about four million dollars. The day he spurned the offer he had to sneak ignominiously out of the waiters' entrance of the Excelsior Hotel, because a dozen irate creditors were holding down chairs in the front lobby. One day I was waiting for Rossellini in that same lobby. Every chair was occupied in the large lounge. Rossellini's assistant indicated the waiting figures.

"Half of those people are here to borrow money from Roberto," he said sadly. "The others are here because he owes them money. I have orders to borrow more from those he owes money to, so he can take care of those who want to borrow from him."

Rossellini is probably the softest touch in Rome. On one of his recent pictures he listed as co-authors four impoverished friends. None of them had contributed a line to the picture, but screen credits are as important in Rome as they are in Hollywood, and within a week the four friends had all received offers and had signed up with other film companies, which then boasted that they had "grabbed four of Rossellini's best writers."

Rossellini was a hard man to catch. They said that he was shy, that he was terrified of being interviewed, and that he was temperamental. His assistant finally said that Rossellini would see me if I promised to leave after five minutes. He was very busy and that was all the time he could spare. We met in the lounge of the Excelsior, sat down, and talked for three hours. Being reasonably honest, I must admit that it was not entirely my charm which kept him in his seat; I had brought Ginny along and his director's eye (well, maybe it was his director's eye) lit up when he saw her and before we had finished even one glass of champagne he had offered her a part in a new picture he was planning, and then, as a rather obvious after-thought, he asked me politely and with charming insincerity if I'd like to help him write the new picture. Rossellini was neither shy nor temperamental nor terrified; he was charming, frank and completely honest in his self-appraisal as well as honest in his opinion of the work of other directors. He was the kind of man you want to meet again.

Although *Open City* made plenty of money in the world film centers, Rossellini lost about six hundred dollars on it. He had to sell everything he owned to finish *Open City,* including his furniture, his watch, his car, and, what hurt him most, a large oversize bed he had always cherished. He borrowed from every-one he knew, and then to satisfy these debts he sold the picture outright to the first person who came along with an offer.

"It is different today," Rossellini told me earnestly. "Today I am wealthy. I do not mean I have any money, but I have credit. Now I can borrow almost anything I want."

Germany, Year Zero, which he made in Berlin, is the current Rossellini picture showing in Italy. It is a stark, tragic picture of Berlin today. The protagonist is a ten-year-old boy who supports his family by stealing. The boy's father is a hope-less invalid, and when a degenerate teacher suggests cynically to the boy that the family would be better off with the old man dead, the boy puts poison in his tea. It is very strong meat, and even Italian audiences, more accustomed to realism

146

than most, squirm at the depths of human depravity portrayed by Rossellini on the screen.

"I don't like the picture much myself," Rossellini said thoughtfully, "but that is what Berlin is like today. A few cigarettes and you can buy anything. Some say that the picture will inspire sympathy for the German people. Why? Everyone in the picture is a monster—even the little boy. I didn't invent these characters. I just found them in Berlin and put them on the screen."

Germany, Year Zero is the most financially ambitious film Rossellini has done. It cost $115,000, but Rossellini explains apologetically that he had to take his staff of nine men to Berlin, and that was expensive. His staff includes his secretary (who also acts as assistant director, assistant cameraman, valet and nursemaid to Rossellini's dog, Micha—which means "cat"), one cameraman, three electricians, two prop men and two friends. Rossellini always takes two friends along with him when he makes a picture outside of Rome.

"I work pretty fast," he explained to me. "I shoot about nine hundred feet of film a day and usually finish a picture in thirty days. But at night, when I am finished work, I want to forget it, so I always have two old friends along and we drink a little wine and talk. Or maybe I wake up one day and just don't feel like working. So my friends and I go to the beach if there is one anywhere around, and swim and lie in the sun."

Rossellini's passion for realism is so great that he seldom uses professional actors in his films. Only one of the cast in *Germany, Year Zero* had ever been in front of a camera before. He believes that actors fake emotions; ordinary people can feel the emotion he wants them to display. If he wishes to portray a parish priest, he gets a parish priest to play the part. Nor does he use make-up on his players. He uses only one camera—he has no camera boom nor does he own a dolly. In Hollywood you often hear someone say admiringly of a

147

director, "He knows how to move the camera." One might say of Rossellini, "He knows how to move people."

Rossellini is gratified but puzzled by the paeans of praise heaped on him by foreign film critics. He squirmed a little when he showed me an article in an English magazine which attempted to explain his technique.

"Technique?" he said. "I have no technique. I get an idea and start shooting. As I go along, the idea develops, or it changes completely. I'm guided only by my instincts, not by any conscious technique. Last month a French group asked me to attend a film conference. I spoke, and then they asked me questions. My God, I was scared! I didn't know what they were talking about. They asked me about my technique of photography and how I managed to bring my characters to life. I was panic-stricken. I couldn't say, 'Look, it all comes from inside. I do these things by instinct, not by technique. I don't know anything about technique.' They would have thought me very ignorant. Then, by some lucky chance, the building where this conference was being held caught fire. Everyone yelled 'Fire!' I was the first one out of there and I never went back."

In Italy they say that Rossellini is a poet who just happens to use the camera instead of the pen. It is a fair estimate.

In our discussion of actors the name of Anna Magnani naturally came up first. It was she who made such a tremendous hit in *Open City*. A bit player until she came under Rossellini's influence, today La Magnani, as she is known to all Italy, is generally regarded as one of the world's foremost portrayers of dramatic parts. Rossellini says quite simply that she is a genius, the greatest since Duse.

"There is no one alive to equal her," Rosselini says emphatically.

A great many critics agree with Rossellini. Magnani at forty has the same genius for projecting tragedy on the screen that Judith Anderson showed us last season on the stage in *Medea*. Rossellini showed us a new Magnani picture which he

148

hadn't finished cutting. No music had been dubbed in as yet, but even sitting in a projection room alone, her performance shook us both. The picture is called *Love*, and it is divided into two episodes. The first is based on Cocteau's *La Voix Humaine*, and it is merely a forty-minute telephone conversation in which Magnani talks to the lover who has just discarded her. Here Magnani does things that perhaps no actress of our time has ever done. During the forty minutes she projects virtually every human emotion possible on the screen. The other half of *Love* is *The Miracle*, and again Magnani carries the whole burden. Unconventional in its spiritual theme, *The Miracle* packs a terrific emotional punch and most certainly takes the props from under those critics of Rossellini who maintain that he is only the master of documentaries.

Vittorio de Sica is of the same realistic school. He was universally acclaimed when *Shoeshine* came out, but the world's acclamation didn't help him to finance another picture, and he was idle for nearly two years. Now he was making *Bicycle Thieves*, another story of human misery in Rome. It is a story of peasants and factory workers, and de Sica uses peasants and factory workers as his players. I watched de Sica shooting some outdoor scenes in front of an old church for *Bicycle Thieves*. A group of shabby workmen and their wives stood waiting for de Sica's word.

"None of these people has ever acted before," de Sica said. "I went to the Breda Factory here in Rome and asked if I could borrow some men and women for a few days. I picked out these thirty and told them to report today in their oldest clothes."

The shooting of pictures has become so commonplace in Rome that no crowds were gathered in front of the church and no police were there to keep the curious out of camera range. It was all done so smoothly that you knew a great deal of preparation had gone before, and that de Sica's assistants were well trained.

"Oh, yes," de Sica said. "I rehearse a great deal. Film costs money, and we can't waste money on retakes. But fortunately these aren't actors trying to hog the camera or intrude their own personalities into the picture. These are just people—and they act like people."

De Sica has his own way of doing things, but he has a great deal of admiration for certain Hollywood directors. His eyes lit up when he talked of Henry King, Frank Capra, and King Vidor. What did he think Italy had that Hollywood didn't have?

"Authentic scenery and sun," de Sica laughed. "Look at that church. Tomorrow we are going to shoot inside it. It would cost Hollywood fifty thousand dollars to build a set of this type. It costs me very little. I give the priest of the church ten thousand lire (twenty dollars) for the poor of his parish.

"If I want to use the Colosseum I have to move my camera only a few blocks and there it is. I pay these people the same wages they get in their factory. We would be crazy to attempt any competition with Hollywood. We can't afford it—and they have learned to do certain things far better than we can. But for realistic pictures with authentic backgrounds, I think Italy is far ahead."

Rossellini, de Sica, Zampa, Soldatti, Vergano, Lattuada, and a dozen others are following this creed of realism. Sometimes the truth is a bit too unpalatable for American taste, and because of that many of the finest Italian pictures will not be shown in New York. Alberto Lattuada's film, *Without Pity,* which deals with the friendship between a Negro G.I. and an Italian girl, is such a picture. Such friendships were, of course, common in Italy during the frenzied days following the liberation, and because they did occur, usually with tragic, sometimes with happy, consequences, Lattuada felt compelled to make *Without Pity.*

The Italian film industry has set a fast pace and a high standard for itself. Whether or not it will be able to maintain it depends upon how flexible the Rossellinis, the de Sicas and the Lattuadas are. Up to now they have faithfully mirrored the crime, the poverty, the anguish of postwar Italy. But Italy is changing. Today the people of Italy are working. De Gasperi, Ambassador James Dunn, and ERP boss Averell Harriman have convinced them that they will receive the benefits of what they, the Italians, call the "Piano Marshall" only as long as they use the material sent them to build an economically strong Italy. Order has come to Italy. Crime, and to some extent poverty, do not loom as large in the Italian scene as they did a year ago. Since the election the country has settled down to back-breaking work.

I had met several Italian working-class families by now and had heard their stories and listened to their hopes and their dreams. The story of the Croccolinos is the story of nearly thirty million Italians who today are feeling their way warily under the system of government which we call democracy. In the long run, the success of democracy in Italy and the country's economic rebirth will depend upon the Croccolinos of Italy. Only a few months ago they rejected Communism in the belief that democracy plus the Marshall Plan would put the country on its feet. If the democratic regime collapses, the Communists will say, "We told you so," and start laying plans for another election which might have a different result. If Giovanni Croccolino decides that he likes democracy and the Marshall Plan is able to drag Italy out of the economic swamp in which she has been mired for years, Italy may eventually become the strongest democratic state in Europe. That is why Signor Croccolino is so important.

Giovanni Croccolino, at thirty-five, has never been able to foresee a secure future. For twenty-three years he lived under Fascist rule and his earliest memories are the sounds of Mussolini rattling his "eight million bayonets" and boasting of worlds which his army would conquer.

When war came, Giovanni was driving a produce truck from Citta Della Pieve to Rome. He had married a slim, attractive girl, Valinda, and they had rented a house in Citta. He was excused from military duty because his job of delivering food was considered essential, and life didn't look too bad. Then came that fateful day in September, 1943, when Italy made a separate peace, and the Germans, from half-hearted allies, became active enemies. Giovanni and Valinda had spent all their savings to furnish their rented house. A few days after the separate peace was signed the Germans fell upon them like a horde of locusts. They stripped Giovanni's house of all its furniture; they ripped the gold bracelet from Valinda's wrist and they took the little gold wedding ring from her finger. They even took the clothes which Valinda had bought for Silvio, their son who was nearly two then. Destitute, Giovanni brought his wife and child to Rome. But he soon found a job—he is a good mechanic—and has been working ever since. Today he repairs cars in the big Fiat garage in the Via Umbria.

I picked up Giovanni at the garage one Saturday afternoon at six-thirty—he had started work at 8 A.M.—and drove him home to a long row of workers' shacks, without heat or electricity. These were to be pulled down soon, Giovanni said, and replaced by modern, low-cost apartments. Silvio, Mario, a younger son, and an excited dog named Musetta, gave Giovanni a tumultuous welcome and his dark face lit up in a smile. We went into the low-ceilinged dining room where Valinda was waiting. Giovanni noticed her purse lying on the table. He picked it up, opened it and laughed ruefully. "Always the same," he said, shaking his head. "Valinda is a good manager, but she can never quite make my salary cover the cost of food."

"I had to borrow three hundred lire this morning," Valinda said. "Thank goodness it is Saturday."

Giovanni makes a salary of eight thousand lire a week (sixteen dollars). Valinda says that it costs one thousand lire (two dollars) a day to feed her family. That leaves only one thousand lire a week for rent, candles, clothing and incidentals. There was a time when the Croccolinos of Italy lived on spaghetti, but today flour is scarce and expensive. Spaghetti is a luxury to be indulged in only once a week.

"What do we usually eat?" Valinda shrugged her shoulders. "We always have the same breakfast. I cook an egg for each of the children and one for Giovanni. With coffee and bread, that is our breakfast. Giovanni takes a sandwich to work with him and the children and I have soup and bread for lunch. At night we have minestrone and fish. I usually get some fruit for the children. And on Sunday we have meat or spaghetti. Cake? Pastry?" Valinda laughed. "We have cake on Christmas Day and on Easter Sunday."

"And we go to the movies, Valinda and I," Giovanni said, smiling. "Once a week we go to the movies and that is our life on eight thousand lire a week. And we are much better off than friends of ours who make more than that because Valinda is such a good manager."

During the elections last April, the Communist Party leaders made glowing promises to the Croccolinos of Italy. They would take the land from the wealthy landowners and give it to the farmers; they would take the factories and give them to the workers. Giovanni listened to the promises but didn't believe them.

"So many workers like myself are ignorant," Giovanni said sadly. "They were fooled by those promises and they voted Communist. It was not because they cared about Communism. But under Fascism we workers had no hope for a better life. During the war and afterward things were even worse. The rich stayed rich and the poor stayed poor. Then the Communists came along with their promises and a lot of poor people believed them. I knew that if they got into power they would forget those promises. I saw no hope in Communism. I voted against Communism. I believe there is only one hope for Italy. That is America. I do not know much about the Marshall Plan, but I hear that it will help industry, give more people work and eventually give us higher wages and more food, and I believe this to be true."

Giovanni Croccolino is not a complicated person. He is an ordinary, decent citizen, proud of his wife and children and willing to work hard to support them. But he is a bewildered man. He has friends in America who write to him quite often and when he reads their letters he is sometimes a little bitter as well as puzzled.

"I have a friend in New York," he said, "who does the same thing I do; he repairs automobiles. But he lives in a five-room apartment. He has electric light and a radio. He has meat nearly every day, and his children have milk and butter. He has a car. Every summer he takes his family to the country for two weeks' holiday. He says he bought war bonds all during the war and one day he will sell them and be able to send his children to college. I know he speaks the truth, but it puzzles me. Why cannot Valinda and I have these things? Why, here in Italy, is there such a big gap between the man who owns a garage and the man who works in one? Is it because you have had democracy for more than a hundred years, perhaps?"

It seemed as good an answer to our relative prosperity as any, and I nodded agreement.

"That is why I voted against Communism," Giovanni said thoughtfully. "If democracy can give my friend who is a mechanic in New York all those things, perhaps in time it will give them to me, a mechanic in Italy. That is why I say America is our only hope.

"Do you not agree, Valinda?" he asked anxiously.

Valinda nodded. "I think so. It is certain that there is no other hope. Today, if we buy clothing we cannot buy food; if we buy food we cannot buy clothing. We are all willing to work hard. We are willing to give our government a chance. There is one thing I will say: there is no grumbling these days as there was under Mussolini or during the war."

"Work?" Giovanni stood up and his dark eyes flashed. "I would work these fingers off. I would starve if I had to for just one thing: just to give my sons an education so when they grow up things will be easier for them."

Croccolino was right. In fact, the only way that Italy can survive is by work—and by self-denial and sacrifice. There are nearly two million unemployed in Italy; the cost of living is almost fifty times higher than prewar; antiquated industrial methods are used in factories and Communists control many trade unions; there has been a terrific increase in population. A casual observer might well throw up his hands and say, "Italy is through. She hasn't a chance."

United States Ambassador James Dunn has made a thorough study of the Italian problem. Dunn has not confined his activities to the drawing rooms of Rome. His figure is as familiar in the factories of Milan or in the agricultural centers of Italy as it is at diplomatic functions.

"If you look only at the balance sheet you get a dismal picture of the economic status of Italy," he told me. "But if you do, you are leaving out the most important factor of all—the people of Italy. They form the real working capital of the country. All the energy and vitality that was suppressed during twenty-three years of 'Fascism are now finding an outlet. The Italians are willing to work their way out of their present plight."

We always come back to our friend, Signor Croccolino and his millions of brothers. If they are willing to tighten their belts and exist on their present admittedly deplorable standard of living for the next three years and if the Italian Government administers the Marshall Plan intelligently, there is every chance that Italy will become self-sufficient—no longer a burden but an independent economic entity able to compete on even terms in the world market. Parenthetically, Italy's recovery is of direct interest to the ordinary American taxpayer. The sooner the nations of democratic Europe get on their feet, the sooner we can stop the heavy drain on our own resources caused by the European Recovery Plan.

Paul Hyde Bonner, economic adviser to the American Embassy in Rome, agrees with Ambassador Dunn that the people of the country are willing to work their way out of national poverty instead of using the Marshall Plan as a temporary belly-filling rain of pasta from heaven.

"The Marshall Plan in its application to a country," Bonner says, "can act either as a vitamin or as morphine. Psychologically, at least, it has acted as a vitamin here in Italy. It has stimulated the people into activity; it has not lulled them into a complacent sleep. It is up to the present government to see that the material sent here under ERP continues to be used as vitamins. I have faith in the integrity and intelligence of this present government and am convinced it will do just that."

"We have a long hard fight ahead of us," says Ivan Mateo Lombardo, energetic Minister of Industry and Commerce. "Naturally, as a coalition government, we have conflicting ideas in the cabinet, but there is one thing we all agree on. That is to use the Marshall Plan in the spirit in which it was offered—not as a temporary stopgap but as a stimulant to building permanent economic prosperity. Some cabinet members believe in completely untrammeled free enterprise. Others believe in a stringent planned economy. My hope is that we will have a happy marriage of free enterprise and planning. Once we have that marriage I believe we will be on our way to recovery. But our greatest asset, I believe, is the willingness of the people to work. Without that, neither the Marshall Plan nor our own governmental planning would be worth anything."

You can't drive around Italy without being impressed with the amount of work already done. During the war more than sixteen thousand bridges were destroyed in the country. Today every one has been repaired or restored. When the Germans retreated they stripped factories of machinery and shipped it back to Germany. In Genoa alone they took forty-three thousand tons of machinery from one manufacturing plant. Some of that machinery was found in the American Zone in Germany and returned, but it was difficult to replace the rest. Yet today the factory is going at full blast.

156

Guido Corbellini, Minister of Transportation, has one of the toughest jobs in Italy, but transport is something he knows. He has been a railroad man all his life and his book, *Technique of Transportation,* has been translated into a dozen languages. Corbellini is typical of the cabinet picked by Premier de Gasperi. With but few exceptions, members of the cabinet are specialists in their fields. I sat in Corbellini's office as he discussed some of his problems.

"The war almost wrecked our whole railroad system," he said. "For instance, we had 150,000 freight cars. Ninety thousand were destroyed. About 80 percent of our passenger trains were wrecked. More than 4,000 railroad stations were destroyed and railroad factories in Verona, Bologna, Firenze and Naples were all damaged severely. Yet we have done considerable rebuilding already and factories are busy now making new equipment. Because of the coal shortage, we hope to completely electrify our railroad system. We think we can do this within three or four years and within that time we expect to have a great deal of brand-new rolling stock. But," he smiled grimly, "it will mean a lot of work."

Many economists will still tell you that Germany in prewar days was Italy's biggest customer. Now that she is penniless, they insist Italy will find it difficult to get new customers. They will point hopelessly to the balance sheet which pictures Italy as mired in red ink.

These economists never meet the Giovanni Croccolinos of Italy nor can they be bothered with such intangible elements as courage and willingness to sacrifice. Maybe the economists will be proved right, but my money and yours (because you and I are financing the Marshall Plan) is on Giovanni Croccolino and the other Italians of good will who, for the first time in their lives, are living with hope in their hearts and faith in the future.

CHAPTER NINE

Averell Harriman came to Rome to discuss ERP with the Italian Government, and while he was in the city he scored a convincing victory over the foes of the Marshall Plan. Harriman held a press conference and when it was over he had representatives of the local Communist papers hanging on the ropes. He answered every question they tossed at him honestly and frankly. He told them bluntly that America was not a charitable institution whose purpose it was to feed the world. He said that America would help Italy as long as Italy helped herself, but that ERP had not been designed to help merely a few industrialists. He talked economics while the frustrated Communist reporters tried to get him to discuss ideologies. He referred them to Secretary of State Marshall's speech of May 7, 1947, at Harvard University, and quoted: "Our policy is not directed against any country or doctrine but against hunger, poverty, desperation and chaos. Its purpose should be a revival of a working economy in the world so as to permit the emergence of political and social conditions in which free institutions can exist."

The Communist paper, *L'Unita,* and the anticlerical paper, *Don Basilio,* couldn't find anything in his answers to attack, so they went to work on him personally. They called him the *"Ambasciatore Gaga."* The word *gaga* doesn't lend itself very well to translation but "fop" would approximate it. *L'Unita* also referred to Harriman contemptuously as one of the ten best-dressed men in America. The Leftist press was hardly accurate in either of these two denunciations (if being a well-dressed man is indeed a denunciation). Harriman hasn't had much time during the past ten years to be either a "fop" or a "well-dressed man." I've been with Harriman in Moscow, London, Washington, Cairo and a few other places during the war, and I would say that only Harry Hopkins ever equaled him in the matter of man hours per week put in at work.

It was rather an amazing commentary on the usually smooth-running Communist propaganda machine that it could turn out nothing more damaging to the Marshall Plan than the fact that Averell Harriman was an *"Ambasciatore Gaga."* Although the election had been over several months, the Communist Party in Italy still seemed stunned by its defeat; they hadn't yet managed to realign their forces.

One night Johnny Perdacari had a dinner party at the Grand Hotel for Ginny. He said he would ask "just a few friends," but when we sat down we found there were twenty-three at the table, most of whom were either cabinet ministers, publishers or diplomats. Ginny sat between Giuseppe Saragat (Vice-President of the Chamber of Deputies and Minister of the Merchant Marine) and Mario Scelba (Minister of the Interior). Neither of the Ministers spoke English, but she managed somehow to make them understand her French. Guido Corbellini, Minister of Transportation, Cesare Merzagora, Minister of Foreign Trade, Attilio Piccioni, Minister without

Portfolio, and Ivan Mateo Lombardo, Minister of Commerce were also present, as was the Count Della Torre, editor and publisher of *L'Osservatore Romano,* the official Vatican daily newspaper.

It was Saragat who had forced the Communists out of his Socialist Party and now he and his fellow ministers were referred to by the Communists as Saragat Socialists. Della Torre, with his high forehead, fringe of thin gray hair, and the neck of a wrestler, looked just what he was—a militant, tough, crusading editor who quite literally feared neither God nor man. Della Torre himself writes all the editorials in the paper and, occasionally, a controversial article.

Ivan Lombardo, Minister of Commerce, who sat next to me, chuckled as he told me of the time the Fascists almost got Torre. The day after Germany invaded Norway, the editor, for the first time, really went to town on Hitler. He called his editorial "The Octopus" and castigated Hitler for throwing the world into war. The vituperative article went all over the world. The Fascist press in both Germany and Italy went after Torre, demanding that he be removed from his job. The Pope remained silent. One day the editor went strolling just outside the Vatican only to be grabbed by two big gendarmes who said they had orders to arrest him. Torre smiled politely and said that he'd be glad to go along with them. The two cops who had expected a fight from the aggressive editor were so relieved that they relaxed their grip on his arms and the Count broke from their grasp and ran into Vatican territory. He never left the 108 acres of Vatican City until Allied troops marched into Rome.

L'Osservatore Romano is undoubtedly the most powerful newspaper in the world. It makes no pretense of being objective. It considers itself a weapon against any foe of Catholicism. Its format is something like that of the *Kansas City Star* or the *Times* of London, but when Torre takes off the gloves and starts to slug it out with *Pravda* he uses invective foreign to both of those staid journals. And Cardinals in New York and Rio and Madrid and London read what he has to say.

There were men representing every party but the Communist Party present that night. The talk was free and unguarded. They even talked freely of de Gasperi, and it was obvious that they all had considerable respect for the Prime Minister.

"When Evita Peron was here we had to receive her," someone remembered. "I had to take her to meet de Gasperi. When the meeting was over, she said in amazement, 'Did you notice his frayed shirt cuffs and the shabby suit he was wearing?' I told her that de Gasperi was a poor man; that he still lived with his family in a three-room walk-up apartment. I told her that he probably couldn't afford new shirts. She looked at me with disbelief in her eyes and asked, 'Poor? Two years in the government and still poor? How can that be?'"

Inevitably, the talk turned to the elections which had put the present coalition government in power.

"What really swung the election?" I asked, and then listened for an hour to the various opinions. The opinion was general (and these were men who had done the active campaigning) that no one single factor beat the Communists. One of them (a Catholic member of the Christian Democratic Party) said that the Church was less of a factor than they had figured. There had been, after all, 8,025,990 Communist votes and virtually all of those voters had been Catholics. The Vatican carried on a campaign that Hague of Jersey City or Kelly of Chicago would have admired. Yet nearly 9,000,000 Italians rejected her pleas. Her best speakers were sent through the country. But just as the precinct captains, working under ward and district leaders, have always been the vital force in any American city election, so the parish priests were the backbone of the Vatican campaign. When Cardinal Schuster of Milan, Cardinal Tisserant of Santa Ruffina or Cardinal Piazza of Venice thundered that Catholics who voted for Togliatti would not receive the sacraments, would not be able

to obtain absolution, and would be refused burial in conse-
crated ground, it was the parish priest who went from door
to door with the warnings. This was especially important in
the rural areas of the South where there were few radios and
few newspapers.

But the Communists continued to make headway. To begin
with, Palmiro Togliatti was (and is) one of the best-trained
politicians in the world. As early as 1921 he organized the
Communist Party in Italy and then, when Mussolini dissolved
the Party, he fled to Moscow for a post-graduate course. He
graduated *cum laude* and for eighteen years acted as a
"trouble shooter" for the Comintern. He returned to Italy in
1944 and found conditions to his liking. The country had been
plundered for twenty-three years and the war had reduced
Italy to chaos. Members of the Italian underground who had
fought so magnificently during the war were persuaded by
him that they belonged with him and the Party. Togliatti
pulled a master stroke when he convinced Moscow to recognize Marshal Badoglio's royalist regime and for this he was
given a cabinet post—the first Communist in history to hold
cabinet rank in Italy. From there on, it was like shooting ele-
phants in a tree.

It wasn't long before his party was the only well-organized,
well-financed and intelligently led group in the country. He
bided his time; he practiced a deceptive moderation in his
policies. He decried the Fascist influence of the Vatican, but
this did not mean that he was anti-Catholic. After all, he reminded his audiences with a friendly smile, his name was
Palmiro. He had been given that name because he had been
born on Palm Sunday. He convinced thousands that Communism and Moscow were not necessarily synonymous. He
was an Italian first and a Communist second. He spoke often
of Communism and democracy and he used the terms inter-
changeably; he converted thousands to the belief that Communism was democracy in its purest form. Meanwhile, he dug
into the labor unions and now he began to use the term "popu-

lar front"—an amalgamation of "all true democratic groups."
Then came his real crowning achievement. He annexed the
left-wing Socialists and thousands followed his Pied Piper,
Pietro Nenni, into the Communist fold. Togliatti called for
land reform, better housing and full employment. He demanded that the government actually collect taxes from the
wealthy instead of merely levying taxes—all much-needed
reforms in Italy. It has always been considered bad form to
pay taxes in Italy. The wealthy (even those of moderate income) have always looked upon the tax laws as we once
looked upon the Prohibition laws.

Togliatti had some pretty good points in his platform (I am
still quoting the talk around the table) and things looked
hopeful from his viewpoint. Togliatti didn't fear the Church
and he knew that the opposition to his party was divided. It is
true that Saragat and his Socialists had moved over with de
Gasperi and his Christian Democrat Party, as had the smaller
Republican Party, headed by Randolfo Pacciardi. But two
months before the election, Togliatti was an odds-on favorite.
Then something happened. The United States suddenly woke
up to the great sales job being done by Moscow through
Togliatti.

"I thought they had us beaten," Ivan Mateo Lombardo
said, and there were nods of assent around the table. "Togliatti wasn't missing a trick. I know about selling. Democracy
is a damn good product, but no one was selling it; no one was
trying to convince the voters how good it was, except a handful of us. Then," he said, "Jimmy Dunn took off his coat."

James Dunn for years has been the whipping boy of the
State Department. He was always loyal to whichever Secretary he was serving under, and an impression (completely
erroneous) spread that he, himself, was the author of much
of the unpopular policy-making. Handsome, suave, impeccably
dressed, he represented the State Department to the press and
the public. He was the lad in the striped trousers and the
morning coat. He was the one who appeased Vichy and Darlan

and gave Argentina a seat at the San Francisco U. N. meeting. Dunn had to take every rap for Cordell Hull, for Stettinius, for Jimmy Byrnes. That was his job and he did it with a smile on his face. Finally they let him out of the gloomy building opposite the White House and sent him to Rome as Ambassador. Here, to a great extent, he actually was his own policy-maker.

"Jimmy Dunn took off his coat and then what?" I prompted.

He began to make speeches, they said. They were moderate speeches at first, but as Communist attacks on ERP intensified, Jimmy Dunn stepped up his rhetoric and let go with a few choice adjectives. He locked up his smooth manner, his friendly smile and his striped trousers in the safe of our embassy and roamed the country selling democracy. He went to the industrial areas and to the rural districts of the South, slugging it out with Togliatti and Nenni. Verbally, of course. He attacked Communism as savagely as Della Torre had ever done. He constantly stressed the benefits which would accrue to Italy under a democratic regime and the chaos which could be expected if the Communists took over.

"Then your private citizens at home took a hand," Lombardo recalled. "That had a great effect."

It was Drew Pearson who started that with a broadcast suggesting that Americans of Italian descent write to relatives and friends in Italy pleading with them to reject Communism. The response was immediate and electric. Mail to Italy from America increased by more than a million letters a week. Thousands of Italian-Americans who had been sending monthly checks to relatives said they'd have to stop the practice if Italy went communistic; that communistic regimes in the puppet states had discouraged such practices and undoubtedly Togliatti (once in power) would call a halt to outside help for the citizens of Italy.

In remote villages these letters were passed from hand to hand. Occasionally they were read from the pulpit by priests.

Meanwhile thousands of CARE packages were arriving and

164

being distributed to the poor, thousands of whom lived in districts which were the chief targets of Togliatti's campaign. The Friendship Train, another bit of salesmanship dreamed up by Drew Pearson, arrived in Italy. It was received with such enthusiasm that even left-wing Rome papers like *L'Avanti* reluctantly had to give its arrival some space. All in all, it was the greatest spontaneous sales campaign ever launched by private citizens anywhere.

Jimmy Dunn was always there when a shipment of CARE packages arrived; Jimmy Dunn rode the Friendship Train. Gradually, in the minds of the people, America and food became synonymous. The Communists offered fantastic promises of what they would do if elected; the Americans distributed food without any conditions attached. It was a high-pressure campaign, but Dunn had nothing to apologize for; his product was good. But people had to be convinced that it was good.

Then the forces of democracy picked up a new weapon against Togliatti—ridicule. The most effective instrument (I strongly suspect that Jimmy Dunn's bright young lads in the American Embassy were behind it) used in this connection was the comic strip. There was one which gained enormous circulation in Italy. The Communists were making a desperate attempt to convince the people that America was Italy's real enemy and that reports of American aid to Italy were sheer propaganda. The comic strip entitled "Togliatti's Day" answered this accusation and the gales of laughter which resulted so infuriated the Communists that they lost their sense of proportion and began shouting really absurd accusations against America which, by their very extravagance, defeated their purpose. And the comic strip continued to appear on fences, factory walls and old barns all over the country.

"They lost their heads," Lombardo said, recalling the last days of the campaign. "Just couldn't take the ridicule."

"You can't kid a man about his religion," I said. "That's why Communists have always been vulnerable to ridicule."

Someone asked me what I meant, and (having been listening now for some time) I was glad to give them my own particular idea of Communism. It isn't copyright (it may not even be true), but it's the concept of Communism I acquired after living ten months in Moscow. Communists can't stand being ridiculed because, to them, Communism is more than a political theory—it is a religion and members of the Politburo are its high priests. Communism is a religion which manifests itself in mass hysteria. Johann Schiller who, as poet, dramatist and philosopher, was certainly Germany's leading triple-threat man in the eighteenth century, once said, "Anyone taken as an individual is tolerably sensible and reasonable—as a member of a crowd he at once becomes a fool." In Moscow you occasionally (damn occasionally) think you have made a Russian friend. You find that he isn't much different from your neighbor at home from whom you can always borrow a cup of sugar, an egg or a bottle of Scotch. He seems to have about the same likes and dislikes. On a Saturday afternoon he's out at the Dynamo Stadium trying to root his football team home; at night he'll take his wife to the neighborhood movie house and he is just as proud as any American father when his son is accepted as a member of the Pioneers (Russian equivalent of Boy Scouts) and comes home with his little button which says on it *"Bud Gotov,"* the same motto as our own Boy Scouts' "Be Prepared." He's a real nice guy until he gets on the subject of Communism. Then his eyes take on a strange glint and, with the utmost sincerity, he'll tell you the damnedest lies about what Communism has done for him and for his country and for the world. He will know that you realize these are lies, but he'll keep it up with a straight face. You finally become convinced that he'll lie and steal and murder, if need be, in the name of Communism.

So it was in Moscow when I was there. So it is with fervent Communists no matter where they are. To them Communism is the gospel according to St. Marx, and the Epistles of St. Paul are no more reverently heard by orthodox Christians than the writings of Lenin are listened to by the devout Communists. And you can't ridicule a man's religion without arousing his blind fury. Were Communism merely a political theory, we could understand it, but it is difficult to understand a religion so foreign to our own concept of theology.

"You're right," Lombardo said. "That's why this battle isn't over in Italy. We're in bad shape economically and we'll be in worse shape before we get better, but I think we can convince the people that Communism is not the answer to our troubles. We can't convince the converted Communists but we can convince those with open minds. Actually, it's against the nature of our people to embrace the regimentation of either Fascism or Communism. I know we put up with it for twenty-three years, but that was because Mussolini did what Togliatti almost did. He caught the nation in poverty and chaos after the last war and grabbed control." He paused, then said, "But democracy was never dead in Italy, as the 70 percent vote against Communism proved. Democracy was asleep—but not dead."

It was Oscar Sinigaglia, seventy-six-year-old president of Finsider who brought up the subject of the unrealistic attitude the trade unions had up to now been taking toward industry. Finsider is the name given to the Italian Steel Industry Financing Syndicate. The gentle elderly man in charge of it had been cast into the discard long ago during the thirties. Sinigaglia is a Jew and Mussolini suffered no Jews in important positions. But the sick steel industry had summoned Sinigaglia back. He had returned from what amounted to exile on his own terms. His terms were that he would work for no salary. An economist, he naturally took a fairly objective view of the mess the steel industry was in, and although Communists would call him nothing but the voice of big business, he is an experienced, capable patriot who has little to gain from his present thankless post except the satisfaction of doing a good job.

He said very bluntly that there were faults inherent in the

167

Italian nature: unreliability, lack of discipline, poor organizing ability, an inclination to make quick superficial decisions, but that the compensating qualities of intelligence, capacity for hard work and sacrifice, and attachment to and responsibility for the family could overcome them. He explained that during the immediate postwar period, with liberation committees and then six- and three-party governments which ruled only by making all sorts of political concessions to each other, a great many economically unsound decrees had been issued. There was, for instance, the absurd ban on dismissal pushed through by the labor unions. Today, he said, factories had thousands of excess workers on their payrolls. There wasn't enough production to justify the retention of these men, but they could not be dismissed. And so the manufacturers did the only thing possible, they passed on the excess wages they were paying to the public. This made the cost of the manufactured product so high that people in Italy couldn't afford it, nor could it successfully compete in the world market. This absence of a world market meant that sources of foreign currency had dried up and you couldn't buy raw material abroad without foreign currency.

It was a stiff dose of medicine that Sinigaglia was asking Italy to swallow. He wanted these excess workers (redundant workers he called them) to be dismissed. Once they were off the payroll, industry could modernize factories, buy the machine tools and equipment so badly needed, and gradually swing into more efficient production. Once industry was producing commodities at a price that made it possible for consumers at home and abroad to purchase the manufactured products, the demand for additional products would rise sharply and then, but only then, could the dismissed workers return.

What would happen to the workers meanwhile? His organization had already offered substantial dismissal gratuities (we would call it severance pay) to such workers. There, too, should be special unemployment subsidies from the government. Finsider was prepared to set up co-operatives managed by Finsider staff men and financed by the corporation. Here, too, special training could be given, for many types of specialists were needed in the steel industry.

"We have one company in Finsider," he said, "which did not have workers belonging to Communist unions. It is the Dalmine Company. They had 1,000 surplus workers for whom they had absolutely no work. Eighteen months ago these 1,000 men were dismissed; either that or the company would have to go out of business. What happened? A year after the dismissal, production costs had dropped something like fifty percent; half the products of that company were being exported; locally, they sold their products easily and within the price fixed by the government. Only recently Dalmine rehired those 1,000 workers because the demand for her products was exceeding the supply. Now they are opening a new factory where another 600 men will be employed. Privately the labor leaders tell me that this is the only remedy for our economic illness. But publicly they still treat labor as a political commodity.

"We have to face the fact that there is only one way to salvation," he went on. "That is to enter a prolonged period of serious and deep privation. No one can dream of returning to the standard of living of peacetime—not for a long time. And, above all, the problem of unemployment must be treated without any political pressure being exerted.

"About 8,000,000 of our people live off the land," he said. "The government must make bold land reforms. It must compel landowners to increase cultivation, switching over from the extensive type of culture to the intensive type. Landowners who say they can't afford this switch-over should be made to sell part of their land to obtain the required capital. Our population increases every year by about 400,000, but the size of our agricultural area does not increase. We can't afford to import food; we must grow it. Small landowners must be encouraged to produce more. The Minister of Agriculture should be given wide powers during this emergency."

The present government has four more years in office. It is going to be a tough four years for Italy. For the next few years individual Italians will need all the help that American relatives can send them. If the Italian labor leaders would realize that there won't be an election for another four years and stop thinking in terms of political expediency and think, instead, in terms of long-range benefits, Italy may pull out of it.

The day after this amazing dinner, a cable arrived from *Collier's*. "We could use a story on present conditions in Greece" was all it said. So we packed up and headed for Athens. The first plane we could get was an American Airliner which left at three-thirty the next morning. I had picked up a bad case of laryngitis but we groped our way to the airport in time to catch the plane. We found we knew two fellow-passengers, John Swope, *Life* photographer and his wife, Dorothy Maguire of the films. Our bags were weighed and I was horrified to discover that Ginny's luggage was overweight to the tune of about twenty dollars. She had two heavy bags and a third small but heavy case I hadn't noticed before.

"What have you got in this thing, bricks from the Colosseum?"

"Drugs," she said calmly. "I hear the Mediterranean is full of germs. I brought a lot of drugs along, just in case."

The big Constellation lifted itself easily from the runway and we were off. I dozed a bit but Ginny's voice woke me.

"You're a great reporter," she said scornfully. "You don't even know who is sitting behind us."

"Sure, I do," I said sleepily. "I noticed them when we got in; a nice-looking young fellow and his wife."

She shook her head hopelessly. "You have great powers of observation. The nice young fellow is King Michael of Rumania and the girl is Princess Anne. They are going to be married in Athens tomorrow."

Just then Michael and Anne arose from their seats and walked toward the front of the plane. Evidently they had asked permission to spend some time in the pilot's cabin. A half hour later the co-pilot came back with a message for John Swope. John had been assigned by *Life* to cover the wedding and he had sent a note to Michael asking if he could talk to him. The co-pilot told John that Michael had nothing to say but as soon as the plane reached Athens, John could take pictures if he wished.

"What in hell do you call a king?" the co-pilot asked.

"He's not a king any longer," I reminded him.

"Well, we didn't know up there," he said, "so we didn't call him anything."

It was about 7 A.M. when we arrived in Athens. Michael and Anne looked like two very sleepy youngsters. When the plane landed, a Greek official came aboard and asked the passengers to wait a few moments. John Swope was having none of that. He was a photographer at work. He merely told the Greek official that he had to follow Michael and Anne and take pictures.

"I'm a photographer, too," I heard a familiar voice say confidently. "I came all the way from New York just to get these pictures."

I looked up to find Ginny purposefully holding her five-dollar Brownie. She and John just walked to the rear of the plane where Michael and Anne were about to leave. Two men in plain clothes looked at them sharply, but Ginny just imitated Swope's nonchalant, confident air. They followed Michael and Anne down the steps while Dorothy Maguire and I watched the show from the window. It was a fairly good show, considering the limited experience royal families have had in recent years in producing extravaganzas. It ran about nine minutes too long, but that is a mistake always made by amateur producers.

The Greek Air Force band was lined up. It woke the early morning with its rendition of the Greek national anthem. King Paul I and Queen Frederika of Greece, all dressed up in costumes right out of *The Student Prince,* stood with the Queen Mother, Helen of Rumania, waiting to receive the two youngsters who blinked sleepily in the glare of the sun. Anne curtsied to the royal trio, a gesture which somehow looked awfully silly at seven in the morning. Then the second team, which had remained decently in the background, greeted them. This consisted of the Greek Premier, Themistocles Sophoulis, and Foreign Minister Tsaldaris. They looked shabby in the shadow of the resplendent white and gold admiral's uniform worn by King Paul. Dorothy and I watched John and Ginny snapping their cameras and I made a mental bet that Ginny had forgotten to put any film in hers.

Now the royal party moved over to inspect the soldiers who were standing at attention. Ginny followed closely on their heels. These soldiers were Evzones, the only fighting men in the world who wear skirts. Traditionally there have always been three regiments of Evzones in the Greek Army. They looked rather cute in their embroidered short skirts, tufted shoes and odd headdress. The travel books refer to this costume as "the picturesque dress of the dashing mountain troops." Many of them wore long sweeping mustaches yellowed at the tips by tobacco stains and this detracted slightly from their girlish appearance. There was twenty minutes of this and Dorothy and I were beginning to wilt as the sun baked our plane. Finally we were allowed to leave.

John was triumphant. The other photographers had been kept back of a barrier close to the Administration Building. Only he had obtained really good shots of the proceedings. Ginny was not exactly overjoyed, however.

"Every time I got set to take a picture," she complained, "there was some silly command given and everyone turned around. This happened a dozen times just as I clicked the shutter. Well, at least I snapped some of the most distinguished derrières in Greece."

The flight had done my laryngitis no good at all, and I was feeling very sorry for myself. We had reservations at the Grand Bretagne Hotel and going up in the elevator I noticed a sign, "There will be hot water only Monday and Saturday mornings." I crawled into bed, unable to talk, unable to hear.

"Do we know either of the Mayo brothers?" I croaked to Ginny. "Get one or both if you can."

Calmly but triumphantly she opened the heavy case which contained her pharmacy. First she took my temperature. It was 103. She phoned the hotel manager and told him to send for a doctor immediately. Then she dug into her case and produced a small can of Sterno and a pan. She filled the pan with water and lit the Sterno. She saw my look of apprehension.

"I'm not going to cook you," she said coldly. "This is to sterilize the needle."

I haven't mentioned that she was a nurse's aid at Bellevue Hospital during the war and is a frustrated doctor. She is never happier than when called upon to treat someone who is sick and her confidence is such that I do not think she would hesitate to perform a prefrontal lobotomy, if no surgeon were available. She sterilized the needle and stuck it through the cork of a bottle.

"What's that?"

"That is crysticillin," she said. "It's just penicillin but it's a new type used for traveling. And this is a bottle of grain alcohol. Turn over, please."

The "please" didn't fool me. I felt the coolness of the alcohol and then waited for the needle. That is always a long moment. I waited and waited.

"If you're going to do it, go ahead," I said through gritted teeth.

"It's all done," she said calmly. "I gave you 300,000 units. You can turn over now."

"I must admit I didn't even feel the needle," I said.

"Good sharp needle," she said, with professional satisfaction. "New type. I brought three of them along. Now I'll heat some water and you go and gargle. I've got some Cepacol Solution with me among these drugs we'll never use."

I gargled and when I came out she was talking to a chubby waiter. "I want a lemon, a spoonful of sugar, two ounces of brandy and a few cloves," she was saying, and the waiter was looking delighted.

"This is a fine time of the day to be ordering brandy," I told her. "People will think we're refugees from Alcoholics Anonymous."

"This is medicinal," she said, and added, "I don't tell you how to run a typewriter. Don't tell me how to treat a patient who may be on the verge of pneumonia."

That scared me back into bed and complete silence. The waiter returned. He watched her light the stove and heat more water. He watched her cut and squeeze the lemon, occasionally nodding and giving out with a delighted, "Okay—okay."

"Why you cook dinner in room?" he asked.

"This is medicine," she assured him, and he roared with laughter.

"Okay. Okay. I am one good waiter. You bet." He sniffed appreciatively when she added the brandy, the sugar and the cloves. "How is your name?"

"Virginia," she told him and he laughed again.

"Okay. I call you sweetheart. Spik English; okay, I spik English," he said happily. "My name Constantine. You call me Constantine."

"All right, Constantine," she said, "you may go now."

"No, no," he protested. "You pretty. I stay here."

"I hope you two kids will be happy," I croaked. She handed me the hot, brandy-spiked lemonade, then dipped into her drug case, came up with a bottle and handed me two white pills.

Then there was a knock at the door and Constantine opened it. It looked as though he had made himself a permanent member of the family. A handsome man walked in carrying a black bag. In perfect English he introduced himself as Doctor Diomiades. He was friendly but brisk and efficient. He took my temperature, tapped my chest, looked at my throat and asked a lot of questions which Virginia answered, and then said seriously, "What you need is an injection of penicillin but, unfortunately, I can't get it for you. We only have a limited supply here in Athens and we keep it in the hospitals for emergencies. I can't do much for you except prescribe a gargle and some aspirin or empirin and codeine compound. Perhaps you can sweat this out."

"Well, I've already given him 300,000 units of penicillin," Ginny said, quite unable to keep the satisfaction out of her voice. "I just happened to have a needle and some penicillin with me. And I made him gargle with Cepacol Solution. Then I gave him hot lemonade and brandy and two empirin tablets. That ought to make him sweat. I also gave him a grain and a half of seconal."

"You don't need me," he smiled. "You did everything I could have done."

"Okay, sweetheart, okay," Constantine chuckled. The doctor said something to him in Greek and he left. "Come back later," he chuckled from the door. "You stay. Okay."

Ginny showed Doctor Diomiades her needles and his eyes lit up. "We have nothing like that left here in Athens," he said. "Our instruments are dull from overuse. The only drugs we have are those we get from America. You seem to have a pretty good supply yourself," he added, looking into her drug case.

Ginny was showing off her drugs the way a woman usually shows off her jewels. She displayed the contents of a dozen bottles and the doctor was as happy as a kid with a box of toys. They discussed drugs and methods of treating ailments the way Toots Shor and I discuss hitting styles of our favorites.

I started to say something but found that I was asleep.

I woke up hours later. Someone was shaking me. It was Constantine, and he was grinning from ear to ear. "Okay, you. Wake up. Look." Proudly he showed me a tray. There was a pot of hot tea and toast on it. "Pretty lady say to wake you at six. Okay? Drink tea. Good. Ah, real good."

I drank the hot tea and ate the toast and felt all right. Ginny came in with her arms full of bundles to find Constantine and myself enjoying a long monologue. The monologue was by Constantine. His eyes lit up when he saw her and he shook with laughter.

"Wait and see what I brought home," Ginny said. "To begin with, I walked to the American Express and changed a hundred-dollar traveler's check. For that they gave me one million drachmas. I could hardly carry that much. And everybody in the street looks like Peter Lorre or Sidney Greenstreet. I'm not kidding, they all look like spies."

"What did you bring home?"

She unwrapped a package. "Look," she cried triumphantly. "Eight detective stories and we haven't read any of them. I also found a place that sold Hershey bars. I bought ten of them. I have a hunch we aren't going to like the food here. And I found a copy of *Time* with a wonderful story about Bill O'Dwyer in it."

"What does the city look like?"

"It isn't Rome," she said emphatically. "I think as soon as you're well you'll want to do your story fast. I found one more thing," she said. "A movie place that shows American pictures. It's only two blocks from here. They've got a real oldie there. We might go one night."

"What's the name of it?" I asked, feeling sure I knew what she'd answer. I was right.

"*Scarface*," she said cheerfully.

CHAPTER TEN

A *beautiful friendship* sprang up between Constantine and ourselves. He would bring our breakfast at eight each morning and hang around until we finished it. He discovered that Ginny liked jam and he brought her a jar of it, laughing uproariously as he told us he had stolen it from the kitchen.

"Strumberry jam," he said happily.

"They really say 'strumberry,'" Ginny said in awe. "I never believed it."

I didn't know a soul in Greece, but an old friend, Ed Anthony, publisher of *Woman's Home Companion,* had cabled to Laird Archer, director of the Near East Foundation, who was an old friend of his. Laird Archer introduced me to a man named Apostoulos Koskinides who took me out of Athens and into the villages and introduced me to modern Greece. Through

177

Laird Archer, we also met Professor Weber, who introduced us to the Greece of antiquity.

During the days that followed we realized that ancient Greece had many advantages over the Greece of today. There was nothing majestic, nothing fascinating about the Greece we saw. The Greece of antiquity was a country of hills crowned with thick forests; a lush land with natural springs that helped the fertile soil yield not merely subsistence for its population but enough excess to make Greece the most envied of all Mediterranean nations. But that was two thousand years ago. Today Greece is a land made barren by erosion and drought. It is a country shunned even by the birds. When you are far out in the hills you never hear the quick scurry of a rabbit or see some brown streak flash over the horizon. There is virtually no wild life in Greece; man began the process of extermination long ago and nature finished the job. Scientists say that a man needs for his subsistence two and a half acres of cultivable land and they warn that this is his minimum requirement. Greece occupies a bare 50,000 square miles of the earth's surface and today less than 20 percent of that can be cultivated. And there are 7,500,000 people living off this 20 percent of the land, which means that there is less than one cultivable acre for each inhabitant of the country.

Suppose we look at Greece through the eyes of one of her own citizens, a well-educated, lovable and gallant man named Apostolos Koskinides. Koskinides is about fifty-five, broad-shouldered, clean-shaven, youthful-looking and strong. He is an official of the Near East Foundation and his life work has been to teach the people of rural Greece how to save themselves from what appears to be certain disaster. When you sit in a jeep beside Koskinides as he drives into a village you know from the joyous cries of welcome that this is a greatly beloved man.

As we drove around the countryside he told me the story of Rizo—a story of what can be done with eighty American dollars.

178

"Greece is a country of villages, you know," he said, smiling. "With us anything that isn't a city—is a village. And there are 10,000 villages in rural Greece, all pretty much the same. Rizo was just another village in the region we call Macedonia. Each year about 15,000 people in villages like Rizo died of malaria and intestinal diseases. In plague years, we have had as many as 2,000,000 people stricken by these terrible diseases.

"Malaria struck Rizo every year, and the people accepted it as something nature had inflicted upon them and there was nothing to be done about it. Their children died young and the adults who survived were too worn out to care whether they lived or died. The women were too exhausted from annual attacks of malaria to bear children. There were only 1,500 people left in Rizo when I arrived.

"As you have probably noticed, our rural communities do not have any water systems at all. Usually there is a well on the outskirts of the village and the women carry the water from the well to their kitchens. In Rizo there was a spring just beyond the village, half-covered by an old stone arch. Occasionally archaeologists would visit Rizo, examine the arch, and say, 'Very interesting. Probably built in the time of Alexander the Great, around 335 B.C.'

"There was plenty of water in the spring. In fact, the water overflowed constantly and the spring had become the center of a ten-acre swamp. Yes, it was a historic old spring, but it was also a death-dealing spring because the water was polluted and rotten with mosquito larvae. I called the villagers together and told them that the malaria which had been killing them and their parents and grandparents came right out of the spring. I told them that if they would co-operate with me I could make the spring as pure as it had been in the time of Alexander the Great. They really didn't believe me but they agreed to help. First, I set them to draining the ten acres of swamp. That took many weeks of work, but it didn't cost anything. Then I got them to help me clean out the spring. We found hundreds of odd objects: ammunition, guns, boots, cats, dogs, and a great many ancient coins. After it was thoroughly cleaned, we cemented the walls and then I chlorinated the water. Finally we built a cover so no stray cats or dogs or children could fall in. I managed to get a brass spigot so the water could be turned on and off. When I tested it I found it as pure as the water of Athens,. or, for that matter, of New York.

"When I returned to Rizo three years later, the priest told me, 'Before you came and cleaned our spring, this was a village without children. Now you can hear them laughing all day long.'

"It cost eighty dollars to perform this small miracle and the money came from the American Near East Foundation. But, mind you," Koskinides said earnestly, "Greece cannot be saved by charity. I am only one of many trying to teach the people of Greece to save themselves. That, not charity, is the only answer to our survival as a people.

"The curse of Greece today is the criminally unsanitary conditions prevailing in the 10,000 villages of my country. If overnight I could magically banish the thousands of disease-breeding wells and springs in rural Greece and if I could at the same time install 4,000,000 sanitary latrines, Greece would be on her way to economic recovery."

Koskinides' face broke into a smile. "You know, if ever I accomplish anything here I will owe it to North Carolina State University. I went there in 1946 for a year to study methods of sanitation. All my life I had worked in the field, improvising and experimenting as I went along. At Chapel Hill I had at my fingertips all the knowledge gained by the world's greatest experts in my field. All this knowledge was available to me. Every Saturday during the autumn I send up a short prayer to Hercules, the ancient Greek god of sport, asking him to look with favor upon the football fortunes of my old college."

It was Koskinides who took me to Magoula, an ancient

village that leans against a rounded, rock-crested hill in Southern Greece.

Let us consider the scant population (650) of Magoula, for, in the long-range picture, they are more important than they realize. There are 5,000,000 of these rural dwellers in Greece out of a 7,500,000 population, and it is to them that the guerrilla leader, Markos, has been directing three radio broadcasts a day from a high-powered station in Yugoslavia. There are probably not more than 25,000 radio sets in all of Greece and not one in Magoula, but the messages of Markos reach Magoula and the other 10,000 villages by word of mouth.

Come with me to Magoula and meet the folks. Maybe we can find an answer or two that is impossible to find in Athens. This is a feast day in Magoula and everyone goes to church today.

The family of Spiros Nikas, the village carpenter, is up early. Katina Nikas is ten, and last Easter her father gave her the first pair of shoes she had ever owned. Today she is allowed to wear them. Her younger brother, five-year-old George, is as excited as Katina and even the four-month-old nameless son gurgles happily. He is nameless because his godfather-to-be is in the hills with the Greek Army and it is his privilege to name the child.

Suppose we share the family's breakfast. It is the same every day—goat's milk and bread. Spiros Nikas owns a brown-and-white goat which is tied to a stake behind his house. He also owns five chickens. In normal times Spiros is a fairly substantial citizen. He is the only mason and carpenter in town and there is plenty of work for him. In fact, he usually makes about 150,000 drachmas ($15) a week. But now he has been put in charge of the village guard and every night he and twenty-five other men guard the roads to Magoula, for even in Southern Greece quick fierce raids by the guerrillas are not unknown.

Spiros receives no pay for his ten hours of guard duty, but he does get seventeen *oka* (an *oka* equals 2.82 pounds) of flour each month, which is enough to keep the family in bread. He also receives seven pounds of sugar. These come from the Ministry of Supply, and the Ministry of Supply gets the flour and the sugar from the American Mission. Spiros has to borrow money from neighbors to buy vegetables and meat, but he only buys meat once in fifteen days.

"I owe my neighbors a lot of money—" Spiros grins, showing fine white teeth—"but they do not care. We are used to borrowing from one another."

Breakfast over, the Nikas family walks to church, two hundred yards away. The dirt road is hard from being baked by 10,000 suns, but there is a cool, early-morning breeze. People are crowding into the church. They all know Spiros and his family and a dozen of them stop to admire Katina's new shoes and the white hair ribbons that hold her braided blonde tresses.

Father Constantine Kokiniotis is just beginning to say Mass. The service is very long and Spiros Nikas, a little uncomfortable in his buttoned shirt and tight coat, edges toward the door. There are as many worshippers on the steps outside as there are indoors. I follow Spiros through the crowd and we sit down at a table in front of the small village coffee shop and drink strong, sweetened Turkish coffee. Spiros, who has lost his earlier shyness, talks of life in Magoula.

"Things were all right until war came," he says. "I was in the army fighting in Albania. I had left a two-month-old son at home. We fought as well as we could and we beat the Italians, too, but the Germans were too strong for us. I came home and found that my baby had died of starvation. Did you know that 55,000 children died of starvation in Athens alone? And here in Magoula twenty died. The Germans had an airfield near here. They surrounded our village well with barbed wire and posted a guard there. You have seen the well? It is a mile from the village and the only one in the district.

"The Germans would not let our women draw water from the well, unless they brought eggs with them. For a gallon of

182

water they demanded two eggs. They had already taken our cattle and our sheep and our goats. My wife had no food for our children, but our chickens kept laying eggs, so she had water. But the little one grew thinner and thinner. Finally my wife had to kill a chicken to keep him alive. Then she had to kill another chicken. Soon she had to kill them all and then there was nothing left to eat. There were no longer any eggs to give the Germans, and she got no water. The little one died."

"Was it better after the liberation?" I ask.

"No." His face, burned a deep red by the sun, hardens. "Then they came down from the hills—the guerrillas. We welcomed them. They had fought well during the occupation. But when these men came down from the hills they carried Communist flags. We could never understand that. They were Greeks. Why did they carry Russian flags?"

By now Mass is over and the square is filled with the chatter of women and the laughter of children. Grizzled old Elias Milos, Mayor of Magoula, joins us. So does Father Kokiniotis, a handsome, erect, black-bearded man with a hawklike nose and large, intelligent eyes. The priest asks if he might send to his house for a bottle of retsina. Everyone nods happily.

"My friend Spiros Nikas has been telling you of our troubles," he says softly. "We have had many troubles. He did not mention the pine trees, did he? In the country surrounding our village we had 50,000 acres of pine trees. The people of Magoula made their living from them and with the money they made they bought sheep and goats and sometimes a plot of land where olive trees grew. Our people would draw the resin from the trunk of the pine tree. That resin has many commercial uses; it is needed for turpentine, paint and retsina."

The retsina has arrived and the keeper of the coffee house brings out half a dozen clean glasses. The retsina is honey-colored and when the sun hits the bottle the wine seems to change color and dance. The priest pours the wine.

"This is the same wine they drank in Greece three thousand years ago," he says. "It is flavored with resin from the pine tree. That resin also takes the impurities out of the wine. That is why our pine forests were important to us. But the Germans used the pine trees for fuel. When they went away they burned all the trees that were left."

"We will be all right when the water comes," Filia Economou, the schoolteacher, says. Smiles light up the faces of everyone at the table and they repeat the word "water" softly, so that it sounds like a short prayer.

By now half a dozen others have joined us. They all greet Koskinides with warm smiles and he asks after their children and their wives. The keeper of the little coffee house comes out with two large plates and a dozen forks. One plate holds hot bits of veal; the other holds slices of tomato and cucumber soaked in lemon juice and olive oil. This is the priest's party.

I had met these people before. I had met them in small villages in our own Southwest and in the towns of Northern France way back in 1940 and in remote villages in Palestine only six weeks before. I had met them in Italy and I had even met such people in small agricultural villages near Vyazma on the road to Smolensk during the war. These were people unconcerned with the complexities of life or with the political strife among nations. Their fight for survival occupied all of their attention.

There was very little kinship between these decent, hard-working men and women of Magoula and the Greek Government in Athens. Many of us in America are under the impression that the government of Greece is democratic. This, of course, is sheer nonsense. But then Greece has never had a democratic government and, if a pundit raises incredulous eyebrows and assures me that the very word "democracy" comes from the Greek and that the Athens of old was, in fact, the finest of all democracies, I can only remind him that there were something like 200,000 slaves in that fabled but spurious

184

democracy. Nor is there democracy in Greece today in the sense that we know it. Today 98 percent of the farmers of Greece (government figures) do not have latrines. A government that does not give the mass of its population such basic necessities as water and elementary sanitation is hardly our conception of a democratic government. But the people seem to bear little resentment.

The people of Magoula have an active dislike for Communism and a conviction that bad as their own government is, it is a lot better than Communism would be. It is Father Kokiniotis who brings up the subject.

"I know you want to ask us what we think of Markos and Communism," he says suddenly. "I will tell you and, if I am wrong, my friends will correct me. We saw what Communism was in 1944. We were too small a village for them to bother with but we saw what happened in Mandra, not far away. They occupied Mandra and killed a great many people there. They brought people out from Athens and took them behind the hills here and shot them. I went and prayed over the bodies. There were hundreds of them. We all saw the bodies."

There are murmured assents from around the table.

"I will tell you," Elias Milos, who combines farming with the job of being mayor, speaks up, "of a man named Athanasios Diakos. In 1820 he led a revolt against the Turks who had occupied our country for four hundred years. They caught him and tortured him. They put his feet in a fire but he laughed and, just before he died, he cried out, 'Better one hour of freedom than forty years of slavery.' That is now one of our national songs. Markos says that the poor people of rural Greece are all on his side. Well, we are the poor people of rural Greece and there is not one person in our village who is on the side of Markos."

Elias Milos stops suddenly and his face is red. His friends clap him on the back and say, "Well spoken, Elias." The priest smiles and fills our glasses for the last time. We clink glasses and everyone murmurs, "To your health," and then I left. •

It is easy for critics outside of Greece to castigate the present Greek Government and to insist that it is not representative of the Greek people. They are right, but when they go further and say that in a free election the present government would be thrown out by the people, they are guilty of wishful thinking.

All the evidence I could gather seemed to indicate that the people of Greece want democracy as we know it. I don't believe they want the Markos brand. Our salesmanship, so effective in Italy, is being tried out on the Greeks. There are about 800,000 citizens of Greek extraction now living in the United States. Nearly a quarter of them were actually born in the old country. The letters they write to relatives in rural Greece tell of this magic land called America where even the poorest villages get water, sanitation, free education and social security.

The heavy-thinking prophets of political prognostication may not like our invasion of Greece, but everyone I talked to in that country seemed to agree that the only alternative to the American Mission was Soviet domination. I admit that I was unable to contact any of the Markos followers, but I have read their publications which were on sale in Rome.

America has been good to the Greeks, and in their minds America and democracy are synonymous. The Near East Foundation, supported entirely by American funds, has brought water, health services and education to hundreds of isolated villages. The Rockefeller Foundation has tried desperately to revitalize the tired, worn-out land, and it is now fighting the Dakas fly, which ravages the olive crop each year. Our Greek War Relief has poured millions of dollars into the country.

The cynical may say that we have bought the good will of the people, but the cynical have never talked to a man like Spiros Rhodopoulos, a village doctor in Mandra. During the occupation, Doctor Rhodopoulos, who is sixty-five years old, went to the hills to care for the guerrilla fighters.

"Our people are as democratically minded as yours," he said, his bright eyes flashing under incredibly bushy eyebrows. "Both you and the British have made tragic mistakes in Greece. In 1944 you crushed ELAS and put into power a complacent, selfish, rightist government. You made us choose between the extreme Left, which few of us want, and the extreme Right, which none of us wants. Yet at heart we Greeks are liberal democrats. We have nowhere to turn right now. We are waiting for a leader to emerge—not a Markos and not any of the present government. My people want a true democratic administration."

Criticism of the present government has been violent by most correspondents in Athens. Sound, thoughtful men like Homer Bigart of the *Herald Tribune* and the late George Polk held back no punches in castigating the highly centralized government. For instance, the government is currently appointing the mayors of all cities, towns and villages in Greece. Even purely local problems are handled by the central government in Athens. The charge made by Markos and his followers that Greece has become a police state has been echoed by the correspondents. It is certainly true that when the Socialist weekly *Machi* ventured to criticize the government for the wholesale execution of ELAS members who had been in jail for three years, two *Machi* editors were hustled off to jail. No one knows how many Communists and alleged Communists have been shot during the last year. It is a fact that the government got panicky early last May (1948), when Christos Ladas, Minister of Justice, was assassinated, and dragged 120 men out of jail and shot them. At the same time a dragnet went out to bring in carloads of Markos sympathizers and a great many of them were shot and hundreds sent to island concentration camps. This had the effect (some governmental officials now agree) of acting as an excellent recruiting stunt for Markos.

Public opinion, privately expressed, was bitter against the executions and imprisonments. People will tell you stoutly that hundreds of those punished were not Communists; they were merely critics of a governmental policy. And hundreds of disgusted young men who until then had no sympathy for Communism fled to the hills to join Markos merely as a protest against the government way of doing things.

Soviet publications insist that betwen 60,000 and 70,000 political prisoners are being held on Makronesos Island, Jura Island and in mainland prisons and concentration camps. I asked Minister of Justice George Melas how close to the truth the Soviet estimate was.

Minister Melas is well known in New York as a representative to the United Nations and he seems more respected in Athens than most government figures. Melas looked astonished at the high estimate given by the Soviet.

"Good heavens!" he said. "That would mean we had one percent of the whole population of Greece behind bars. The figure is absurd, of course. We have perhaps a little more than 20,000 prisoners in jail. And we've executed quite a few, and, while we're on the subject, we are going to execute some more. Every man we've executed deserved it; each one had a fair trial, competent counsel and was found guilty. These men were enemies of the state. Don't forget that we are fighting for the life of our country."

When Melas touched on the subject of the recent killing of George Polk of the Columbia Broadcasting System, his eyes narrowed with anger. Melas was in charge of the investigation into the murder of the American correspondent.

"What made me absolutely sick," he said, and his voice trembled, "were reports that we in the government had a hand in the murder of George. My God, what a monstrous lie! You can accuse us Greeks of a great many things and you would be justified, but no one ever accused us of being downright stupid. For our government to instigate the murder of an American correspondent would be downright stupid. We are depending for our very existence on America today.

"We've been working hard on the killing of George Polk. We've explored every possibility. To my mind there is only one

188

answer. The Communists murdered him to embarrass our government."

No one in Athens seemed to have any real evidence or knowledge as to who killed George. The Communists, of course, accused the Greek Government and there were many who agreed with them. The whole question had developed into a political cause célèbre, but to two stony-eyed women it remained a personal tragedy. George had been married for eight months to slim, lovely Rea, who was twenty. George's mother had come from California to be with her. Young Rea, a Greek citizen who had been brought up in Alexandria, was bitter against the government police.

"They question me and question me," she said wearily. "I tell them I know nothing. I ask them not to waste their time with me. I ask them to find the ones who killed my George."

I asked her if she thought the Communists had killed her husband.

"I don't know," she said stonily. "There aren't many Communists in Salonika—virtually none. Why should they kill George? The Greek police say they did it to embarrass their government. That does not make much sense to me. But I don't know—I just don't know. They have been trying to make me sign a paper saying I am sure the Communists did it. This I will not do because I do not know. I only know that I want to get away from Athens. I want to leave forever," she said bitterly.

The loyal mother of George put her arm around the youngster. "We'll get you out of here soon, darling," she said soothingly. I asked her what she thought of the government's accusation.

"I don't know," she said sadly. "It doesn't much matter, does it? Even if they discover the murderers it won't bring George back to us. I found one thing that has given me peace of mind. I talked to doctors who examined George's body and they tell me that George never suffered a moment. That's the important thing. Now I want to get Rea home with me so she can start a new life."

"I want to get to America." Rea looked up. "I have nothing in common with Greeks any more. My friends are George's friends. They have been so kind to me. Greek officials only want to question me. George worked for CBS, you know. Ed Murrow has done everything possible to help me. He was a good friend of George's."

Lieutenant General James A. van Fleet, ranking American officer in Greece who now virtually runs the Greek Army, was none too sanguine about immediate military success against Markos. Today the Greek Army is engaged in a full-scale offensive against Markos—an offensive planned by Van Fleet. "But from here on in it won't be easy," Van Fleet said, pointing to the big map on his office wall. "Look at those mountains. There have been bandits in those mountains for 2,000 years. Not even the Turks could drive them out and they had something like four hundred years to do it. However, I am hopeful that within a few months the army will have broken up Markos' big concentrations. Once that is done the big military phase of the fighting should be over and it should develop into a police problem."

The Greek Army is using American guns, aircraft, rations and leadership. The *andartes* (revolutionaries) are using Yugoslav and Albanian equipment and Moscow-trained military leaders. Russia supports Markos; we support the Greek Army —but only Greeks are killed. And a lot of Greeks are being killed or made homeless.

If I have dwelt overlong on the shortcomings of the Greek Government it should by no means be construed as any championing of Markos. Let's take a look at this character. He is Moscow-trained. So is Nikos Zachariades, the real brain of the Markos movement. Zachariades has been described as the most brilliant student ever to attend the Moscow School of Oriental Studies. As Secretary-General of the Greek Communist Party he is responsible for the policy of the group which is called, in typical Soviet terminology, "Markos' Provisional People's Democratic Government."

Like any Soviet-dominated group, this one relies a great deal on propaganda as a weapon, and from the looks of the propaganda turned out to date it seems obvious that the second team is in there. On May 27, 1948, the Geneva newspaper, *La Voix Ouvrière* (*The Voice of the Worker*), published a harrowing photograph which depicted ten starving children. The caption under the picture read: "These are victims of Athens monarcho-Fascists. Their parents have been deported, arrested or shot by the Athens monarcho-Fascists in the pay of the Yankee imperialists. They were found roaming the Greek countryside and were saved by the people's army of General Markos."

The same picture, with a similar caption, was used in the press of Hungary, Czechoslovakia and France. There was one slight error in the caption. The picture was actually taken in 1941, not in 1948, and it showed Greek children who were starving under the German occupation. It was then reproduced in a book, *The Greek Trilogy*, written by Colonel W. Byford-Jones and published in 1945 by Hutchinson & Company of London. I found the book in an Athens bookshop. The pictures were identical.

The "provisional people's democratic government" broadcasts a great deal, and some of the broadcasts are models of hysterical invective. May I present a sample or two? When a Markos attack had been repulsed in the Sterea Hellas area of Greece, the radio blasted, "Van Fleet ordered the vassal criminal generals of the monarcho-Fascists to slay and exterminate all the noncombatant population of Sterea Hellas." Another time the radio droned: "As soon as he arrived in Greece supermurderer General van Fleet inaugurated the policy: 'Kill all prisoners of war.'"

And one day the radio told the world: "The murder of George Polk was inspired by the American imperialist Governor Griswold and the supermurderer Van Fleet." Yet one more: "The American and Athenian tyrants will not spend money to care for refugee children. Instead they march them naked and shoe-less through the streets of Athens to attract sympathy."

This kind of hysteria is dished out three times a day. The Greek Government isn't very good at propaganda itself but it never descends to such depths. The most effective Greek prop-agandist I know is a thirty-three-year-old engineer named Constantine Doxiadis. A graduate of the Architectural College in Athens, he took his doctor's degree in engineering in Berlin.

Young, dynamic Doxiadis is just about the only Greek alive who is not a politician. He belongs to no party and has respect for none. His title is Director-General of Reconstruction and his immediate job is to rebuild the 1,700 villages destroyed during the war by the Germans. Doxiadis began his recon-struction in the most devastated region, the section close to the Bulgarian border in the North. He designed the houses and stayed in the North until they were completed.

Markos and his men were always threatening this region but Doxiadis kept on building.

"When you say that a man loves the soil of his country it sounds very nice," Doxiadis told me in sharp, clipped collo-quial English, "but it is also a lot of bunk. You won't love the soil long if you have to sleep on it with nothing over you but the stars. Now, a home is the link between a man and the soil. Give him a home and he'll love the soil. Once we'd rebuilt the villages up North we moved out. Markos came in then, trying to get recruits. The people laughed at him. What did he have to offer them? They had homes. Give all of our people homes and you won't find many Communists in the country."

Doxiadis knows what it means to live in the hills. Because he had studied in Berlin and knew German, the Germans thought he would be a useful man during the occupation. They approached him. He told them to run along and then he lit out for the hills. Doxiadis is young, vital, honest, and he loves his country. He's working under great difficulties now but he ignores political pressure and goes right ahead building. When the government says it needs every cent for military uses he tells them coldly that new houses for the homeless are the best possible weapons to use against Markos. And everyone has such respect for young Doxiadis that he gets his way.

There is an old proverb which says, "Greece and poverty have always been sisters," and most Greeks accept this as the truth. They'll have to accept it as the truth for many years. But they are awfully nice people and some day they may remember that the word "democracy" was coined by their forebears and they may decide to try it themselves.

CHAPTER ELEVEN

It *was* an octopus that drove us out of Greece—a dead octopus. Muriel King, the fashion designer, was in Athens on a special job for the American Mission. We told her we'd like a real Greek meal, and Muriel knew just the place.

"This is not '21' or the Colony," she warned us, "but if you want to try the food the Greeks really eat this is the place."

The restaurant was in Piraeus and it held a half dozen wooden tables and there was sawdust on the floor. There was no menu; the waiter merely started to bring a succession of dishes. First came a huge fish swimming in oil. The head, complete with what looked like upper and lower plates, had eyes that seemed to gaze at us reproachfully. Then came another dish of what looked like soft-shell crabs; this was octopus, considered quite a delicacy by Athenian gourmets. When you cut into the rubbery tentacles, black ink spurted out.

"I've had it," Ginny said, getting a little pale.

"It takes some time to get accustomed to it," Muriel admitted.

"I haven't got that much time," Ginny said. For the next two days she ate nothing but toast and tea which solicitous Constantine brought to our room.

"Let's go to Paris for a decent meal," Ginny moaned. "I'll starve to death here."

I refuse to attempt any description of the city that has been described by the great writers of a dozen ages. Fortunately we had a few Parisian friends, which meant that we could get away from the conventional and dreary Maxim's-Tour d'Argent-Ritz Bar merry-go-round on which so many Paris visitors travel. I have been to Paris a dozen times, but I have never summoned up courage enough to ride to the top of the Eiffel Tower. I have a horror of high places and the thought of shooting up some hundreds of feet in a swaying elevator is not my idea of heaven on earth. This time I was determined to make it.

One day, in a spirit of high adventure, we reached the second level of the Tower (about 300 feet above the ground), and I suggested that we stop for lunch. The second-level restaurant is as good as any in Paris. During lunch I told Ginny how absurd it was for us to fear the remaining few hundred feet. People did it all the time—even without oxygen. The head-waiter, overhearing me, interrupted to give us some statistics.

"Several hundred people go up to the top each week," he said. "Mothers bring babies up there. Schoolchildren ascend alone. There is no reason for anyone to fear the trip. There has never been an accident. It only takes a few seconds from here and then you have the greatest view in the world before you."

"I suppose working here as you do you have a chance to go up every day?" I asked him.

"Me?" he said, startled. "Oh, no! Not for anything would I make that trip. I was in the underground with the Maquis during the war, but I admit the thought of getting into that lift and climbing into the sky frightens me."

We never got to the top either, but we liked the restaurant and the view from the second level so much that we went there often. We usually brought some French friends with us and we discovered that not one of them had ever gone even as far as the second level. It seemed incredible that native-born Parisians had never visited the Eiffel Tower. Our friends, in turn, took us to amazing restaurants, small neighborhood bistros where the food was infinitely better than in the expensive tourist traps.

Then Ken Downs and his wife, Marie-Therese, arrived from Berlin on a holiday, and I knew that from now on we'd spend a lot of time at the track. Downs was once I.N.S. chief in Paris and, during the early years of the war, he and I worked together as correspondents in London and Egypt. Now Downs was working in Berlin as one of Colonel Frank Howley's civilian assistants and doing occasional magazine articles. Howley is in charge of the American sector in Berlin. Marie-Therese possessed all the beauty and chic of the traditional Paris girl, and, in addition, she was highly intelligent, gifted with a sense of humor and a knack for languages; her English and her German were almost as good as her French. Ken Downs is one of the few men I know who likes horse racing. Most people go to the track merely to bet. Downs goes to watch the horses run. Harry Hopkins and Heywood Broun are the only other two men I ever knew who went to the track because they actually enjoyed horse racing. Downs is also uncannily successful in picking winners.

Ken's idea of a really good time was to get up at daylight and drive out to Maison Lafitte to watch the horses work out. I made a few trips with him and stood in drizzling rain as the beautiful horses owned by Marcel Boussac streaked around the track. We met Boussac's trainer and visited his breeding farm. Downs, like most race followers, had one dream horse. His horse was Souverain, and it wasn't long before I, too, had become a member of the Souverain cult; in Paris it is a cult. Each week hundreds go to the Ali Khan stud farm about twenty miles from Paris to see Souverain, just as the faithful made pilgrimages to Lexington to see Man O' War.

My acquaintance with Souverain began in a restaurant named L'Etrier on the Avenue de Villiers. L'Etrier means The Stirrup, and it is a very attractive spot indeed, with walls of paneled cedar and a dozen pictures of a big bay horse framed upon the walls. The slim, dark, good-looking man who greeted Ken so warmly when we dropped in one day was Monsieur Ferdinand Schmitt. Monsieur and Madame Schmitt, together with a fabulous Parisian boulevardier known as Lulu the Chestnut, own the horse. They also own the restaurant and those two properties constitute quite a parlay.

When Monsieur Schmitt heard that I wanted to meet Souverain, he beamed as though I had said I would like to meet his child. Monsieur Schmitt asked to be allowed to order our lunch. Ginny and Marie-Therese were out looking for bargains somewhere, so Ken and I were alone. When Ken suggested that we dispense with cocktails, Monsieur Schmitt was delighted. Like Downs, he disapproved of cocktails and believed that a meal should begin and end with champagne.

After a memorable meal, we made a date to meet Souverain early the next day. Souverain, we found at seven the next morning, lives unostentatiously but comfortably in an ivy-covered stone barn at Marly-la-Ville on the enormous breeding and training farm owned by Ali Khan. The word "barn" hardly fits the present domicile of Souverain. It is more like a chateau. The retired champion has two huge stalls, an indoor track where he can exercise if the weather is bad and a private outdoor playground where he can cavort to his heart's content. Trainer Henri Mueller brought Souverain out of his stall, and the champion looked at us with large, eloquent eyes and frowned.

"Souverain is disappointed because you have no camera with you," Monsieur Schmitt said. "He loves to have his picture taken. Give him a little run."

Trainer Mueller detached the lead from Souverain's halter

and the big horse looked at him questioningly. The trainer spoke a few quiet words to the horse and Souverain wheeled and started to trot around the paddock. He obviously knew that he was on show and he hammed it up with the flair of any great actor, general or king, despite the absence of the newsreel boys. He held his head erect, and flashed the whites of his eyes in what European racing fans call the "double-whammy" look. You felt that he was well named, for Souverain, of course, is French for Sovereign.

Champion race horses are traditionally highstrung, nervous, and apt to get very annoyed if the wind blows a leaf across their vision. Souverain showed none of these usual attributes. He acted more like a huge pet dog. It may be because right now Souverain is a happily married man who in his first year at stud has had twenty-two brides.

Watching Souverain practically purring with pleasure, it was hard to realize that he saw more actual fighting during the war than many G.I.'s. The story of how he was brought back from the fighting front to become the idol of French racing circles begins with a gentleman named Lucien Chataignoux. Because his last name so closely resembles *"châtaignier,"* the French word for "chestnut tree," he has always been known to his intimates as Lulu the Chestnut.

Lulu the Chestnut is a tall, lean man with the ruddy complexion that indicates good dining and wining, and little round green eyes that don't miss much that goes on around him, especially at the tracks, where he spends most of the time. His origins are somewhat obscure, and there are some who think he was just born full-grown, polo coat, pork-pie hat and all, at Longchamps or St. Cloud. Lulu always cut quite a figure around the paddock and on the boulevards and at the night clubs, but until he met Souverain, he never was exactly a part of the rigid social circles of Paris racing. You would never see him in the clubhouse hobnobbing with Prince Ali Khan or Monsieur Marcel Boussac, the Warren Wright of France. But when a race was over you would almost invariably spot Lulu the Chestnut's polo coat up near the head of the line at the cashier's window.

During the occupation the Germans continued to operate the Paris tracks. By some odd coincidence, a French jockey on a horse that was heavily backed by German or collaborationist money often found that he was unable to get his horse to put forth its best efforts. Lulu the Chestnut was frequently among those present at the cashier's window when the long shots scored. His acquaintanceship with jockeys and trainers was large and, of course, his knowledge of horseflesh considerable.

During the last year of the war Lulu the Chestnut found himself in pretty fair financial condition. But what good were francs when you couldn't get a good steak? Of course, there were black-market restaurants, but the prices they charged were outrageous and sometimes they went out of business overnight. To put an end to uncertain eating arrangements, Lulu the Chestnut decided to open a restaurant of his own. He formed a partnership with his friends, Monsieur and Madame Schmitt, and L'Etrier was the result.

In the summer of 1944 Lulu heard that horses were going very cheap in Normandy, the Blue Grass region of France. You could buy the finest colts at bargain basement prices. There was just one slight hitch: the owners could not guarantee delivery. Three tough gentlemen named Bradley, Patton and Montgomery were operating a quite different kind of race in Normandy and there was a great deal of shooting going on. In Paris, Lulu had heard of a magnificent young colt called Souverain. Lulu knew breeding and he knew that Souverain, by Maravedis out of Jolie Reine, had the blood lines that might possibly result in racing greatness. So with Monsieur and Madame Schmitt he bought Souverain for 500,000 francs (less than $1,700) and then sent a couple of brave souls (who were unemployed at the time) to Normandy to pick up the horse. They drove right into the melée in a truck Lulu had hired and finally located Souverain running around the countryside not one bit awed by the diving P-47's, booming howitzers, and the other confusions of a very noisy war. They loaded him into the truck and started for Paris. They used back roads, and ran smack into a German tank detachment. The Germans were moving fast—away from Generals Bradley, Patton and Montgomery—so they let the horse go but seized the truck. Lulu's two friends grabbed Souverain and started the hike to Paris.

It was a long and not uneventful trip. The American Air Force was shooting at anything that moved in those hectic days and the main roads were clogged with the swollen tide of the German retreat, but the three footsore travelers made it safely across country to Paris.

Lulu the Chestnut and the Schmitts were delighted with their purchase. The horse was immediately put in training, but he didn't seem to show much interest in hurrying. He would gallop, but only if prodded. Lulu the Chestnut wondered whether racing was just too tame a pastime for a horse who had been living on the world's greatest battlefield. But when Lulu entered Souverain in his first race all doubts were settled. Souverain had been kidding all the time.

The excitement of the crowd seemed to communicate itself to the horse. They had trouble saddling him. In the paddock he reared and his eyes flashed wildly. On the way to the post his jockey had difficulty holding him in check. When the barrier went up all his jockey had to do was hang on. He won easily and Lulu the Chestnut knew that he had a horse, not a goat.

He only ran twice as a two-year-old and won both races. Then his three owners astutely withdrew him from competition. French owners do not follow the American and English practice of tossing two-year-olds into one race after another, and the result is that the older generations of French horses are sounder.

As a three-year-old, Souverain showed what the boys around the track call "promise." He was beaten once and then won three consecutive races, but the opposition wasn't much. His owners weren't putting him in against the first team as yet. They were shooting for the moon and were doing nothing to jeopardize the colt's chances. In French racing circles the moon is the Grand Prix de Paris.

Lulu the Chestnut felt that Souverain was capable of winning the big event, but he didn't appear overconfident when asked about it. In fact, although he had entered Souverain in the Grand Prix he had also entered him in a race against cheaper horses on the program of the same day. He wasn't sure, he said coyly, whether Souverain was good enough to compete with the best horses in Europe. It wasn't until the last possible moment, on the day of the race, that the owners withdrew Souverain from the cheaper event and declared him for the Grand Prix. Prince Chevalier was the favorite. Souverain was very lightly regarded. After all, his owners had so little confidence in him that they had almost withdrawn him from the race to put him in an event with a lot of platers. And so Souverain went to the post as the rank outsider at one hundred to one.

Souverain won from Prince Chevalier in a photo finish. No one knows how much his owners won on the race, but it is certain that they were somewhat more affluent after the event. As a matter of record, no one was allowed to pay for a drink at L'Etrier for the next week.

Three months later they took Souverain to England for the King George VI Stakes, the great autumn international classic. This was no contest. At one time during the race, Marcel Lollierou, Souverain's French jockey, had a moment of panic. He looked around and, seeing no competition anywhere near, had the horrible thought that he must have strayed off the course. But he hadn't. Souverain won by five lengths with Jockey Lollierou holding him in. Airborne, winner of the 1946 Derby and the darling of the British racing public, was second. This was quite a day for the three owners of Souverain. Once again they had wagered heavily on their pet. And it was the King of England who handed them the victory cup. Lulu the

Chestnut had come a long way from Montmartre and the boulevards of Paris. He could now trade his polo coat and green pork-pie hat for a cutaway and gray topper.

In 1947 Souverain won the Ascot Gold Cup by four lengths. The British were understandably annoyed at the idea of a French horse copping two of their most prized classics. The *Daily Mail,* militant guardian of all sacred British traditions, including the supremacy of British horseflesh, was highly indignant. It sent a man to Paris to learn the secret of Souverain's success. He was given access to the barn and allowed to talk freely with trainers and grooms and Souverain. What he learned there prompted him to dash for a phone and call his editor, Frank Owen. His discovery was headlined in the *Mail* and read by two million indignant readers. He reported that Souverain was trained on "sweet milk and tender carrots." This was at a time when austerity was the word for living in England. The newspaper implied unpleasant things about those tricky French who would feed sweet milk and carrots to a horse at times like these. It wasn't until the roar of laughter arising from Paris had echoed across the Channel that the *Daily Mail* realized that Lulu the Chestnut had been guilty of a bit of leg-pulling.

The answer to Souverain's success was simple—he was indeed what the French call a "super-crac." That sounds like basic, or at least Belmont Park English, but it is a French expression reserved for the great champions and it hasn't been used to describe a horse in France for many years.

He won them all, from six-furlong sprints to two-and-a-half-mile route events against the hottest competition of the racing world, barring the Americas. Like Man O' War or Citation, he could win them any way he pleased. He could sail out in front and stay there or he could loaf behind the field until the stretch and then turn on a blazing burst of speed. The latter tactics were usually employed and it was an unforgettable thrill to racing fans to watch his "change of foot" when he began his killing final spring.

Souverain's racing greatness was established in 1946 when he won the Grand Prix de Paris in France, the King George VI Stakes in England, and followed those by copping the Ascot Gold Cup in England in 1947. No other horse in history had ever done that. It was a tougher test than the one Citation passed in 1948 when he won the Kentucky Derby, the Preakness and the Belmont to win the American triple crown. It was tougher because Souverain not only had to beat the best horses on the continent; he had to cross the Channel and polish off the best that England and the wealthy Maharajas of India could produce. It is said that half a dozen horses, after trying vainly to beat Souverain, went out and hung themselves.

Lulu the Chestnut, Ferdinand Schmitt and happy Madame Schmitt held a conference. Souverain had won the biggest stakes in Europe. Should they send their one-horse stable to America for the rich dollar stakes? Twice Souverain had been flown to England and the trip hadn't bothered him. But a trip by air to the United States might be too risky. It would take about eighteen hours—a long time for a horse to stay on his feet. There were other considerations. Even a great race horse is highly susceptible to injury and, with the possible exception of smoker's throat, a horse can contract just about any disease that a man can. On the other hand, the owners had received fabulous offers for the horse. The Maharajah of Baroda had offered $600,000 for him and had been turned down. They would never sell Souverain and they decided not to ship him across the Atlantic. Instead they would retire him to stud. He was only four and he had years of great racing left in him, but there was always that chance of an injury that might end not only his racing days but his life. So they sent him to a lovely farm for a life of remunerative ease and romance. He receives four hundred guineas for each romance. Even in France stud fees are traditionally based, not on francs, but on guineas.

In a couple of years the sons and daughters of Souverain will be trying out their young legs on French and English tracks. If they are successful, Souverain's stud fees will be hiked considerably. As a stallion, Souverain should earn many millions of francs for his three owners. Now Lulu the Chestnut sits in the clubhouse chatting amiably with Prince Ali Khan, Marcel Boussac, or the Baron de Waldner. No one ever calls him Lulu the Chestnut any more. Today he is Monsieur Lucien Chataignoux to one and all, and he is considered to be a highly respected character.

Horses, wine, food, girls—these four commodities are not dismissed as casual frivolity by Parisians or even the country's economists. It is these four (plus clothes, a subject which I will leave strictly alone) that attract thousands of tourists each year, and without the dollars they leave in Paris the city would be really from hunger.

What of the girls of Paris? This question immediately evokes thoughts of night life and its traditional institution— the Folies Bergère. Ginny and I sat through the show twice and met the owner of the Folies and he invited us backstage. So we went backstage and met Yvonne and some of the other girls.

Yvonne is just twenty. She doesn't have much of a voice and her dancing is only passable, but every year she attracts nearly a million paying customers to the Folies Bergère, the fabulous musical show which is as much a part of Paris as the Eiffel Tower, Mona Lisa or onion soup.

Tired American businessmen who come to Paris to "relax" hurry right to the Folies Bergère even before they have bought that bottle of perfume for the little woman or sent the boys back home postcards. Afterwards they will tell you what a great show it was; they will rave about the singing of dimple-kneed Nita Raye, the comedy of the baggy-pants deadpan comic known only as Dandy, and the magnificently costumed Chinese ballet. When they do this they are lying in their teeth —they go to see Yvonne and her forty professional sisters. Yvonne is the girl who takes her clothes off and waves her lithe body all over the stage of the Folies Bergère, and only a cad would mention the fact that she cannot sing or dance well.

Monsieur Paul Derval, producer of the show since 1918, shakes his head sadly when you mention that Yvonne is really the one the public pays to see. Derval, a highly intelligent man with very good taste, likes the nude part of his show least of all, and it is a source of constant irritation to him that nudity and not artistry has become the trademark of the Folies. Derval, in fact, thinks so little of Yvonne and the other *nues* that he only pays them 24,000 francs a month, which is eighty dollars.

He gladly pays singer Nita Raye 400,000 francs ($1,300 a month) and he has paid stars like Josephine Baker and Maurice Chevalier far more than that, but these, he says, are artists. Derval often pays as much as 300,000 francs ($1,000) for a dress to clothe a Josephine Baker, and if Monsieur Michel Gyarmathy, his author, director, stage manager and dress designer writes a sketch in which a girl is to wear a silver-fox cape, Monsieur Derval insists that the cape be silver fox and not long-eared rabbit. Derval spares no expense to make his Folies the most glamorous and artistic show in the world, and he is sick at heart because after months of painstaking effort to produce such an extravaganza his customers only come to see a lot of silly naked girls parading about the stage.

Yvonne Menard, however, feels differently about it. If people did not pay to see the female form innocent of the disfiguring adornment of clothes, girls like Yvonne would be standing behind counters at the Galleries Lafayette or trying to convince plump American women that they really look divine in that stunning little toque with the peacock feathers.

Yvonne is grateful to the tired businessmen and she likes her job very much indeed. She lives in the northern part of Paris in a three-room flat with her parents, and each night (well, nearly every night) when the curtain has rung down she puts on her clothes and gets into the subway for the half-hour trek home. In addition to her nude routines, Yvonne was recently given a speaking part in a sketch with comic Dandy, and so she receives 28,000 francs a month.

Yvonne Menard is tall and slender and she has a pert face and light-brown hair. It must be admitted right at the start that although Yvonne is perhaps the best-looking girl in the show, she is a bit thin and slightly—what shall I say?—undeveloped. This is not Yvonne's fault. The upper architecture of most twenty-year-old girls in France is slightly skimpy and undeveloped. During the occupation years, milk and butter were too precious to be wasted on growing young girls. The German military authorities had other uses for milk and butter. Even today Yvonne never gets any milk, for milk in Paris is only for children and the hospitalized ill. When visiting foreigners meet Yvonne and take her out, they try to impress her by buying champagne. Yvonne would be much more impressed if they would give her just a glass of powdered milk. No Parisienne in her right mind would even dream of a glass of fresh milk. One sees milk *nature* only in the farming districts.

But the tired businessmen who fill the large 1,600-seat theatre each night do not seem to mind Yvonne's mammalarian deficiency. When she and her forty undraped sisters dance up a flight of stairs and then leap into what is supposed to be the fires of hell, the tired businessmen applaud with gusto. It might be mentioned that the customers are not limited to American visitors at the Folies Bergère. In fact, during the winter months, when virtually no foreign visitors are in Paris, the show still sells out every night. There are tired businessmen in Normandy and Picardy and Flanders, too, who come to Paris for fun and frolic.

Yvonne was surprised that I had picked her out. After all, Nita Raye was the star of the show. She was also about to marry Maurice Chevalier, which made her just about the luckiest girl in Paris, for Monsieur Chevalier is one of the town's wealthiest citizens. Or (Yvonne suggested), why didn't I write about Mademoiselle Fortunia, who was the *première danseuse*? I didn't explain to Yvonne that Ginny and I had picked her because she seemed to be the one fresh, young-looking thing in the whole show.

Yvonne told us that she had been studying dancing since she was fifteen. Her eyes lit up as she talked. "Dancing was fun. Oh, it was hard work, especially after working in an office all day, but I loved it."

"When did you give up typing in favor of dancing?" I asked her.

"I haven't given up typing at all," she said. "Two years ago I heard they were having an audition at the Folies Bergère. There must have been a hundred girls trying for the few jobs vacant, but Monsieur Derval and Monsieur Michel picked me. I was certainly surprised. My mother and father just couldn't believe it. Of course I had to start as a *nue,* and that doesn't pay very well. So my father told me to keep my job as a secretary and I have. I still work in the same office, but they let me off on days we have matinees. I make about the same salary at the office that I do here at the Folies."

I reeled at this cosmic revelation. It was beyond belief that a Folies Bergère dancer should spend eight hours a day pecking away at a typewriter. Ginny, reading my thoughts, said coldly, "Don't be so suspicious. Look at her fingernails."

Yvonne smiled a little ruefully as she noticed my startled glance at her short, stubby nails.

"I have to keep them short," she said. "I used to glue on false nails, but it took too much time. And then," she added in a matter-of-fact tone, "I guess people don't come to the Folies to see a girl's fingernails. Do you think?"

I hastily changed the subject. "How do your parents feel about your working as a *nue*?"

"Why should they mind?" Yvonne seemed honestly puzzled at the question. "Of course they worry a little during the winter because it is so cold here in the theatre. Last winter it was very bad. It wasn't Monsieur Derval's fault; he got all the coal he could, but the government would only allow him so much. That is why most of us had colds all winter. It was especially difficult for those of us who are *nues*."

Girls in the chorus of Broadway musicals usually consider themselves to be serving an apprenticeship which will one day lead to star parts or Hollywood. Most girls in the chorus of the Folies Bergère think they have already arrived—their dreams seldom soar higher than this.

"Wouldn't you like to be a star?" I asked Yvonne.

"Yes," Yvonne said, and then she added with complete honesty, "but I don't think I sing well enough. Everyone would like to be a star—like Mistinguette. Naturally. But meanwhile, I am very happy."

Discipline backstage is rigid and although the girls like and respect Michel Gyarmathy, who is complete boss backstage, they say that he has eyes in the back of his head. All the girls have to be in their dressing rooms ready to go on at eight each night. A girl who is fifteen minutes late is fined 5 percent of what she receives each performance; a girl who is absent is fined 25 percent. There is always a long waiting list for jobs in the Folies, and girls who miss cues, make late entrances or who are habitual absentees don't last very long.

"I have to keep a close watch on the girls," Michel said gloomily, as though this were the most distasteful job in the world. "This present version of the Folies has been running for three years. Monsieur Derval and I have a completely new production written, costumed, and ready to produce, but we can't put it on until people are tired of this one. And we sell out every night. Derval has one very strict rule. He believes that the audience which pays to see the performance tonight is entitled to the same enthusiastic, exciting performance the first-night audience saw three years ago. If I find a girl keeps showing up tired and unable to do her best, I investigate. If she has been ill, I let her rest a few days. But if I discover that she has been keeping late hours and not getting enough sleep, I discharge her. But the girls who work hard are rewarded. We give them speaking parts in sketches or we raise their salaries."

American visitors watching the nudes prance about the stage often get a slightly cockeyed idea about them. Not that the girls are prim, convent-bred recluses, but it is a fact that nudity and immorality are not synonymous on the Paris stage. Hundreds of G.I.'s found this out to their great surprise. A girl who takes a job in the Folies Bergère merely as a front for less legitimate but higher-paying activities which keep her up late doesn't last long with keen-eyed Monsieur Michel Gyarmathy.

The Folies Bergère is quite definitely big business. It costs Derval about one hundred thousand dollars to put on a new edition of the Folies, and his running expenses are enormous. For instance, when Michel engages a girl he immediately has three pairs of shoes made for her. Poorly fitting shoes can give even the most glamorous-looking girl bunions or ingrown toenails. When the shoes show signs of wear they are not repaired, but replaced by new ones. In all, there are twelve hundred costumes hanging on racks in the big dressing rooms. In addition to the nude numbers (which comprise about a third of the show) there are a half dozen lavish scenes which feature really beautiful and expensive clothes. Twice a month these twelve hundred costumes are cleaned. Derval maintains a permanent staff of dressmakers to repair the costumes and make new ones. This is under the supervision of Madame Derval. There are 350 men and women on Monsieur Derval's payroll and many of them are the highest-paid specialists in Paris.

If there is such a thing as a national theatre in France, it is the Folies Bergère, even though such a statement will shock members of the French Academy and cause devotees of the Comédie Française or the Opéra-Comique to choke angrily on their apéritifs. It would, of course, horrify the ever-increasing followers of Jean Paul-Sartre. However, the truth is that the rather tired old theatre on rue Richon has not been dark a single night since 1918, when Monsieur Paul Derval took it over. It has run 365 days a year and continued through two wars and a few depressions. It never had a losing year. No theatre in the history of show business has ever created the records made by the Folies Bergère.

The truth is that an American eye finds the Folies a pretty old-fashioned revue, and an American ear gets no pleasure out of the corny tunes or lyrics. Only the nudes differentiate it from the routine Broadway revue of the 1920's. There are a dozen places in Paris where you'll hear better music and see better-looking girls. You can take a girl to the Monseigneur, one of the nicest night clubs in the world, listen to a fine orchestra, have a bottle of champagne and get a bill for five dollars. But when the best clubs are half-empty the S.R.O. sign will be up at the Folies Bergère. And Monsieur Derval, incidentally, charges about $1.80 for standing room and about $2.20 for a good seat. Translate that into francs and it means that the ordinary French customer must lay out a day's pay to see Yvonne and her colleagues. And the ordinary French customer is the backbone of the success of the Folies. The visiting tourists may fill up the expensive seats, but it is Monsieur Jacques Doakes of Paris who fills the *promenoir* and the cheaper seats. It is difficult for an American, accustomed to the magnificent Broadway productions, to understand the amazing hold this revue has on the public.

It seems a great pity to disillusion those happy warriors of World War I who still talk of the glamorous days when they spent their evenings at the Folies. Honestly, they could do much better by dropping into the neighborhood Bijou where they might at least see their dreams come true on the screen.

CHAPTER TWELVE

*O*ne of the best newspapers in Europe is, I believe, the *Herald Tribune* European edition. The editor is Geoffrey Parsons, Jr., son of the chief editorial writer of the *New York Herald Tribune* and one of the truly great adornments of the journalistic profession. Geoffrey Parsons, Jr., does the kind of job on the European edition of the *Herald Tribune* that his father has been doing for what young Geoff always called "the New York supplement."

Geoff and his wife, Drue, own a farm in the country and their table is always laden with fresh fruit and vegetables. So we went to Geoff's for dinner with Averell and Marie Harriman and we listened to Parsons and Harriman talk, and it was talk that made sense.

"If you want to learn something about France, get out of Paris," Harriman urged. "Go to some of the smaller cities and see how the people are thinking and working."

Parsons suggested, "Go to some city that took a bad beating during the war and where there hasn't been much reconstruction as yet. There you'll hear France speaking."

So I went to Dunkerque because I wanted to hear the end of a story which had begun in Dunkirk, New York, about a year after the war ended. Dunkirk is an ordinary American city of some 20,000 ordinary men and women, but this city that sprawls comfortably on the shores of Lake Erie in upper New York State did something extraordinary for Dunkerque, France.

One day a group of men were sitting around the luncheon table at the St. Francis Hotel on Main Street. Someone casually mentioned that he'd seen a short piece in the *Dunkirk Observer* about Dunkerque, France. It seemed that Dunkerque took quite a beating during the occupation. The Germans had appropriated all the livestock, all the farm tools and implements as well as all the surgical instruments and dental equipment.

One of the men mentioned that their Dunkirk was named after Dunkerque, France, way back in 1810 when a French trader noticed how similar the lake harbor was to the North Sea harbor of the French port.

"Nice if we could help them," another said casually. And that's how it began. Today they don't even remember whose idea it was. But people started talking about it, and one day Wally Brennan wrote a piece about it in the *Observer*.

The idea began to grow. It grew to a point where a committee was appointed to study the possibilities of helping Dunkerque, France. The Chamber of Commerce and the City Council approved a plan to raise $2,500 and it was presented to the people. There was a howl of protest. Why only $2,500? The hell with that! Let's really do this well. That's how the people talked as they gathered at the soda fountain in Monroe's Drug Store (est. 1859), and as they walked out of the First Baptist Church on Washington Avenue or gathered in front of St. Hedwig's Catholic Church on Doughty Street.

"What can they do with money over there?" someone said.

212

"Why not send them things they need? Let's send them shovels and pitchforks and seed and livestock and surgical equipment and . . ."

Mayor Murray called a mass meeting. Industrial Commissioner Roman Wiate, Wally Brennan, editor of the *Observer*, and Attorney Joe Rubenstein proposed a plan. Each civic society, lodge, union local, club, veterans' organization would be assigned a specific task. At the meeting, the Mayor said each organization would be notified by mail as to what its specific job would be. But that wasn't good enough.

Nels Currier, President of the C.I.O. local, United Steel Workers of America (he worked at the Alleghany Ludlum Steel Plant), got up and bellowed, "Tell us *now* what you want Local 2693 to do and it'll be done. Give us our orders."

Across the hall, Charlie Rudolph, president of C.I.O. Local 767, jumped to his feet. "What do you want from us at the American Fork and Hoe Company? You want shovels, money, or just work from us? Name it and you can have it."

His boss, Neal Benton, manager of the plant, cried out, "We'll go along with anything you want our men to do. As Charlie says, 'Name it, you can have it.' "

Jux Weinberg, department-store owner, said, "You can have anything you want off the shelves of my store."

Something was happening there in that hall. Man after man got up demanding his assignment then and there. Farmers from outlying districts pledged calves, pigs, chickens; their wives got up timidly to suggest that the people of Dunkerque might like some strawberry or blackberry preserves. The president of the Elks, after conferring briefly with a few members, got up to announce that the Elks would donate a bull to the cause. Tongues weren't talking that night, hearts were.

"Dunkirk to Dunkerque Day" was scheduled for Thanksgiving, 1946. The firehouse on Eagle Street was the warehouse for the goods that were donated. There were canned goods, clothing, dental and surgical supplies, all sorts of farming implements and seeds, toys, blankets, cooking utensils.

213

A few items came that couldn't be conveniently kept in the firehouse: a herd of breeding cattle, ten young heifers, two bulls, a dozen goats and a dozen pigs. They were moved to Fritz Schweyen's farm. Eighteen kids belonging to the Hi-Ya Club (a boys' club organized by high-school teacher Paul Reber) saved up enough money to buy and contribute a microscope; Charlie Rudolph's local and the plant got together to contribute fifty dozen shovels. School kids brought in hundreds of pencils and school supplies.

Well, the great day came. Ambassador Henri Bonnet came to accept the gifts. There was a parade, with the Ambassador, Mayor Murray and Charles Boyer on the reviewing stand. Eighteen big trucks went by, laden with the gifts for Dunkirk's sister city. The committee had set out to raise $2,500. The value of the goods collected was close to $100,000.

A hundred things happened that day that the people of Dunkirk still talk about. But the really big thing that happened is the thing that none of them has been able to explain. This wasn't just a momentary flash of generosity quickly forgotten. Something happened that seems to have left a permanent mark on every man, woman and child in the city. Dunkirk grew up; Dunkirk realized that it wasn't just a pleasant little city on Lake Erie. Dunkirk realized that it was a part of the world.

A new kind of thinking had come to Dunkirk. People asked themselves questions: "Why did the Polish population come through a hundred percent to help a French city? What did our Poles have in common with those people over in Dunkerque? Our Italian population and our German population knocked themselves out to help. It's the first time our Protestants, Catholics, Jews really got together to work for the people of a city nearly 4,000 miles away. Why? And the rest of us upstate hard-bitten Yankees, what made us go overboard the way we did? Not many of us ever met a Frenchman, and yet . . ."

Dunkirk, without being quite able to put it into words, was embarking on a program of direct contact with the people of the Old World, with no middleman in the form of government or diplomat involved. Dunkirk, in short, was giving Europe a practical demonstration of democracy in action. Hundreds of letters of thanks came from Dunkerque, and when they were translated and printed in the *Observer*, the people of Dunkirk said thoughtfully, "Why, these are our kind of folks. They're no different from us. Maybe people all over the world are just like us. If they are, they don't want any more wars. . . ."

How about the people in Dunkerque, France, who had been helped? How did they feel about America? How did they feel about democracy? I went there to find out the answers. I went there to hear France speak.

When the last shot was fired, Dunkerque took inventory and found that 80 percent of the city had been destroyed. Even today, after three years of peace, the city looks as though some giant hand had picked it up, shaken it angrily and then dropped it carelessly on the white sands of the Dunkerque beaches. Only 5 percent of the people of Dunkerque were able to return to their original dwellings, when peace came. Today, more than 13,000 men, women and children live in ramshackle, makeshift temporary dwellings, in tiny prefabricated homes or in partially destroyed houses. Even today there is not a bathtub operating in Dunkerque, for the city doesn't have the electric power to pump the water.

The only part of the city which does not show the ghastly scars of war is the beach known as the Molo Plage. It was here, on the white sand and in the shallow water, that thousands of British soldiers died on June 6th and 7th in 1940. But it was from here that 310,000 of them were picked up by every conceivable kind of boat and returned to England to fight again. Today the waters of the Channel curl peacefully over the beach. Water and sand obliterate even the most horrible scars, and today only a couple of grotesque-looking concrete blockhouses on the beach remind you of perhaps the most horrible forty-eight hours of the whole war. The thousands of broken tanks, armored cars and guns which once dotted the beach have all sunk mercifully out of sight, and now children, whose memories are happily short, wade out into the cool water and play on the sands. But back of the beach there is nothing but desolation and destruction.

Let's meet some of the people who live here. Suppose we drop in to see Sister Claire. She runs the Dunkerque dispensary, a low, one-storied temporary shack made of plaster board. Before bombs leveled it, this was a fine brick-and-concrete hospital. Sister Claire is about as big as a whisper. Her eyes are blue and soft and young-looking, although the little sister must be almost sixty. Twelve hours a day Sister Claire takes care of the sick, and, because doctors are few and overworked, she does a great deal more than the ordinary nurse does. Her dispensary is close to the harbor, and dock workers and seamen off ships who are injured are often brought in to the little sister. She makes comforting sounds to them and her small hands work busily, and finally, she smiles and says, *"Voila, tout ira bien maintenant."* One morning I watched her treat a sailor whose arm had been burned. It was not until she had finished and he thanked her that I realized he was an American seaman.

"It doesn't hurt a bit," the sailor said.

Sister Claire picked up the tube of tannic acid ointment she had been using on his arm.

"Ceci vient de Dunkirk," she laughed. It was indeed from Dunkirk and so were the sulfa drugs and the jars of vitamin tablets and the bandages and the rubber gloves and the syringes and needles that filled a large white cabinet.

"All this came from your American Dunkirk," she said. "And the good it has done! Hundreds of our people have been helped by these medicines. It is hard now—almost impossible—to get medicines in France. Many people who were very sick are well today because of what your Dunkirk sent us. And the vitamins we give to the children. We have very little milk for them and the vitamins help so much. There is no way I can thank the

216

people of Dunkirk, but I remember them in my prayers always."
And then she added shyly, "They will not mind that?"

The material which was sent from America's Dunkirk was
distributed very intelligently under the auspices of "American
Aid to France." It was earmarked and put in charge of Anne-
Marie Perret, a Swiss girl, and all the material was allotted
according to her discretion. It was smart to allow an outsider
to distribute the goods, for no one could charge that either
personal or political pressure was exerted. You only have to
walk through the streets and out into the fields beyond the city,
and hear the warmth of the greetings when people see her, to
know what a great job Anne-Marie did.

There was, for instance, the matter of the wheel chair. Who
would receive the one wheel chair that had come from Dunkirk?'People in the North of France are apt to be proud and,
until you know them a bit, unbending. (There are those who
say the same thing of the people of upper New York State.)
Anne-Marie was told of two elderly sisters who lived with their
uncle in a small house on rue Jules Degroit. Anne-Marie asked
the two sisters to come and see her at American Aid to France
headquarters on the Avenue des Bains. It was a sweltering day,
but the two sisters arrived in heavy black taffeta high-necked
dresses. Anne-Marie Perret said they shouldn't have put on
their Sunday clothes just to visit her office, and the older sister
said calmly, "But these are the only dresses we own."

Anne-Marie Perret knows how to handle women, and within
a few moments she had them trying on dresses that not long
before had been hanging on racks in Jux Weinberg's store in
Dunkirk. Anne-Marie noticed that even while they admired
the dresses, their eyes kept stealing furtively toward the wheel
chair that stood in the corner of the room. Finally, she asked
them why they were interested, and they told her of their uncle
Jules Beck who, they said, was very old. Arthritis had crippled
him badly. He had been bed-ridden for nearly a year, but if
only he had a wheel chair . . .

217

I dropped in to see M. Beck and the two sisters. It was a little like turning the clock back a hundred years. Their neat Flemish-type house with its tiled floors had been untouched, although eight bombs had fallen in the garden. The house and the garden were enclosed by a brick wall and the air was strong with the scent of the white reseda blossoms which hung heavily from the trees. It was Jules Beck's 90th birthday and he and the two sisters were sitting at a small table in the garden, having tea. Just tea. There was no sugar or milk and there was no birthday cake. Monsieur Beck sat in his wheel chair smiling contentedly.

"This has given me new legs," he smiled, patting the wheel chair. "For this I will always be grateful to America. I can enjoy my garden now."

He talked of the horror of the occupation when the Germans had stripped their home of everything. Chiefly he resented the fact that they had chopped down six trees that had stood in the garden for a hundred years. There was something familiar about the thin, strong face of the old man. When Anne-Marie Perret mentioned that he was a cousin of General de Gaulle's mother, I saw the family resemblance. Even in the wheel chair you could tell that Jules Beck was well over six feet tall and he had the nose and the piercing eyes of de Gaulle. The two sisters were wearing serviceable blue dresses trimmed with white, and one of them shyly showed me the label at the back and asked me what Safe Store meant. I told her it meant that a man named Jux Weinberg, who owned the Safe Store on Main Street, Dunkirk, had a very big heart.

The seeds which Dunkirk once sent are now potatoes and carrots and beans and radishes and beets. Albert Barbary has a neat little red brick house beside the canal which is called in Flemish the Noort Graf. He is a cheerful, apple-cheeked man with a drooping mustache and a pleasant smile. He is a farmer six days a week, but on the seventh he is "mayor" of Petite-Synthe. Petite-Synthe is one of the six districts of Dunkerque, and each has a "mayor" who is a member of the City Council.

Sixty-seven-year-old Albert Barbary showed me his beans and his carrots and his white radishes with pride.

"Our soil likes your American seed," he remarked. "See how fat the beets and the radishes are. This soil was old and ruined by the powdered cement and brick from the debris of the bombed buildings. But the fertilizer Dunkirk sent made the soil bloom again."

The old gentleman took me to the outskirts of the city. Here an area of about four square blocks was completely leveled. The debris had been cleared away and the whole region was aglow with the bright greenness of growing things. Occasionally an ugly wall or chimney still firmly attached to the ground arose from the green plain, but beans were already creeping over them as though nature was trying to hide their ugliness.

"When the seeds came," he said, "we decided to allot a plot of ground to everyone who wished to plant and care for a garden. Hundreds of our citizens planted the seeds and here you see the result. Dunkirk sent us shovels and hoes and we passed these around from one family to another as they needed them."

Some five hundred men, women and children were working here in this communal garden which was merely one of a dozen in the city.

"We are giving prizes tomorrow for those who have the best gardens," Albert Barbary said suddenly. "It will be at the Salle des Fêtes on the Avenue de la Republique. Will you come? You will be interested to see what prizes we are giving," he said with a sly smile.

The Salle des Fêtes, a low wooden building which serves as a sort of community center, was crowded the next morning. Because it was Sunday, the men were dressed in their best clothes and nearly all looked a little uncomfortable in their white celluloid collars and detachable ties. Their wives and children sat beside them primly, trying hard not to look expectant. They all relaxed when the band started playing Flemish tunes, and then huge "Mayor" Vanmairies of the Rosendael district ascended the platform, cleared his throat and began to speak. The judges sat in chairs behind him, looking a bit embarrassed as they stared into the faces of nearly a thousand of their neighbors. Finally the winners were announced. As he mentioned a name, there would be a happy squeal from the children of the family, and then the farmer who had been declared a winner would smile self-consciously, get up and walk to the platform to receive his prize.

The prizes? The prizes were pitchforks, spades and hoes made by the men of C.I.O. Local 767 in Dunkirk's American Fork and Hoe Company back in 1946. The winners (there were thirty of them) clutched the spades tightly as they left the platform. They would no longer have to borrow these precious tools; these they would own for life. When it was all over, Monsieur Vanmairies made a very nice speech about the generosity of the people of America. The people of Northern France are traditionally stolid and unemotional, but they weren't on that bright Sunday morning in August. They applauded and then they roared their thanks and their children joined in. Then the band played the only American song it knew—"God Bless America." Gratitude trembled in the air of that low-ceilinged room; you could feel it coming from the hearts of everyone there.

You couldn't go anywhere in Dunkerque without seeing some of the goods which were collected and paraded through the streets of Dunkirk, New York, on Thanksgiving Day, 1946. The Dunkirk Hospital had contributed an examination table. I found it in the office of Dr. Fernand Fievet. I also found a dozen patients waiting for the doctor.

"The Germans took all of our medical instruments," Dr. Fievet said bitterly. "When the war ended, I found nothing left in my office but a broken-down couch. This table," his hand went unconsciously to stroke its gleaming whiteness, "is busy many, many hours a day. I don't know what I would have done without it."

The microscope used by Dr. André Rommel in the small

hospital, 24 rue des Fusilles, is another precious gift from Dunkirk. I found blond, keen-eyed Dr. Rommel bending over the microscope when I dropped in to see him.

"A young woman brought her three children in here this morning," he told me. "The microscope says all three have tuberculosis. Without the microscope we wouldn't have known it for some time. I would have had to send the sputum specimens to Lille or somewhere else to a laboratory. Now at least with this microscope we can find out the truth quickly."

Dr. Rommel told me that the children of Dunkerque have never lived normal lives or eaten the food of normal childhood. Their undernourished bodies find it difficult to fight the deadly bacillus of tuberculosis. But many of these children are saved because the microscope gave its warning in time.

Eighteen children in Dunkirk, New York, saved their spending money for weeks to buy this microscope. These eighteen boys are three years older now. They might like to know that the spending money they contributed is saving the lives of children in Dunkerque today.

For twenty years Father Pierre Lestienne has been principal of a boys' school in Dunkerque. A bomb completely wrecked the wooden building where the children of Dunkerque had learned their reading, writing and arithmetic. But today five hundred youngsters are studying in a new schoolhouse. I stood with Father Lestienne watching a dozen youngsters kicking a football around.

"That came from your Dunkirk," Father Lestienne said. "That football is the only one in town and it gives the boys a lot of pleasure. Our children had forgotten how to play. Now they are learning again."

We stepped into Father Lestienne's office and he showed me supplies of pencils, crayons, notebooks, painting sets.

"The children of your Dunkirk schools sent these," he said. "As you will see, we still have some left after nearly two years. We give the crayons and the paints as prizes to the best students each month. Dunkirk sent us a great many books in your language and my pupils are so curious to read these stories that they are studying English very hard."

We went into a classroom. It was not unlike a classroom in a Dunkirk school, except there were long wooden benches and tables instead of individual desks. At the back of the classroom were twelve pairs of rubbers, each bearing the name of the boy who owned them.

"They are very proud of these rubbers," Father Lestienne said. "We have a great many sudden showers here in the North, and now the boys can splash around happily in the mud with them. Yes, the rubbers all came from Dunkirk."

Twice a day the boys of the school receive powdered milk, all contributed by American Aid to France. Very few of these children have ever tasted anything but powdered milk, and if it were not for America they would have little of that.

Yes, you can go anywhere in Dunkerque and see evidence of American generosity. On the docks where men are engaged in the backbreaking work of rebuilding, you will see a man filling his pipe from a tin of tobacco with a familiar label—tobacco from Dunkirk.

"There are three things a man cannot live without," a husky, bearded dock worker told me, laughing deeply. "Bread, wine and tobacco. We work hard here on the docks, but a pipe or two a day helps the hours pass more quickly. Yes, they gave the tobacco you sent from your Dunkirk to us—the workers."

You can drop into the municipal library and you'll find more than five hundred books—gifts of Dunkirk. You can drop into any one of a thousand tiny prefabricated shacks, and the housewife will point proudly to the wallpaper—a gift from Dunkirk. You can watch a man trying to make his half-ruined farmhouse a bit more attractive by painting it, and you'll notice that the paint and the brush he uses are from Dunkirk. You can drop into the little hotel known as the Chapeau Rouge and you'll find four or five men playing cards or chess to kill the long evenings, and if you look at the cards and the chessboards, you will find that they were made in America—a gift from Dunkirk.

Gustave Robelet, a thin, active, intense man, is Mayor of the City of Dunkerque. His eyes light up when he tells of the excitement when the first gifts arrived from Dunkirk.

"Things were very bad then," he said, shaking his head thoughtfully. "We were feeling discouraged. We didn't see how we could ever dig ourselves out of the ruins of the city. The gifts from your Dunkirk had a terrific psychological effect. We were not forgotten, after all. There were people thousands of miles away who were worried about us and who were trying to help us. And the things which came were things we needed so badly, especially the medicine, the powdered milk, the seed and the farming utensils. America has been very good to us and, believe me, we are grateful."

Usually the Communist Party in France (as everywhere else) sneers at American help and calls it an instrument of "American imperialism." In Dunkerque, as in every devastated city, the Communist Party is fairly strong. People who are hungry, without heat or shelter or adequate clothing, are often apt to believe the promises given so blithely by Communist leaders, and in sheer desperation turn toward the party which promises most. In Dunkerque during the last election, about 25 percent of the vote went to the Communist candidates, but even they refrain from criticizing the aid America has sent their city.

"In distributing these essentials of life which America sends us," Mayor Robelet says, "no one was discriminated against because of his political beliefs. When the Communist leaders saw their own children drinking milk and wearing clothes sent by generous American communities like Dunkirk, they could hardly attack America for any imperialistic aims. As a matter of fact," the Mayor said, "your generosity gives people a new faith in democracy, and here in Dunkerque the Communists are losing ground rapidly because of the gratitude people feel toward America."

The Chapeau Rouge was not a very pretentious hotel nor was the food served even faintly reminiscent of any Paris restaurant, but it was the best hotel in town and I stayed there. One night I was trying to phone Ginny in Paris and I found the operation a complicated one. There were only two "trunk" lines leading out of Dunkerque and neither seemed to be working. It is amazing how quickly an inoffensive telephone becomes one's enemy. I determined to sit in the tiny dining room of the hotel until my Paris call was completed. A half dozen others were there at a table. Two of them were playing chess —the others were watching and giving occasional unsought advice as is the custom with kibitzers the world over. The game was finally done with. By now they were my allies in my one-man fight against the French telephone system and they took turns barking quick and angry Flemish-French into the mouthpiece.

One of the chess players was a high-school teacher named Pierre Landret. There was something about Pierre Landret that made you look at him twice. He was dark; his hair, his eyes, and the shadows under his eyes were dark. There was only one electric-light bulb in the room, and when Pierre Landret moved, it seemed to throw dark shadows across his lean, gaunt face. But he had a quick, bright smile, and when he showed his fine white teeth in a grin, the somber darkness seemed to leave his face. I finally gave up the impossible when the operator said that she might get Paris for me in the morning. The Frenchmen, having watched the unequal battle, decided to leave and I went out into the street with them. It was midnight, and a brilliant moon softened the desolate ruins of the city. They all had bicycles except Pierre Landret. He was staying with a friend about half a mile from the Chapeau Rouge, he said, and I fell into step with him.

He seemed to enjoy practicing his English on me, and he talked with animation. He asked if I had seen the beaches by moonlight. He lived near the beach, he said, so we set off through the quiet city.

He had been a Lieutenant in the French Army. He had been wounded early in 1940, and was discharged from the army. "Not serious," he said. "It was my right arm. You see, a bullet smashed the bone but a skillful doctor fixed it nicely." He rolled up his sleeve to show me the scar. "However, I would not be able to bend the arm or use the fingers for some time. That is why I was discharged. And so I came home to Dunkerque, only a few weeks before the horrible battle began here. My uncle owned a tavern outside the town and the Germans didn't trouble us too much because they thought they were winning—even though the bulk of the British Army had escaped. They made my uncle's place an officers' tavern and they needed us to run it. To them, I was merely a cripple with only one good arm, and at night as we served them cognac and mirabelle they would talk quite a lot. That is how I learned that it was here on the beaches of Dunkerque that they lost the war."

We had reached the beach now and we sat on a sea wall. All around us was silence except for the waves as they crept up on the sand. Pierre Landret took one of my cigarettes and nodded his thanks.

"They lost the war here?" I dug my shoe into the sand and threw up a cascade of it in the air. "By letting the British Army get away?" I asked a bit puzzled.

"That was only part of it," he said. "And only men escaped from these beaches; men in the war were pretty much expendable. It was equipment which could not be replaced, and the British left most of their equipment here. But had the Germans destroyed both the equipment (which they did) and the British Army, which they could have done easily, and then immediately invaded England the war would have been over. Had Hitler listened to his generals, this would have happened. It is interesting to reflect on this possibility.

"The British Army was trapped here on the sands," Pierre went on. "The German armoured divisions under Generals

Guderian and Reinhardt were on their way here with all opposition destroyed. They reached the Aire-St. Omer Canal only some fifteen miles from where we are sitting now, and then you know what happened? I know because I heard German officers discussing it angrily for the next three years in my uncle's tavern. Hitler gave an order that the armour should stop and remain where it was. Out there," he flung a careless arm inland, "at Bergues and Hazebrouck, only a few miles from here. *Mon Dieu*, those German tanks could have walked in and pushed almost half a million British soldiers into the sea. They had nothing left but light stuff. They had no air cover worth the name. They had nothing. The order to remain on the other side of the canal came from Hitler himself. One reason he gave was that he didn't want his German tanks to be lost in the Flemish marshes; but that was nonsense. I am merely quoting," Pierre Landret said apologetically, "German officers who argued this point in our tavern. In any case, while the German Panzer forces remained there, the British escaped.

"Believe me," he said, "that is when Hitler lost the war. Had he destroyed the British Army he could have walked into England under cover of the Luftwaffe. For some reason or other, Hitler hesitated. His paratroop generals pleaded with him. They had visualized all this long before. They were ready for an invasion of England by air. Their paratroops were veterans of a long campaign. Remember, they took over Holland in something like thirty minutes. The English terrain was to their liking. It was made to order for their airborne attacks. And yet, Hitler never gave the order to go ahead. None of the German officers whom we heard discuss this could understand it. Perhaps Hitler thought the British would make a deal with him. I don't know. Nor did the German officers know. In any case, Hitler lost his big chance. Yes, he could have won the war in June, 1940, and been ruling the world by now. And, if you'll forgive me," he said softly, "that includes your country. Don't forget, your country didn't come into the war until you were attacked."

"That's true enough," I said, "but there was Lend-Lease and there . . ."

"Please," he interrupted, "don't think I am criticizing America. It is the only hope now. It is the only hope of the world. What is the alternative here in France? Communism or de Gaulle. Either is horrible to contemplate. One is evil, the other is selfish. One means death as an independent nation, the other means the kind of ultra nationalism none of us wants.

"There is no reason for the present inflation," he said earnestly. "France is not like Italy or Greece or Holland, overpopulated to the point where the land cannot sustain the people. Structurally we are a sound country with plenty of good farming land and, potentially, plenty of industry. Yet, every day you read in the paper of new strikes, of new demands for higher wages, of a new government taking over. Our political parties are hopelessly divided. Only the Communist Party is well organized and well disciplined. If the other parties would unite and show a strong front a great deal of Communist support would disappear.

"You cannot get milk or butter in Paris or Dunkerque, but go into the country, especially in the South, and you will find plenty of milk and butter and fresh vegetables. The farmers will not bring these products to the cities to market. What can they do with the few francs they get? So they hoard their produce and barter it for commodities they need. They do not trust the government. They fear further inflation when the franc will be worth nothing. But food will always be worth something and they would rather have this food than the money. Many blame the Communists for the present chaos. This is nonsense. They are not the cause; they are the beneficiaries of the present economic conditions. The coal miners do not strike because they are Communists. They strike because they only make about forty dollars a month. If they made enough to maintain a decent standard of living, they would forget Communism quickly enough.

"Unfortunately, we only have one strong man in the country—de Gaulle," Pierre Landret said gloomily. "Have you ever met anyone in this country who actually liked de Gaulle? No? Nor have I. But there is no doubt that sooner or later he will take over. If he could only get rid of the idea that he is a male Jean d'Arc he might prove good for the country. Some say he is a Fascist. I do not believe this, but I do know that he is a strong-minded, ambitious man who will not compromise even if it would help the country. And some of the men he has around him are pretty terrible.

"It is not going to be pleasant to be a Frenchman during the next few years," he said grimly. "Our only real hope is ERP. Above all, we need coal, factory machinery and tools. Once we have these under ERP, our factories can really get to work and once they are producing at full capacity, maybe things will adjust themselves. But I do know one thing: our future will be decided by us—the people. However," he laughed, "we cannot straighten France out sitting here on the beach at Dunkerque. And I have a date with twenty-five youngsters at nine in the morning."

Little Dunkirk on Lake Erie really started something. You don't have to be big to have big ideas, and it was a big idea that Dunkirk came up with. Other cities followed what soon became known as the Dunkirk Plan. Denver adopted Brest; Los Angeles now helps to care for stricken Calais; Chicago adopted Coutances, and the whole state of Texas has taken the horribly mangled city of Le Havre to its warm heart. And San Francisco has adopted Beauvais.

I walked back to the Chapeau Rouge thinking of the things that Pierre Landret had said. The man who ran the little hotel, a big somber-faced man named Marcel Depinet, was sitting at a table reading the Dunkerque afternoon newspaper.

"That Pierre is a smart man," he said. "I saw you walk off with him. He knows what he is talking about. He is a cute one," Marcel laughed. "I suppose he told you of his short-wave set."

228

"No," I said.

"Pierre's uncle owned a place outside the city," Marcel chuckled, "and the German officers made it their headquarters. Pierre played very stupid. He made believe he knew no German and they thought him too dumb to learn. They talked freely in front of him and then early every morning Pierre would go down into his cellar. He had a short-wave radio set there and each day he would send reports to London as to what he had heard the night before. Yes, Pierre became one of our best underground fighters. He fought with his brain and it is a good brain. And after the war de Gaulle himself decorated Pierre with the Legion d'Honneur."

I told Marcel that I was leaving the next morning for Paris.

"That is too bad," he said with disappointment in his voice. "Some very good fish came in today. Besides, it is Monday and every Monday our cinema changes its program. It is true that we seldom get new films. We get a great many old American films and they are very good. Tomorrow one of these will be shown. It is a film about your Chicago." He held the newspaper out to me. "You see the announcement? It is a picture called *Scarface* with Paul Muni. Have you heard of it?"

CHAPTER THIRTEEN

It *was* time to go home and we were ready for it. We were getting homesick for New York and our daughter Joan. So we booked passage on the *Queen Mary* and two days before it was to sail, a cable came from *Collier's* saying they wanted a quick story on Queen Wilhelmina, another on the Frankfort to Berlin airlift and how about doing a story on Norway or Sweden?

"Those stories are important," Ginny said thoughtfully. "You better do them and come home later."

After I put Ginny on the boat train at the St. Lazar Station, I went back to the Hotel Plaza-Athénée and the doorman was sympathetic and the chasseur was sympathetic and a bellboy handed me a letter.

It was a short note from Moshe Brilliant. Moshe wrote that David "Mickey" Marcus had been killed in combat and that

230

Paul Blauner, the waiter I liked so much, had been killed when an Egyptian bomb had hit his home. He and his whole family had been wiped out.

I was in no mood for any more of Paris now. I phoned Jackie de Maudiut, an experienced and clever newspaper-woman, and told her I wanted to get in touch with someone in Amsterdam or The Hague who could help me with a story on Queen Wilhelmina. Wilhelmina had announced her intention of abdicating within a few weeks in favor of her daughter, Juliana. *Collier's* wanted a personality piece, plus a round-up of her influence on the country and how the people of Holland felt about her.

"I don't care about seeing the Queen or Juliana," I told Jackie. "I want to see people who have been close to the Queen for some years. Servants in the palace or cops who have guarded her or some of the underground men who were with her in London and some of her cabinet ministers. And I'm in a hurry, Jackie," I added.

Jackie, who would make a good bureau chief or magazine editor in any league, understood just what I wanted and proceeded to make arrangements for me.

I flew to Amsterdam the next morning and was met by a highly intelligent citizen of Holland named F. M. S. Donders. He had made appointments with a dozen men and he put himself as well as his car and chauffeur at my disposal. Within a few days I had learned quite a bit about Her Majesty, Queen Wilhelmina, and the country she had ruled for so many years.

Mynheer Frans van Heuven owns a pleasant tavern just outside of Haarlem. The tavern had been in his family for three generations and, Mynheer van Heuven said, a little sadly, he was going to retire soon and turn the tavern over to his son, Johannes. He lowered his huge body into a large chair, put his huge right hand around the tall, white-collared glass of Amstel beer that stood on the table, and sighed ponderously.

231

"We will retire together, the Queen and I," he said, nodding his enormous white-thatched head slowly. "I will tell you a little story about her. Her mother, Queen Emma, was making a public appearance on a holiday and the streets of Amsterdam were packed with people. Wilhelmina was with her mother. She was about fourteen then. She looked at the great crowds of cheering people and then peered up at her mother and asked, 'Do all these people belong to me?' and the Queen Mother said to her gravely, 'No, my child. You belong to them.'"

Mynheer van Heuven took a deep draught of beer, wiped the foam from his heavy white mustache with the back of his sleeve, and chuckled. "That was more than fifty years ago and I am sure she still remembers it. She never forgot for a moment that she belonged to us."

Queen Wilhelmina of Holland, who had reigned for fifty years, was about to relinquish the royal crown to her daughter, Juliana. Virtually everyone in Holland felt a close kinship to the sixty-nine-year-old monarch, and they felt that her abdication would mark the end of an era during which Holland proved her greatness. The future is uncertain and dark, for today Holland is almost economically bankrupt, but the past fifty years have been, for the most part, glorious. Holland emerged from the war badly hurt and filled with weariness, but she took a deep breath and set about the difficult task of rehabilitation. The abdication of Queen Wilhelmina would make the job of rehabilitation the more difficult because she was the one person in Holland in whom all political parties (even the Communists) had faith. Wilhelmina occupied the same place in the affections of the people as did Queen Victoria during the closing years of her reign.

But Wilhelmina was tired now; not only physically tired, but mentally and spiritually tired. The fifty years of responsibility culminating in the dreadful burden of having to rule her people from her London headquarters during the war, had taken their toll.

There were those in The Hague last summer who thought that the abdication of the Queen was prompted by something more than physical ailments. Wilhelmina is one of those who actually believed the Atlantic Çharter to be something more than a bit of rhetoric. Right after it was made public, Wilhelmina promised independence for the Dutch East Indies. Her government, backed by powerful business interests, disagreed with her on this policy, insisting that economics, not ideals, should be the determining factor in Holland's foreign policy. The disagreement between Queen and government was too fundamental to admit of compromise, and one heard whispers that Wilhelmina was retiring rather than give tacit approval to what she believed to be a repudiation of a promise she made to free the Dutch East Indies. But those close to the Queen scoffed at this. The Queen never ran away from a fight, they reminded you; she was abdicating only because she knew that her mental and physical strength were not equal to a fight.

The people of Holland always had great respect for their Queen, but it was not until the war years that this respect matured into veneration.

When the Germans entered Holland in 1940, the Queen hurried to London to set up her government-in-exile. She ordered her ministers to accompany her and from London she ruled with the same vigor and intelligence that she had shown in her palace office at The Hague. It was not easy, for the constitution of Holland clearly defined the duties of the sovereign and just as clearly defined the prerogatives of the Parliament. Wilhelmina found herself in London without a Parliament, and she found that she had to make independent decisions without the direction or approval of the Parliament. All her life she has had an almost mystic reverence for the constitution, and it was not easy for her to take over alone during the grave emergency. Circumstances had virtually made her a sovereign with dictatorial powers.

The first thing she did was to fire her Prime Minister, Jonkheer de Geer. De Geer had been an advocate of appeasement, and now that Holland was occupied he was a firm believer in the Petain policy of collaboration. Wilhelmina dismissed him and went to the radio to tell her people at home the reason why. By now the Germans had begun a systematic campaign of propaganda against the Queen. She and her ministers had shown themselves to be cowards, they declared, by running to London. The bewildered people, miserable under the ill-fitting Nazi yoke, didn't know what to believe, but when the Queen, in her strong vibrant voice, told them that she had dismissed de Geer because he was unworthy to represent them, they took heart. Her judgment on de Geer was correct. He made his way back to Holland and became one of the Nazi puppets.

Henceforth, Wilhelmina made periodic broadcasts to her people and they listened eagerly, drawing strength to survive and even to resist, from the calm voice. When the Germans began to bomb London, her ministers tried to persuade her to move to the country, but the doughty sovereign only gave them impatient looks. One night a bomb fell in front of the modest house she occupied near Victoria Station. It killed two guards and damaged the house badly. She still refused to move, and the story traveled quickly to Holland. The stolid Hollanders chuckled proudly and looked upon their conquerors with contempt. The resistance movement in Holland grew.

Although the Queen was living in London, the people sensed a new and warming relationship between themselves and their sovereign. She was actually directing the work of the resistance. She was not hesitant about ordering sabotage or murder if the results justified it. And the people recalled with pride that since William of Nassau founded the House of Orange, back in the sixteenth century, no one with that royal blood in his (or her) veins had ever shown lack of courage.

In London, Wilhelmina had picked for her Prime Minister the law professor and Minister of Justice, Peter S. Gerbrandy. Today Gerbrandy is leader of the opposition in Parliament, a

Dutch equivalent of Winston Churchill. Stocky, paunchy Gerbrandy has the incredibly light-blue eyes you see so often in Holland and he has a drooping walrus mustache, white, except where it is stained yellow by nicotine, for Professor Gerbrandy is a confirmed cigar smoker. Today he lives comfortably in a charming house in The Hague, and he often talks of the difficult but, in a way, glorious days in London.

"We discovered a new Wilhelmina," he told me as we sat in his spacious living room. "She had always worked hard, but in London she drove herself furiously. Often I would meet her at eight in the morning to find that she had already been at her desk for two hours. When we would decide on a policy, her first question always was, 'Is it constitutional?' To her the constitution represents the people, and never once would she sign a decree unless she was sure that it was the will of the people.

"Some people found the Queen difficult." Gerbrandy's blue eyes twinkled. "Conferences with her were never routine affairs during which she automatically approved the suggestions of her ministers. She would listen and then ask questions. If you didn't know your subject thoroughly, the Queen could be difficult. She was intolerant of stupidity and carelessness. Things were bad then, very bad, but she never lost faith in the final outcome even when the rest of us could not see the way to victory. I will tell you something about the Queen. She had one great love—her country—and never in her fifty years of rule did she ever do anything that she did not firmly believe to be best for Holland and the people of Holland. She was the greatest patriot of her age, and no one ever served her country with the integrity and honesty of purpose she showed."

Gerbrandy suddenly stopped and bent over to pat his black sheep dog which bears the unlikely name of "Scotty." He was silent for a moment and I felt that he had suddenly realized that, all unconsciously, he had been talking of the Queen in the past tense. When he raised his head his eyes had lost their twinkle and he too looked old, and his apple cheeks had lost their color.

"Those terrible years took their toll," he said sadly. "I saw her yesterday and—but never mind. She is tired, so tired. Well, she has earned a rest."

Once the resistance movement was well organized in Holland, lines of communication were established between the underground fighters and Wilhelmina's London headquarters. The underground established a newspaper that was distributed clandestinely, and the Queen wrote many articles imploring her people to have faith in the eventual outcome of the war and to have the courage to resist and die if need be. After the bombing of her home, the Queen sent Juliana and her children to Canada. Juliana objected, but no one in fifty years has been able to stand up against the will of the Queen if she thought her decision to be one which would further the interests of the people. Were she killed it wouldn't matter, she confided to her ministers, but Juliana, last of the Orange line, must be saved at all costs to carry on the royal tradition. Had the Queen and Princess Juliana both been killed, a not unlikely contingency in the days of nightly bombing, it would have stunned the people of Holland into a complete surrender to the Nazis. With Juliana and her children hustled off to Canada, Wilhelmina intensified her activities, keeping to a schedule that often made hollow-eyed wrecks of her younger but less durable ministers. She, for instance, read and often criticized eve·y issue of the underground paper which arrived every day in microscopic film. And she insisted upon receiving every underground member who had to flee from Holland. As the Germans redoubled their efforts to break the spirit of these stubborn, unyielding Hollanders by executing hundreds of resistance fighters for acts of sabotage, the exodus to England increased.

Wilhelmina saw every one of them. These were not formal, empty sessions. She carefully picked the brain of every Hollander who arrived in London. She questioned each one, sometimes for hours, and thus she had an overall knowledge of what was going on which surpassed that of anyone living in Holland. Until then she had always dealt with the people through her ministers and her Parliament. Now for the first time she really came into contact with them, and it was a rewarding experience for both.

She founded a club for them in London called "Het Englandvaardens" (The men who have come to England) and she supported this not out of state funds but out of her personal exchequer. Here they could relax and drink their beloved Holland gin (which is, of course, not gin at all) that somehow or other she managed to get from Holland. More than once I visited this club during the war years. It was always filled with lean, hard-sinewed young men. A great many of them were incorporated in the Dutch Navy and in the Dutch air force still fighting on from Britain. When they raised their glasses, as often as not they would murmur, "To the Queen!"

Occasionally, the Queen, impressed by one of the resistance men who had escaped, would make him a member of her household. One of these was Gerard Rutton, who in civilian life had been a writer and photographer. I found Rutton living in quiet, charming Bussom, which is between Amsterdam and Utrecht. Bright rambler roses climbed up the brown brick house, meeting the red tiles of the roof. It was a peaceful setting in which to find one of Holland's renowned resistance fighters. We drank tea (tea, more than gin or beer, seemed to be the national drink in Holland) and Rutton stretched out his long legs and talked of his Queen.

"None of us will ever forget her concern for us in London," he said thoughtfully. "You know, we had always respected the Queen, but now there was a new warmth about her. She was under a terrific strain but she questioned those of us who had escaped not once, but again and again. We found that usually she knew more about what was going on in Holland than we did. We found too that she was living on the same rations the Germans forced us to live on in Holland."

She made Rutton one of her A.C.D.'s. He accompanied her on her return to Holland in March, 1945. Three-quarters of the country was still occupied by the Germans, but she insisted upon returning for a short visit. She went to the completely destroyed village of Eede-Aardenburg and immediately began to discuss the rebuilding of Holland with the small group of ministers who had come with her. She wasted no time in grieving over the destruction she saw all about her. She was getting old, and time was running out. She remained on Dutch soil ten days and then went back to London to plan the rehabilitation of her country. She returned again on August 4th of the same year (one day before the Germans capitulated) and she immediately took over active charge of rehabilitation. The first thing she did was to ask Parliament to consider the decrees she had issued during the war and to ratify those it approved of. In effect, she was asking the people for a vote of confidence. Had she by act or spirit violated the constitution during those years when circumstances made her rule alone, without Parliament? This is what she was asking the people. The Parliament ratified every one of her decrees. Then she got down to the serious business of rebuilding a stricken, ravished country.

"I would go on tours of inspection with her," Rutton said, smiling. "Believe me, these were not routine affairs. In one village the burgomaster showed the Queen how the damaged church was being rebuilt. He was very proud of that until the Queen asked him sharply what he had done about rebuilding the damaged homes. 'Nothing,' the burgomaster said in amazement. 'We thought it necessary first to rebuild the church.' The Queen looked at him and said, 'Homes are more important than churches at the moment.'"

"Yes," Rutton chuckled, "the Queen is a realist. She strips a problem of its non-essentials and goes right to the heart of it. And since the war she has been very close to the people and their problems."

She was seriously ill in 1945, but her iron will triumphed over a body that was beginning to show the strain of nearly fifty years of intense driving. She refused to allow that body a moment's rest.

For fifty years she had spent most of her time at The Hague. The housing problem in Holland was acute; so acute that virtually every family that owned a house had to take another family in to share it. Wilhelmina owned two palaces in The Hague, but she refused to live in either. She moved to an unpretentious eight-room house on the Nieuwe Paaklaan, half a mile from the traditional palace of the House of Orange. As always, she would share the discomforts of her people. It took weeks for her ministers to convince her that this was an impractical solution to the housing problem. The little red-brick house bulged under the presence of ministers, visitors and secretaries (she staggered her secretaries in ten-hour shifts). Finally an ingenious minister told her that although the people could not occupy her palace they could occupy the house on Nieuwe Paaklaan (New Park Lane) and that she would actually help the housing shortage if she moved back to one of the palaces. Reluctantly, she did so.

During her long reign Wilhelmina had never spent more than one month a year in Amsterdam. Now she began to take an absorbing interest in the big city. She began to spend four months a year in Amsterdam, the commercial and cultural center of Holland. She developed a habit of daily walks, which presented a bit of a problem to Holland's police force. Amsterdam is the only city in Holland where the Communists are strong, and the police were understandably apprehensive for her safety. For twenty years she had always been accompanied on trips around the country by Sergeant Johannes Krabber of the Amsterdam police force. She would allow him to accompany her on her walks around Amsterdam—no one else. She stipulated that Sergeant Krabber wear plain clothes. Soon the dowdily dressed Queen (Hollanders actually boast, "Our Queen is the worst-dressed woman in Europe") and the broad-shouldered, 240-pound, six-foot-seven-inch policeman became familiar figures on the streets of Amsterdam.

"Worried about her safety?" Huge Sergeant Krabber blinked his pale blue eyes in astonishment when I asked him. "Of course not. No one in Holland could possibly wish harm to Her Majesty. We have walked everywhere, in the Ransdorp district, the Durgerdam district where the workers live, and in shopping centers like Kalverstraat and Leidschastraat, where she would stop to buy presents for her grandchildren. We went everywhere and never was even an unkind look given the Queen. This I know because I am what you Americans call a copper," his clean-shaven face broke into a smile. "Yes, I look for unfriendly glances, but never found them on our walks. She was always stopping to talk to people. She purposely went to the poorer sections to ask the people if the meat and bread rationing was sufficient for them and their children. They always answered her honestly, and sometimes she would say to me, "Mr. Krabber, make a note of that." Sometimes she would want to go to the Volkstomeel, a theatre which puts on old plays the people like. She didn't watch the actors; she watched the audience. Always she was interested in her people. Only a few weeks ago we took her grandchildren to the circus. The children loved it and the Queen loved their enjoyment of it. The Queen never misses anything. Never. She always knows what is going on. But," Sergeant Krabber said anxiously, "I am talking too much. I am only a policeman, but I have a great admiration for her."

Wilhelmina made a habit of asking to tea political groups antagonistic to the conservative Protestant parties she favored, and she urged them to present their views. One day she exploded an ecclesiastical as well as political bombshell by asking twenty Catholic priests and twenty Calvinist ministers to tea. In Holland most clergymen are unabashed, avowed politicians. The Catholic Party, for instance, ranks second only to the Socialist Party in power—30 percent of the Parliament are Catholic Party representatives. Bringing the priests and the ministers together in one room to discuss affairs of state could only be compared in American terms to asking the Daughters of the American Revolution to sit down in amiable friendship with the cast of *Carmen Jones* or a barnstorming Negro baseball team. The priests and the ministers glared at each other—and an hour later were busy trying to outdo each other with constructive suggestions designed to pull Holland out of the economic and political chaos into which the war had plunged her. Nor was Wilhelmina afraid of the word "Communist." There was a left-wing group of artists and writers in Amsterdam and she invited them to tea one day. One of her ministers had the temerity to object and she said to him coldly, "Remember, these men are Dutchmen just as we are. And remember, 10 percent of our people voted Communist in the last election."

Jan Reyndorp, a young artist I met in Amsterdam, told me of that historic tea. "She was amazing," he said with reluctant admiration. "There we were, all avowed enemies of the monarchist system. We were Communists and proud of it. She talked to us and reminded us that we were young; we were the ones who would have to rebuild Holland. She told us that she didn't care what our political affiliations were—that was something she had never in fifty years interfered with—but she did care about Holland and did want us to realize that this was the time to build and not destroy. We, the young men of Holland, had to do this, she and other leaders of her age were too old and too tired. Well, by God, within half an hour she had us convinced that even though she was a product of a system we did not like—she was a great patriot and a great woman. She gave us credit for being sincere and for being honest in our convictions, and we gave her credit for the same qualities. It is impossible for any honest man to believe in anything as absurd as a monarchy, but I tell you, it is not impossible to believe in the greatness of this woman."

The casual visitor to Holland might spend a week end at the seaside resort of Scheveningen near The Hague and, hearing the happy laughter of the people who jam the hotels and cafés, might be pardoned for thinking that this was again a happy and prosperous country. The casual visitor, watching Hollanders humming and dancing in the Casino to the music of "La Vie en Rose" (which was played everywhere in Europe last summer from Tel Aviv to London) might feel that Holland was one country which had come back quickly. The casual visitor at the lush Hotel des Indies at The Hague or at the Hotel Victoria in Amsterdam would never think that Holland was in economic difficulties. The casual visitor driving around Haarlem on a Sunday and seeing thousands of Hollanders bicycling along the neat country roads (70 percent of all Holland owns bicycles) might envy them their apparent prosperity. But this would not present the true picture; this would not be the Holland of today.

The textile industry has always been Holland's big source of foreign revenue. The mills are there today, but there is little raw material to work with and there is a desperate shortage of manpower. The first cotton to come to Holland arrived in September under ERP auspices. In 1939 a huge building program was inaugurated. Today the bare skeletons of half-finished office, factory and apartment buildings rise nakedly wherever you go. Under its neat, placid surface, Holland is writhing in economic agony. Her neighbor, Belgium, has managed to recover and is now holding up her head again, but Holland is in the position of a tired, half-drowning swimmer crying piteously for a lifebelt. The only lifebelt in sight is the ERP, and Holland is reaching for it gratefully. Whether it will suffice to keep the tired swimmer from going under remains to be seen. The problem now belongs to Juliana and the Parliament dominated by Socialists and Catholics.

It is a tough problem because not only circumstances are against Holland—geography is against the country. A quarter of her land lies under sea level. But this seems to have instilled a strong community feeling among the people. They know that the threat of the encroachment of the sea is a danger common to them all and in the past when the sea did break through, the people fought shoulder to shoulder against catastrophe. It gave them a feeling of dependence on each other and more than that it taught them that when real danger came no one could help them but themselves.

When Moscow sent some of its brightest men to stir up the people in the last election with promises of help that would be forthcoming from Russia if the country went Communist, the people only yawned with boredom and the Dutch Communists themselves hurriedly asked the "foreigners" to please go away.

ERP is a different proposition. To exchange their labor for material which they needed—this made sense. You hear no nonsense (not even from the Communist papers) about "American imperialism" in Amsterdam or Haarlem or The Hague. Holland would never accept help if her integrity were to be compromised or if there was any interference with her present framework of government. Holland is a monarchy but, paradoxically, it is a country of independent people in whom the democratic spirit burns brightly. Like the Italians, the Dutch are willing and anxious to work their way out of their present unhappy position. But they'll work out of it under their present constitution which, except for the business of a monarchy, is as democratic as our own. It is too bad that Wilhelmina isn't twenty years younger. She's quite a battler, whether the fight be against foreign invaders, the sea, or economic plague.

Wilhelmina has nothing left but her indomitable will and her great integrity. Her body and her mind are weary unto death and she cannot help solve these problems, none of which were of her making. But she retired, knowing that a nation of nine million people sincerely regretted her passing. She could look back to that portentous day fifty years ago when at eighteen she stopped being a girl to become a Queen. The pictures of that occasion show that she was slim then, though you might not know it now, and her hair was golden and her short bangs were clipped straight across her forehead. Perhaps sometimes she remembers the oath she took. With her hand resting on a Bible she repeated in her thin but even then confident voice, "I swear to safeguard the Constitution and to defend the Kingdom and its territories. I swear to protect the rights and liberties of my subjects and I shall use all lawful means at my disposal to maintain general prosperity."

She can look back over the fifty years and know that never once did she deviate from that solemn oath. She can look any fellow Hollander in the eye and can say with clear conscience, "I have done my best for Holland." And there is not a living Hollander who could disagree with her. Wilhelmina has been a good Queen.

CHAPTER FOURTEEN

I *hurried* back to Paris and the next day Ken Downs, Marie-Therese, Tony and I took off for Berlin. Tony was a three-year-old French poodle who enjoyed the automobile ride very much. Because Ken had a few favorite restaurants he wanted us to visit on the way, the trip took four days, but it was a rewarding delay. Ken knew this man at Verdun and a second at Metz and a third at Nancy, and we sat over long, leisurely lunches listening to these men talk and they all talked as Pierre Landret had talked that night sitting on the beach. When we stopped at villages there was always the milk, butter, fresh vegetables and fruit so scarce in Paris (except at a few luxury restaurants). We never met a man who liked de Gaulle; we never met anyone who didn't profess great respect for him. Every man we met was convinced that only ERP stood between France and economic chaos; we didn't meet a single person who seriously thought that France would ever submit to Communism. And finally, just north of badly damaged Strasbourg, we crossed the Rhine and were in Germany.

We drove a hundred miles on the magnificent Autobahn which led to Frankfort, and during these hundred miles we never saw another car; mute testimony to the scarcity of gasoline (or of automobiles). I hadn't been in Frankfort for nearly three years, but it hadn't changed much. True, the rubble had been cleared from the streets and the sidewalks, but there was no sign of any rebuilding. Frankfort is an important news center in Germany and the Park Hotel had been converted into press headquarters. Here the unmarried members of the American and British press were quartered; married correspondents rented houses from the American Military Government authorities. Frankfort was important because it was one terminal of the air lift and it was at near-by Wiesbaden that General Curtis LeMay had his headquarters. We walked into the lobby of the Park Hotel.

"You'll find your colleagues in there." The German desk clerk pointed to a room opening off the lobby.

We opened the door and I stopped. A familiar voice was raised in excited argument. Now and then another voice tried to break in but the first voice never faltered.

"Larry is still here," Marie-Therese said, and Ken and I laughed. I had heard the voice of Larry Rue of the *Chicago Tribune* hundreds of times. He and I had lived at the Savoy Hotel in London during the early days of the war. Larry could out talk any man in London. Years before, Larry had been one of Floyd Gibbons' ghosts and I always thought that Floyd had picked up his staccato, nonstop-talking style from Larry. Once in London two other correspondents and I had cornered a couple of cabinet ministers from whom we wanted to get some information. They were A. V. Alexander, First Lord of the Admiralty, and Duff-Cooper, then Minister of Information. We asked them to dinner and had the Savoy trot out its best. In the midst of dinner a waiter came up with two

246

bottles of Lanson, '28. "Compliments of Mr. Rue," he said. Larry and Toots Shor live according to the same Golden Rule.

"I don't want to be a millionaire," Shor once said, and the line has been oft quoted, "I just want to live like a millionaire."

Larry has always been like that. In 1940, when France fell, he was seriously alarmed—this would mean that no more champagne would arrive in England until the war was over. So Larry took every cent he had and bought up all the Lanson, '28 he could find. 1928 champagne is a little old now, but in 1940 it was considered by connoisseurs to be the best vintage. He stored his champagne in the wine cellar of the Savoy and it was always available to his friends. When the cabinet ministers had duly tasted and expressed their appreciation of the champagne, genial Alexander asked, "But where is Larry? Why doesn't he join us?"

"He will; he will." I knew Larry. The five of us sitting at dinner would prove a potential audience too tempting for him to resist. Larry arrived with the coffee. He immediately began to tell Alexander some of the things that were wrong with His Majesty's navy and then switched to tell Duff-Cooper how he should run his Ministry of Information. The two ministers enjoyed it tremendously. Had any of us attempted such criticism they would have resented it—Larry's effervescent good nature anesthetized any barbs of criticism he threw. He went on at great length, never allowing Alexander or Duff-Cooper to get in a word. By now I had despaired of ever getting the information from them which had been the reason for our dinner. After two hours of monologue I made a mild protest to Larry Rue.

"Larry," I asked, "why don't you ever stop talking?"

Larry didn't pause for a moment. He took my question in his stride, turned to me and said, "Whenever I do, I find that the conversation immediately gets very dull."

Walking into the comfortable-looking lounge of the Frankfort Press Club I saw that Larry was in his oldtime form. Jack Raymond of the *New York Times* was sitting there, so was

Colonel Anthony Drexel Biddle and his wife, Bob Cooper of the *London Times*, Ed Hartrich of the *New York Herald Tribune* and one or two others—but only Larry was talking. I walked up behind him and whispered in his ear, "Larry, why don't you ever stop talking?"

Without stopping for breath, he half-turned and said, "Whenever I do, I find the conversation very dull. . . . My God! Quent, Ken, Marie-Therese—sit down, you know everybody. That's a nice dog. What's his name? Tony? Come here, Tony. Did I ever tell you of the German shepherd Floyd owned? This was in Shanghai, back in 1933, and Floyd had . . ."

It was the Savoy all over again. We just became part of Larry's audience, and there are worse fates. An hour later Larry reluctantly tore himself away. He had a story to write. Tony Biddle, whom we had all known when he was acting as ambassador for the various governments-in-exile during the war, was as charming as ever. So was his lovely bride, Margaret.

The next morning the Downs and I hitch-hiked to Berlin on the air lift. There were two air fields, Rhein-Main (just outside Frankfort) and Wiesbaden. We left from Wiesbaden. The whole operation was on a wartime basis. We had to have travel orders "cut." (I hadn't heard that phrase since traveling with the Air Transport Command.) The C-47's loaded with flour and coal took off from Wiesbaden. No weight allowance was made for passengers on what was becoming known as The LeMay Coal and Feed Company. The planes were, of course, overloaded by any ordinary standards, but this overloading was part of the "calculated risk" the Air Force assumes when flying under wartime conditions. We thought we might have trouble getting Tony and Marie-Therese transportation, but when the pilots saw Marie-Therese and then started playing with Tony, we realized that if there was to be any jettisoning of passengers, Ken and I would be the ones unloaded. There is an informal friendliness about our Air Force, whether you meet its generals in Washington or its pilots in Germany. The Public Information Officers at Wiesbaden (all pilots themselves) fitted us out with parachutes, always rather a ghastly operation, and then assigned each of us to a different aircraft. Tony would go with Ken Downs. Marie-Therese laughed when the commanding officer said in a slightly embarrassed tone, "They got a rule here that any women we transport have to wear pants."

"Honest, Major, I am wearing pants," she said sweetly.

"I mean slacks." He blushed furiously. "That's because of the parachute. The straps go between your—I mean in case you have to bail out the straps . . ."

"I know. I know," travel-wise Marie-Therese soothed. "I have worn parachutes before. It won't take me a minute to change. I have slacks with me."

We listened to the briefing the pilots received just before the take-off. This of course was a routine operation where latest weather reports were given, but today there was something else added. They were warned about a hill a few miles from the field; two of their group had been killed the night before when their C-47 crashed into the hill.

Within a few minutes we had been assigned to planes, had met our pilots and were in a jeep that took us to the far end of the field. The pilots all wore the green-gray overalls and peaked caps they wore during combat days.

"We've got Number Five," my pilot said. He was young Lieutenant Gerald Kercher of Cass City, Michigan. His co-pilot was Lieutenant Cloyd Pearce. I asked him where he had ever got that first name. He shook his head gloomily and said he didn't know. He asked me where I'd ever got my first name and I shook my head gloomily and said that I didn't know. We climbed into the tired-looking C-47 that was fifth in line. It had already been loaded. Large boxes of powdered milk and dozens of flour-filled sacks were lashed to the floor of the cabin. The manifest was lying on top of one of the boxes.

Kercher picked it up, looked at it and blinked. "Eight thousand pounds," he said to Pearce. "Think this old crate can lift that much?"

"That's your problem, chum," the co-pilot said cheerfully.

They took their places, and Kercher put me in the navigator's seat. Our propellers started to whirl, and the plane shook and seemed to snarl in protest. Gerry Kercher looked back, grinned and yelled, "Hang on!" We started to roll. Gerry wasn't sitting back, relaxed. The skin was tight on the back of his neck. The plane gathered momentum slowly. It creaked and groaned with the effort. I felt that I wanted to lift it by main force, and then, after what seemed an eternity, it lurched drunkenly and we were airborne.

About two hours later we landed at Tempelhof. Kercher and Pearce had time to hurry into the snack bar at Tempelhof for a milk shake before the loudspeaker told them it was time for the return trip. Usually the pilots make two round trips a day, but quite often they had to make three.

Plump, middle-aged Marie, the Downs' cook, was waiting to greet us in their lovely home on Wildenow Strasse in Berlin. She took one glance at Tony and a look of ecstasy spread over her face.

"Come here, dog," she said. "What is his name?"

"Tony," Marie-Therese said with relief. She had been worried lest Tony precipitate a domestic crisis.

It was a pleasant house with a charming garden which Ken had rented from the American Military Government. Civilian officials had to rent houses and hire servants through the Military Government officials. Rent and wages were fixed and paid by the officials in dollars, and the American housing authorities then paid the German servants in marks. Every effort was made to keep dollars away from the civilian population of Berlin, and on the whole the attempt was fairly successful. A shower of dollars in Berlin would lead to immediate and disastrous inflation.

Downs had phoned Colonel Frank Howley, and the Colonel

had suggested that we drop over. As we were about to leave, Marie-Therese came out of the kitchen with an expression of amazement on her face.

"Just take a look in there," she said. "We've lost Tony. Tony, who never heard a word of German before, understands everything Marie says to him." We peered into the kitchen.

"Good Tony." Marie was talking to the dog in German. And the big poodle, with his head cocked to listen, seemed to understand every word. When Marie said, "Come here, Tony," the dog walked over and put his head in her lap.

"Really, Marie-Therese, Tony has all the earmarks of a collaborator!" I said. "Imagine a French dog obeying a German!"

"During the war we had many French dogs who obeyed Germans," she said bitterly. Marie-Therese was a real diehard and I loved her for it. Her grandfather had fought in one war against the Germans; her father had fought in another.

Colonel Frank Howley, American Commander of Berlin, is a wiry, good-looking man who moves quickly. He has spent some forty of his forty-five years on the back of a horse. He has the lean, tanned face of the cavalryman, but his voice is soft and engaging and he is extremely articulate.

"What do you want to know about Berlin?" he asked, smiling.

"Everything," I said.

"Then you've got to start from the beginning," he said. "It was July, 1945, when I came into Berlin with the first contingent of military government. Remember, the Russians had been here for two months alone. They had Berlin all to themselves and a lot of our present troubles stem from that time.

"The Russians say I'm tough, uncompromising," he smiled. "Well, we tried every other method of getting along with them. We tried appeasement, we tried seeing things their way, but eventually we found that we just didn't speak the same language. For instance, in their zone and in their Berlin sector they make all of their appointments on a political basis. If they have a vacancy for a factory manager, they'll appoint a

German who will string along with them politically; it doesn't matter if he can run a factory or not. This goes for schoolteachers, policemen, even preachers. They only want stooges in all appointive positions. We've tried hard to return government to the German people, but the Russians have no intention of doing anything like that.

"A strange thing has happened here in Berlin," Howley went on. "The people are showing an amazing liking for democracy and I'm all for encouraging this feeling. Now I'm not going overboard on this. After all, we came in here as conquerors— not as liberators. There are still plenty of tough Nazis around here who hate our guts—and I hate theirs. But there are people like Ernst Reuter and Frau Louise Schroeder, and Dr. Otto Suhr and Professor Kurt Landsberg and Karl Hubert Schwennicke and Eric Reger and a lot of others who are convinced that if Germany is to survive she must do so under a democratic regime. And if you want to meet them and talk to them, Ken can arrange it. . . . Damn it, there go the lights."

At eleven each night all electric current (except in hospitals) was turned off in Berlin. Mrs. Howley came into the room bearing a candlestick. Berlin lived by candlelight after eleven. After six weeks in Berlin trying to read at night by the light of a candle, I began seriously to doubt those stories about Abraham Lincoln doing all his studying in front of a fireplace with nothing but a candle to light the pages of his book. Nobody's eyes could take that beating.

I saw General Lucius Clay the next day. I had met him on previous trips to Berlin and he was as interesting and as charming as ever. I asked him about Reuter and the others Howley had mentioned, and he agreed emphatically.

"These men are actually risking their lives fighting for a democratic Germany," he said. "Mind you, we've screened them all thoroughly. They are not recently reformed Nazis. They've been battling against totalitarianism for many years. I must say I never thought we'd have Germans on our side," he laughed. "You'll see what I mean when you watch these men and women in action and hear them speak at political rallies. These people are all under sentence of death. If we ever move out of Berlin—God forbid—those executions would be carried out."

I did meet them all, not once but many times, and I did hear them speak to huge crowds while Russian photographers snapped their pictures. And after a month in Berlin I, too, felt as Howley and Clay felt: democracy had found some unexpected allies in the last place on earth one would think of looking for them. Allies, for instance, like Jeannette Wolff.

Jeannette Wolff is a gray-haired little woman who looks like everybody's grandmother. She peers at you calmly out of large blue eyes, and when you talk to her it is difficult to realize that she is under sentence of death—and knows it. When you mention this to her she shrugs her shoulders a little impatiently. She has been sentenced to death before. In fact, when the American Army liberated a concentration camp at Stutthof in 1945, they found Jeannette Wolff in the death house awaiting execution. The Nazis had sentenced her to death then; today the Soviet Union has done the same thing and for the same crime. Jeannette Wolff is a believer in democracy, a hater of totalitarianism, whether it take the Nazi or Communist form, and that, in Berlin today, is a crime punishable by death. The Soviet Union was merely waiting impatiently for the Western powers to move out of Berlin so it could carry out the executions necessary to stop the advance of this absurd, unthinkable nonsense called "Western democracy."

Jeannette Wolff is not a very important person. Twenty years ago she was an obscure kindergarten teacher in an obscure little town in Westphalia. The people elected her town councillor in charge of health and social welfare. Then came 1933, and the Nazis made it a criminal offense for anyone to be either a Jew or a democrat. By birth Jeannette was a Jew; by choice she was a member of the Social Democrat Party. Since then she has spent half of her life in hiding and the other half in concentration camps. But somehow she survived, and in October, 1946, the people of Berlin elected her to the city assembly. She has been one of those whose voice has been raised in protest every time the Soviet officials or the members of the Soviet-dominated Socialist Unity Party tried to bring Berlin's four-power status to an end. Late last June, the Soviet officials served unmistakable notice on Jeannette Wolff that she had incurred their displeasure.

The weekly meetings of the city assembly are held in the Stadthaus on Parochialstrasse in the Russian sector of Berlin. As the members emerged after this meeting they were greeted by a crowd of two thousand people making a "spontaneous" demonstration against the members of the assembly who were not conforming to Soviet policy. These two thousand had all been brought to the spot in Soviet trucks, and a dozen Russian officers and Russian sector police stood by as the demonstrators screamed invective at Louise Schroeder, Mayoress of Berlin; at Professor Ernst Reuter, a militant fighter against Soviet policy; and at other leaders of the parties opposed to Soviet domination. They managed to get through the crowd unscathed, however. Jeannette Wolff was not so fortunate. As she emerged from the building, she was greeted with a chant, "Jewish swine—Jewish swine." A dozen voices cried out the same phrase, "They should have finished you in the concentration camp." She looked at them calmly and said, "They're mad. This is 1933 all over again."

They knocked her down, kicked her into unconsciousness, and then, their mission accomplished, hurried to the Soviet trucks which waited to return them.

The next day an anti-Communist rally was held in the French sector of Berlin. Sixty thousand Berliners appeared to protest the "spontaneous" demonstration against their duly elected representatives. They cheered the speakers, and then Jeannette Wolff, leaning heavily on a cane, hobbled to the speakers' stand. The crowd unloosed a roar of approval. They called on her to speak. Her body was battered and bruised but her voice was strong as she cried out, "Those who summoned the mob to serve them yesterday have lost the last bit of respect among the people of Berlin. They can knock us down and kick us, but they cannot keep us down. This is not Prague, this is Berlin. Political courage is the special virtue of the democrat. We shall not fail nor shall we weaken until freedom is secure."

Democracy is something new to Berlin, and it would be absurd to say that the whole population is as willing to fight for it as Jeannette Wolff. But every day more followers flock to the democratic cause. Sheer physical courage is something that appeals to the Berliner. The Berliner knows that Jeannette Wolff and dozens of other leaders will die if the Western nations move out of Berlin, and the fact that these leaders show no concern at all for their personal safety has fired the imagination of the Berliner. There must, he is beginning to think, be something in this thing called democracy, after all.

Even today Berlin looks like an ant heap that some giant foot has kicked viciously. Yet nearly 4,000,000 people live in the ruins and rubble of the city. Today Berlin is one spot on earth where the power of democracy is really being tested. This test was not of our choosing. It was forced upon us when the Soviet representatives walked out of the Kommandatura; when the Soviet announced the blockade of Berlin. The odds are all in favor of the Russians in this test. It must be remembered that Berlin is geographically almost in the center of the Russian zone. The city itself, of course, is divided into four sectors, supervised by American, Russian, French and British units. Ever since June, when the blockade was put into force by the Soviet High Command, the only access to Berlin from the American zone has been by air. We cannot move food, fuel or men on the railroad, nor can our trucks and cars use the great highway that extends from Frankfort (in the American zone) to Berlin. Berlin is just a tiny isolated spot in the Russian zone, and our position in the city is, of course, untenable from a military point of view. The combined military strength of the three Western powers in Berlin would not amount to more than a combat team and a few light tanks.

If we were compelled to leave Berlin, it would be one of the greatest triumphs the Soviet Union ever achieved. Soviet prestige, a bit dimmed this past year by defeats in Italy, by Tito's lapse from the sacred Kremlin line, by anti-Soviet demonstrations in Czechoslovakia, would be reestablished to such a degree that it is likely that all opposition would vanish in the satellite states, and Communist minorities in the sixteen so-called Western countries of Europe would be handed fresh and powerful ammunition to use in their anti-American campaigns.

It was thought by practically everyone that twelve years of Nazi rule had effectively destroyed all remnants of the democratic spirit that had once manifested itself in the establishment of the ill-fated Weimar Republic of the 1920's. But Hitler had erred. True, he had killed 5,000,000 Jews and thousands and thousands of political opponents, but he had not exterminated them all and they began to emerge right after the fall of Berlin. Clay and Howley looked upon them at first with understandable suspicion, but investigation proved that these men and women who were now voicing democratic principles at great personal risk had always been fighters against National Socialism. These were not Johnny-come-latelies, discarding the cloaks of Nazism hurriedly in order to curry favor with the Western powers. And these individuals have grown in stature and in power. There is, for instance, Ernst Reuter, a huge, sad-eyed man who looks like an unhappy spaniel.

As a young man Reuter (now sixty-five) was fired by what he thought to be the idealism of Lenin, and he joined the German Communist Party. Closer acquaintance with the practice as opposed to the theory of Communism revolted him, and he renounced the Communist faith in 1919.

Reuter was prominent during the days of the German Republic. Highly intelligent and a fine administrator, he founded the unified transit system of Berlin during the 1920's. He served as Mayor of Magdeburg until 1933. As one of the leaders in the fight against Hitler, he had to flee. He found his way to Turkey and remained there, teaching municipal administration in the university until 1946, when he returned to Berlin. The people of Berlin remembered him, and Reuter was elected Mayor. There the Soviet representative to the Kommandatura promptly hauled out his well-worn but serviceable veto. It begins to look as though all Russians were born with a veto in each hand. In any case, Reuter was rejected, and Frau Louise Schroeder, also a member of the Social Democrat Party, who had been elected Deputy Mayor, was installed. Reuter retained his membership in the City Council and he was put in charge of public utilities and transportation.

Reuter is perhaps the most popular man in Berlin today, and one of the finest speakers in Germany. He has an amazing gift for establishing an immediate contact with his audience, and he is as effective facing a crowd of 70,000 at the Brandenburger Tor, as he is at a meeting of the City Council. I asked Reuter what would happen to him if the Western powers left Germany.

"I never thought of that," he said slowly, as though puzzled at such a frivolous question. "The usual thing, I suppose."

Had the people of Germany showed the same kind of courage in the early 1930's, when their democracy was blasted out of existence, there might never have been a Fascist Germany. The danger to men like Reuter and Suhr and Franz Neumann and Jacob Kaiser is a very real and ever-present one. Professor Reuter, for instance, has a wife and son. The boy is a student at the University of Berlin, which is in the Russian sector of Berlin. Each night Frau Reuter waits for the return of her husband and her son. These waits must seem interminable to the gray-haired elderly woman. She has heard the threats made by the Russians against her husband; she knows they are capable of carrying them out. But there has risen in Berlin a spirit of what we called "resistance" during the war. To Reuter and the others this is a war for survival. They do not believe that the German people in themselves are evil; evil was thrust upon them and they were too weak to resist it. Finally they have awakened. This whole spirit of resistance is embodied in the person of Ernst Reuter.

"Do you think you and Frau Schroeder and the other leaders can ever teach democracy to the people of Germany?" I asked him.

Reuter considered that for a moment. Then he said, "No. I don't believe that you can ever *teach* democracy to anyone. You see, the people of Germany have had propaganda pounded into them ever since Hitler came into power. Then came a time when they found out it was all false. Everything they had been taught was false. Today they can be impressed only by positive action, not by political theories. They are watching the fight between the Western powers and the Soviet with great interest. They are seeing democracy in action. They hear your planes day and night, and they know these planes are bringing them food and coal to keep them alive. They are grateful, but I think that democracy would make an even stronger impression if you would send this food and fuel on trucks through the Russian zone. That would show them how strong democracy can be."

The Soviet-controlled press in Berlin has been bitter in its denunciation of Reuter, Frau Schroeder, Dr. Otto Suhr, President of the City Assembly and editor of a Socialist magazine, Professor Kurt Landsberg, leader of the Christian Democratic Party in the City Assembly, young, good-looking Karl Hubert Schwennicke, leader of the Conservative Liberal Democratic Party, and others who have taken the viewpoint of the Western powers, and has accused them of being mere puppets activated by General Clay or Colonel Howley. Actually, this is not the case. Reuter on more than one occasion has been sharply critical of lack of aggressiveness in the high echelon policy of the Western nations.

"For three years," Reuter said mildly, "we have watched the Western powers indulge in the most incomprehensible policy of appeasement toward the Soviet authorities. By now the patience of the most indulgent democrat must be spent."

Reuter is not alone in his criticism of our reluctance to take the initiative (at least the diplomatic initiative) against Russia. Eric Reger, editor of the American-licensed daily Berlin newspaper, *Der Tagespiegel*, is not backward about what he thinks American policy should be. Reger, like the others, is sure to face a firing squad should Berlin be turned over to the Russians but, like the others, he dismisses that possibility with an impatient gesture. A husky, strong-faced, dark-eyed man of fifty, Reger is highly regarded by both Clay and Howley, but he most definitely is not a "yes" man.

"What the Western powers should do," Reger says calmly, "is to tell the Russians to get out of Berlin and out of Germany. There is reason enough for this. At Yalta the details of the Quadripartite occupation of Germany were agreed upon. The first aim was to pull the fangs of the German military potential. This was done in short order. Then the four contracting powers agreed that they would bend every effort to make Germany a democratic nation. In their own zone and in their sector of Berlin the Russians have not lived up to this commitment. They have outlawed the democratic parties in their zone. They have taken over the trade unions and staffed them with their own puppets. Germans in the Soviet zone are slaves today, just as they were under Hitler. Those who object are eliminated or thrown into concentration camps. Today there are 25,000 German political prisoners in Sachsenhausen alone. Most of them dared to oppose the totalitarian view of the Soviet leaders. The Russians have done nothing at all to give democracy a chance in Germany. They have broken the agreement they made at Yalta and should be dismissed from Germany."

Slim, shrewd-eyed Frau Schroeder, who was with us, nodded thoughtfully. She has been a lifelong member of the Social Democrat Party and represented Schleswig-Holstein in the pre-Hitlerian Reichstag. During the Nazi era she hid herself in Berlin. Her eyes twinkle when she tells you that she became a welfare worker among the poor of the city and so escaped notice by Nazi authorities. But today, as the first woman ever to act as Mayor of a major German city, she is a real power. Usually the Communists have a group of hecklers planted at all political meetings. The slightly built, sixty-three-year-old Mayor merely waits calmly until the abuse has stopped; then she speaks, and her quiet sincerity has an electrifying effect on crowds. Frau Schroeder is very high on the Soviet "drop-dead" list. Like most of the leaders of the three democratic parties, Frau Schroeder talks excellent English.

"Reger is right, you know," she said mildly. "The Soviets have shown that they have absolutely no respect for their own promises. They just don't understand the language of democracy. If you compromise with them, they merely take it as a sign of weakness. I am afraid," she added, "they only understand the strongest of measures."

Others of the condemned squad have different ideas. One of the most respected men in Germany is a stocky, beetle-browed, balding man named Jacob Kaiser. Kaiser ran the Christian Democratic Party in the Soviet zone. This is the conservative, predominantly Catholic party. When the Soviet authorities took over his party and asked him to play along, Herr Kaiser skipped out of the Soviet zone and headed for Berlin. A union leader of the Walter Reuther type, his influence among workers is great.

"There is only one real solution," Kaiser told me bluntly. "Let all the four powers get out of Berlin and let us sink or swim as best we can."

"A lot of people would starve if the Western powers moved out of Germany," I suggested.

"A lot of people are starving now," Kaiser said grimly. "No one in the Soviet zone has had oil or fats for three months. Children can't live without fats."

Whether or not the people of Berlin are anxious to embrace our conception of democracy might be an arguable point, but there is no doubt that their hatred of Russia and Communism is sincere and bitter. One day I went to watch a motorcycle race being held on a highway near the Wannsee district outside Berlin. A crowd of about eight thousand gathered near the finish line. Four Russian officers, wanting to get a better view of the finish, drove their car through the crowd. The car drove slowly and there was no danger of anyone being hurt, but for some reason the incident inflamed the German spectators. A few in the crowd began chanting, *"Komm, Frau, komm, Frau."* Others began calling, *"Uri—Uri."* Soon the whole crowd was grimly chanting.

During the two months (May, June, 1945) when the Russians held Berlin alone while our American Military Government units cooled their heels at Halle waiting for an invitation to enter the city, the Red Army did a thorough job of raping and looting. Their approach to the women of Berlin was blunt and brutal. They merely pointed a gun and said, *"Komm, Frau,"* and the *Frau* (or *Fräulein* or *Mädchen*) either went— or else. *Komm, Frau* were two of the three German words learned by the Red Army men. The German word for "watch" is *Uhr,* and the Red Army men prized watches even above *Frauen.* They roamed the city demanding watches from the citizenry. They merely demanded, *"Uri—Uri"*: their own version of the word *Uhr.*

Those who survived those two months of terror (I might add, the same kind of terror visited upon Russian cities by the German armies in 1941, when they invaded the Soviet Union) will always associate the Red Army men with the phrase *"Komm, Frau,"* and the word *"Uri."* At the motorcycle race practically everyone in the crowd took up the cry. It was a spontaneous cry of hatred and protest. The incident happened in the American sector of Berlin, or the concentration camps might have been augmented by several thousand additional guests. Ridicule is one weapon the Russian cannot face.

Part of the unhappy situation in Berlin today is due to the military necessity which enabled the Russians to reach Berlin first in the spring of 1945. Their final assault against the German capital resulted in horrible casualties but eventual victory.

Had our army been in charge of our State Department or the British Foreign Office, there is no doubt that we would have engaged in a rat race to reach Berlin ahead of the Russians. That is what they wanted. So did Winston Churchill. At that time the Russians were firmly established on the banks of the Oder, only thirty miles from Berlin. The American forces were three hundred miles from the German capital with the Elbe River presenting quite an obstacle. Had General Eisenhower given the order to take Berlin at all costs, several thousand American parents would be without sons today. Fortunately, Eisenhower acted like a general instead of a diplomat; to Eisenhower, American lives were not expendable. And so, in accordance with the military logic of the situation, the Russians reached Berlin first.

Anyhow, the Russians did get there and they took full advantage of their advantageous position. Even in Berlin you found men who insisted that Roosevelt had agreed at Yalta to allow the Russians to take Berlin. I have asked several men who were at that conference and every one of them agreed that no decision had been made on this point.

There are those who criticize the concessions made to Russia at Yalta. They forget that in February, 1945, we needed Russia more than she needed us. Japan remained to be beaten and at that time not one of the scientists working on Manhattan Project would guarantee that the atomic bomb would work. If it worked, fine; if it didn't, we faced an assault on the mainland of Japan that would result in casualties horrible to contemplate. With Russia in the war against Japan those casualties would be reduced. So we weren't too demanding at Yalta, but I have never heard anyone who attended that conference say that one of the things demanded by the Russians was the exclusive right to expend a hundred thousand lives or so in the final attack on Berlin.

But the Red Army did move in and did suggest that we wait outside the city until they had mopped up and quelled all resistance. This was according to accepted military procedure. In addition to exacting retribution from the German populace for every obscene crime committed by the German Army in its swift advance into Russia in 1941; in addition to the wholesale and organized looting which left Berlin as bare as Mother Hubbard's cupboard—Russia also moved very fast in a political sense. They brought twenty-five Moscow-trained German Communists back to Berlin and installed them in key positions. They organized a German Communist Party which was afterwards named the Sozialistische Einheitspartei Deutschlands (The Social Unity Party of today). Wilhelm Pieck, a Communist Party member since 1918, was taken off the ice and made its leader. When our Western Military Government teams were allowed to enter Berlin in July, 1945, they found the city government well organized and staffed with personnel eminently satisfactory to the Soviets.

Russia knew that eventually the Western powers would insist upon a free election in Berlin, so she put most of her stooges in positions that wouldn't be affected by elections. Then, at the first meeting of the Kommandatura, the Soviets asked the three Western powers to ratify all official acts and appointments made during the two happy months. This was during the phase of love-up-our-brave-allies, and the Western representatives were pleased to oblige. In effect, we thus approved the appointment of many Communists to key spots.

The heads of the various municipal departments were all elected to office in October, 1946, but the second man in each department retained his appointive office. So today we see the strange spectacle of a really fine democrat like Dr. Walter May heading the all-important department of education, being consistently hampered by the efforts of his deputy, Ernst Wildangel, one of the early Soviet appointees. The incongruously named Wildangel does all he can to spread Communist doctrines throughout the school system.

There are men in important spots, like Johannes Becher, head of the Kulturbund, which the Soviets insist is nonpartisan. There is Hans Jendratsky, a pretty good borer-from-within, holding an important official position, and there is Karl Maron, strong man of the Socialist Unity Party in Berlin. There is Paul Pieck (son of Wilhelm), head of the personnel branch of the German Economic Commission, and then there is Walter Ulbricht, member of the Comintern and the real behind-the-scenes boss of Communism in Germany. It has been said that he even gives orders to Soviet officials. These are some of the men who learned their ideological a.b.c.'s in the Moscow centers of learning. All of them are in vital spots, and any time we made a gesture of protest the Soviet representative at the Kommandatura playfully rattled his veto. Then finally they vetoed the Kommandatura itself.

If we move out of Berlin, these are the men who would be in command of the situation. The Soviet-controlled papers in Berlin have been directing a propaganda barrage of vilification and abuse against the Western powers and those Germans who believe in democratic principles. During the summer of 1948 they printed what purported to be an exposé of Secret Plan L. This was supposed to be the plan for evacuating the Western powers from Berlin—a plan, they said, already in operation. It scared a great many Berliners, even though there wasn't a word of truth in it. The papers also sneered at our air lift, saying, "No wonder the American pilots know their way so well to Berlin. After all, it was they who reduced Berlin to rubble with their bombing." Berliners were amused by this, because for three years the Russians had been telling them that the Red Army and Air Force alone conquered Germany. All in all, an exquisite war of nerves was and is being waged in Berlin, but luckily, neither Clay nor Howley seems to have any nerves.

The situation in Berlin is bound to get worse before it gets better. Each day the Russians bob up with something new in an effort to create the chaos and confusion in which the seeds of Communism seem to sprout so well. At one of the last meetings of the Kommandatura, Colonel Howley, usually the most patient of men, protested against the Soviet tactics which were rendering the Kommandatura impotent. General Alexander Kotikov, Soviet representative, had just blandly repudiated an agreement he had made the week before.

"Will General Kotikov kindly explain this amazing change in policy?" Howley snapped.

"Colonel Howley should know," Kotikov said calmly, "that Soviet policy has not changed for thirty years."

For once a word of truth was spoken by a Russian representative to the Kommandatura. Thirty years ago Communism spoke of itself as an international movement. It is still international, and for the past three years Berlin has been its target.

CHAPTER FIFTEEN

I*t is* very seldom that you see a man walk up to a very tough cop, throw his arms around him and belabor him with kisses. Some people, in fact, might spend their whole lives without ever witnessing such an amazing spectacle. However, I saw this happen in Berlin, and the cop, instead of starting one from the floor and landing it on the chin of the affectionate laddie who was doing the kissing, just blushed a little and stood quietly with his hands at his sides. The tough cop was Orazio Raymond Carlucci, of Montclair, New Jersey, and the character who did the kissing was General Jean Ganeval, of Paris, France.

It is true that the General kissed the cop only twice—once on each cheek—but even that is enough to inspire the ordinary cop to mayhem. Just before he went into his kissing act, General Ganeval had pinned two medals on Ray Carlucci. One was the Croix de Guerre with palm and the other was the Legion of

266

Honor, medals seldom seen on the broad chests of gendarmes from New Jersey. This ceremony took place in the military compound of the French sector in Berlin, and, when General Ganeval had finished, the onlookers broke into applause. French high officials applauded; American generals clapped loudly; British officers (showing proper restraint) applauded politely, and, so help me, a dozen high-ranking Russian officers applauded more vociferously than all the rest.

The band played the "Marseillaise" and five hundred French infantrymen stood at attention, and then it was over and everyone (including the Russian officers) rushed up to the tough cop from New Jersey and shook his hand and then, finally, he and I walked away to find his car.

Carlucci was walking on clouds and he had the look of a dazed sleepwalker. He kept muttering to himself, "How do you like that? How do you like that? Me—a dead-end kid from the docks—ending up with these medals. How do you like that?"

I lead him to his car, found the keys in his pocket and told him I'd drive. In his bemused condition he would not have known the Brandenburger Tor from Pier No. 9, Hoboken, where he had played as a kid. So we drove back to his office.

"Did that French General give you the whole routine, Ray?" Miklos Strauch, the second toughest cop in Berlin asked. "Did he kiss you on both cheeks like in the newsreels?"

"Yeah, Mike, he did," Carlucci said proudly. "Is that all right?"

"Sure, it's all right," Strauch laughed. "We got a report while you were out, Ray, that four cars were stolen last night. You want I should go out and get them?"

"Yes Mike, you go out and get them. Take three of the boys with you."

"What for?" Mike protested. "I can do this alone."

"You got to have someone to drive the cars back," Carlucci said mildly. So Mike left and we were alone in the office of the Director, Criminal Investigation Division, Department of the Army, Berlin. That's Carlucci—Director of the C.I.D., which makes him the top cop in the American sector of Berlin. There are a million and a half Germans living in the American sector, and any time any of them commits a crime against Army personnel or property, it is up to Carlucci to bring him to justice. It is also his job to bring to justice any G.I. or officer who commits a crime against the German citizens in the sector. This, however, was not the job for which the French Government gave him the Croix de Guerre (with palm) and the coveted Legion of Honor.

Ray Carlucci began the war as a private. He emerged as a captain. The Army was smart enough to put him in its Criminal Investigation Department and he did a lot of work with the French in North Africa and with the Italians in Naples. The Army gave him the Bronze Star for that. Later he was handed the unenviable job of cleaning up Marseilles, and, if you knew Marseilles in wartime, you knew that this was not a job for a Milquetoast. They slapped an 11 o'clock curfew on the city.

"They thought we were kidding about that curfew," Carlucci said. "Life was usually getting started in Marseilles around eleven at night. But I had two big boys with me. Nice boys, too, who could hit very hard indeed, if necessary. Both of them were Negroes and they'd never heard anything about fear. We'd go into a joint at eleven and I'd say, 'Everybody pay their bill and scram outa here.' We didn't have much trouble with the G.I.'s. Sometimes the people who ran the joints objected and tried to ease us out. My two big boys didn't like to get run out of places. Me, either. So now and then we had a little trouble, but, I will say, we never had to use guns.

"Sometimes a character would pull a knife, but my boys were brought up on knives. They could throw a punch faster than anyone could throw a knife, and they always tossed the knife-thrower into the clink. Well, we cleaned up Marseilles pretty good, and not many of our G.I.'s got hurt. Anyhow, that's what the French gave me these medals for."

When the war was over, Lieutenant General Lucius Clay heard about Ray's record and assigned him to act as C.I.D. chief in Berlin. Carlucci has held the job ever since, and virtually everyone in Berlin (except a few characters who now languish in non-air-conditioned jails) will tell you that the boyish-looking thirty-eight-year-old gent with the quick grin and the soft voice has done very well.

When Carlucci says that he was a dead-end kid he is not fooling. Some months ago Communist newspapers in America attacked Carlucci savagely. They dug up the fact that before the war he had been an undercoverman who occasionally wangled his way into Communist-controlled unions for the purpose of blowing a very loud whistle. He was then working for Joseph P. Ryan, President of the powerful International Longshoremen's Association, American Federation of Labor. With their usual fine restraint they screamed that Carlucci had been a "fink" and a strong-arm guy who went around busting the skulls of honest laboring men with a baseball bat. A headline in the *Daily Worker* yelled, "Army's Top Cop in Berlin Was Labor Spy." They reported that he had run afoul of the law as a young man and that he had broken his probation.

The Secretary of War sent General Clay a message suggesting that he get rid of his "top cop." The General told them in Washington that Carlucci had never made a secret of his past. Clay also handed the Army brass a copy of Carlucci's war record with commendations from every commanding officer under whom he had served. He told them of the fine job Carlucci was doing in Berlin. When Clay goes to bat for one of his men he takes a full swing.

"You know, the Communist papers weren't too far off," Carlucci says frankly. "Except for that crack about the baseball bat. I was a dead-end kid, as I told you. I got mixed up in a crap game once and then got in a fight, and the first thing you know I was in court. I was sixteen and got a suspended sentence. I was supposed to report to a probation officer, but I skipped one report and went to a reformatory for fifteen days. After that I held all sorts of jobs around the docks in Hoboken and Union City.

"Yeah, I did a lot of things as a kid I'm not proud of. Who hasn't? But then I got into the Army. Some guys maybe the Army is no good for. It made me grow up. You work for men like General Clay and Colonel Howley and you're bound to grow up. You're bound to develop a sense of responsibility."

Carlucci took over the job of running the C.I.D. in Berlin in 1945, right after Colonel Howley and his American Military Government men moved in. The job was one which might have discouraged a more experienced cop than Ray Carlucci. He was thirty-four then, well built, but he only weighed 140 pounds, which is all he weighs today. Berlin was filled with dubious characters with no papers, no visible means of support, and no affection for, or inclination to obey, the Ten Commandments or the law as set forth by American Military Government. For the most part, these were not Germans; they were members of the Spanish Blue Division, which had fought against Russia, or they were French collaborationists who quite rightly feared to go back to France. They were renegade Poles and Yugoslavs and Greeks, and they were Italians who felt that the pickings would be better in Berlin than in Rome. Most of them had managed to steal American uniforms and all of them had larceny in their hearts.

"We didn't have much trouble with the Germans then and we don't now," Carlucci says. "But these other characters would steal the fillings outa your teeth. They were very good at stealing automobiles. They would steal them in our sector and hustle them over to the Russian sector. They'd repaint them, get new license plates for them and sell them."

This posed a delicate problem for Carlucci. If you followed a stolen car into Soviet territory the Russians might not like it. They were showing increasing signs of touchiness. Carlucci didn't know anything about protocol. Hell, he was a cop. So he just stormed into Russian C.I.D. headquarters and asked for the head man. He told the head man the situation. He explained that he was no political cop. He was just a guy who wanted to nab anybody who was stealing or murdering, and how about a little co-operation? The Russians, who seem to understand the direct approach better than they do the diplomatic, liked Carlucci's attitude. Henceforth, he could follow stolen cars anywhere he wanted.

"Funny thing," Carlucci says, as though puzzled by it himself. "Me and the Russians hit it off fine. You see them all there when I got these medals?"

Carlucci has thirty American agents and ten Germans working out of his headquarters at Andrews Barracks. In addition, he can call on the American M.P.'s any time he needs them or he can use any or all of the three thousand German police in Berlin. On one occasion he used not only all of these, but the air force as well, to solve a murder mystery.

One day on the list of G.I.'s who were A.W.O.L. he found the name of Corporal Stanley Claycomb. Several days went by and the Corporal's name remained on the list. There was no reason why Carlucci should take on what was a routine job for the M.P.'s, but he found himself thinking about the young Corporal, and one day he went to see the men in Claycomb's outfit. They all expressed themselves as being amazed at the Corporal's absence.

"He just ain't that kind of a guy," a sergeant told Carlucci. "Besides, he had a girl. Not one of these *fräuleins* you can have for a couple of cigarettes, but a real nice girl."

"Maybe he ran off with her," Carlucci suggested.

"Not a chance. This girl can't run," the sergeant said. "She's a cripple. Yeah, she's in the hospital now."

Carlucci went to see her and she was a nice girl. She was horribly worried about her Corporal, too. She had been stricken with osteomyelitis and Corporal Claycomb had sent her to the hospital and was paying the doctor's bills. One of Claycomb's pals told Ray that the Corporal never smoked or ate candy or used any of his Post Exchange rations; he sold everything to pay for his girl's doctor's bills. There was some

Kraut dentist near Tempelhof who bought chocolate syrup from the kid, someone remembered. Matter of fact, Claycomb had mentioned that this dentist owed him quite a bit of change.

Carlucci sent his boys out to round up any dentists who lived in the Tempelhof area. They came in with Dr. Werner Raabe, a calm, cool customer who had been a paratrooper in the German Army during the war. Yes, he remembered Corporal Claycomb, a very fine young man. Claycomb had sold him a few cans of chocolate syrup and he had paid the soldier.

Carlucci and his boys examined Doctor Raabe's apartment, which also included his professional office. Carlucci noticed what appeared to be bloodstains on the wall. Could be, Doctor Raabe said easily, sometimes a patient did bleed. There was a balcony outside the living room of the flat. Ray found a small hatchet there and the back of it was rusted.

"Maybe you hit the Corporal on the head with this and then washed the blood off with water," Carlucci said. "It's only the back of the hatchet that's rusty."

"Really," Doctor Raabe laughed, "this is absurd! You accuse me of murder and you haven't any proof that the Corporal is dead."

"That's right," Ray said softly, because he just isn't a loud-voiced character. He told Mike Strauch and John Weber (once a cop in Baltimore) to go over the flat carefully. He told Pat Gallagher to analyze anything that looked suspicious. Gallagher is in charge of the well-equipped C.I.D. laboratory in Berlin. Then Carlucci went looking for a body. He asked the Air Force to help. They sent low-flying airplanes searching the Tempelhof area. Ray asked the infantry and the M.P.'s for a thorough search of the neighborhood. A week later, they found the body under the rubble and debris not far from Raabe's home.

Meanwhile, Pat Gallagher had turned up something in his laboratory. He had found plenty of Claycomb's fingerprints, but he had also found a small thatch of bloodstained hair under a splinter of wood a foot above the doorjamb in the opening between the dentist's office and living room. The blood was the same type as Claycomb's. He found a suit of Raabe's at the cleaner's. It hadn't been cleaned yet and it, too, showed bloodstains. Carlucci, who had been keeping Raabe on ice on a technical black-market charge, brought him into his office.

"You got into a fight with Claycomb," he said quietly. "You hit him with this hatchet and killed him. You dragged him through the doorway and his head hit the side and a splinter picked up some of his hair. You carried him downstairs on your back but some of the blood got on your coat. You brought him out in back of your house and piled bricks and debris over him. You oughtn't to have done that, Doctor."

"We were having a drink," Raabe said, sweating now. "He swung at me with a bottle and I took the hatchet and hit him to save myself. It was self-defense."

"But Dr. Raabe," Carlucci said mildly, "this boy was hit on the back of the head. And Doctor, he was sitting down when he was hit. It isn't self-defense when you hit a sitting man on the back of the head with a hatchet. Now, Doctor Raabe, you and I are going to sit right here until you tell me the truth."

It went on for eight hours—persistent, endless questioning. Raabe was an ex-paratrooper. You couldn't have beaten a confession out of him with a lead pipe. But he finally broke down. He had owed the Corporal several hundred marks for canned chocolate syrup and he killed him to escape paying the debt. He was tried and sentenced to death. I have told this story at length because I think it demonstrates something important. An unknown G.I. was reported missing and the search for him could not have been more thorough had he been a four-star general. A G.I. is a V.I.P. to Clay, Howley and General Huebner (who is in command of combat troops in Germany). To them he's the most important person in the country. It's nice to know.

The black market has always been one of Carlucci's biggest headaches but, with a few exceptions, illicit traffic in Army-rationed goods never really reached astronomical proportions. There were (and are) a few big operators, but Carlucci has caught up with most of them. What is still loosely referred to as black-market operations is as often as not a method of barter which custom has made legitimate.

"It's like this," Carlucci went on. "The Russians keep yelling in their newspapers that the Americans are a bunch of black-market operators. All our boys have always done is to barter their own cigarettes, soap, candy and watches for luxury goods; things which do not deprive the German economy or population of vital commodities.

"Thousands of German kids are eating chocolate today and drinking powdered milk because some American would rather have a bit of Meissen china than he would the chocolate or the milk. I really enjoy," Carlucci said, "going after professional black-marketeers whose activities actually deprive German civilians of essential commodities, but you'd be surprised how few of them there are.

"You know," Carlucci went on, "there is still a lot of anti-Semitism around here. Some of these Krauts hate Hitler but they hate him because he lost the war for them. And they hate the Jews. Why? God only knows. It's a hangover from the propaganda they heard all those years. You show me a Jew-hater and I'll show you a no-good goddamn lousy yellow rat. I like to get my hands on characters like that. Some of these *Fräuleins* around here have sold that bill of goods to our G.I.'s, too. You see, these Krauts got to blame someone for the loss of the war, so they blame the Jews. Well, in one way, they're right; we had Jews in every outfit I was ever with during the war, and I never seen better fighters.

"You hear stories that the D.P.'s are the biggest black-market operators in Germany. That burned me and I went through the D.P. camps with a fine comb. Those Jewish D.P.'s had all come from great distances. They carried everything they owned with them. Some had a few dollars relatives in

America had sent them; some had a couple of pieces of china or maybe a dozen silver spoons. I mean that is all they had in the world. But the only clothes they had were the clothes on their backs. So, naturally, they sold or traded the china and the silver they had so they could get clothing for their kids. We are moving the D.P.'s out of Berlin now and they put in a rule that none of them could bring foreign currency with them. So before they get into a plane at Tempelhof, I got to search them. Well, for God's sake, I wish you could see what the poor devils have with them to start a new life somewhere. Nothin'. Nothin'.

"Sure, now and then we have grabbed a big operator among them, but in every case we found he was a professional black-marketeer disguised as a D.P. Yet, you still hear these stories. They're all planted by Krauts or some poor dopey G.I. who gets to believe what the *Fräuleins* say. There are a lot of good Germans, believe me. Take my German cops. They are fine but I had a little trouble training them. They didn't know about search warrants and writs of habeas corpus, and they didn't know a man is considered innocent until proven guilty, and they didn't know you can't beat a confession out of a suspect. We give the Germans here every protection that we give our citizens at home. It's new to them and they like it. Some of them never heard of a trial by jury. We try them and a German jury finds them innocent or guilty. I guess that's democracy at work, hey? But I would like to get my hands on those Jew-haters who spread those phony stories."

I went to a D.P. camp one day to watch Carlucci and his boys shepherd the D.P.'s into trucks to take them to Tempelhof. I watched Ray and his men search their pitiful belongings. Three years ago when I had been in D.P. camps, I was horrified by the numb listlessness of the men, women and children who had survived. They didn't seem to care whether they lived or died. The horror of the years of torture had entered their souls and you wondered if it would ever leave. Now they were alive again. They were, for the most part, headed for

Israel and the joy they felt was almost embarrassing to watch. The Joint Distribution Committee (an agency of the United Jewish Appeal) had done an intelligent job in the D.P. camps. First, they kept the D.P.'s alive with food and medical attention and then they gave them something to live for. They taught them trades so that they would never become economic burdens. Now they were qualified mechanics, radio operators, textile workers, machinists, carpenters. Henceforth, they would be independent and this showed in their bearing.

"These people are all right," Carlucci growled, as though fearing he'd be accused of sentimentality. "They had been pushed around for years. How in hell they kept alive, I don't know. Yeah, I'd enjoy getting my hands on those Krauts who say they're black-market operators."

"How would you enjoy going after the guy who stole the boss's rug?" I asked.

Carlucci winced and looked very pained. "I was hoping you didn't know about that," he said. "It was like this. General Clay had been in Frankfort for a couple of days. When he came back to his office, damned if his rug wasn't gone. So he called me in. I questioned every workman who had been in the building while the Boss was away. I couldn't get a thing out of any of them. The rug is still missing," Carlucci said unhappily, "and every time I meet General Clay he says, 'Carlucci, when are you going to return that rug of mine?' "

He shook his head. "You know what the rug was worth? Maybe ten bucks. That's all. And when I leave here that's what they'll remember me by. They'll say, 'Carlucci? They stole the General's rug right from under his nose. That's the kind of a cop Carlucci was.' "

Maybe some day General Clay will break down and confess to Carlucci that the whole thing was a gag and that the moth-eaten rug was not stolen but thrown away. But I won't tell Carlucci that. You don't catch me blowing the whistle on a four-star general.

The American Press Club on Sven Hedin Strasse was the center of whatever social life there was in Berlin. The bar was presided over by an old friend, Fred Bauermaker. Back in 1933, when I lived in Berlin, Fred occupied a very important position. He was then bartender at the Adlon Hotel bar. It was Fred who extended credit to us when we were broke; it was Fred who sometimes whispered, "That man at the next table has been planted here to listen to you men. Be careful what you say in front of him."

Attached to the club were two tennis courts and they were occupied from morning to night by correspondents and their wives trying hard to fashion some kind of a normal life in a ruined, desolate city. During the summer and fall of 1948, there was always a feeling of tension in the air. There was always the possibility (by no means remote) that the Russians would abandon their diplomatic attacks in favor of more direct methods. The wife of a correspondent who had a couple of children to take care of found it impossible to dismiss this thought lightly. Yet none of them left Berlin.

American newspapers, press associations and "news" magazines had sent their first teams to Berlin. Drew Middleton of the *New York Times;* Marguerite Higgins of the *Herald Tribune;* David Nichol of the *Chicago Daily News;* Wes Gallagher of the A.P.; John Thompson of *Newsweek* (who had lost an eye at Dieppe); Emmett Hughes and John Scott of *Time* were only a few of the really first-rate correspondents who were in Berlin. Feature writers like brilliant Sonia Tamara (*Herald Tribune*), Judy Barden (*New York Sun*), Joseph Fleming (*Stars and Stripes*—an excellent paper) and a dozen others were always hustling around the city looking for stories. The blockade of Berlin meant that gasoline could only be brought in by air and it was strictly rationed. Correspondents who owned cars had to put them in mothballs and use the jeeps from the correspondents' pool. Wives couldn't do their shopping by phone; the commissary did not deliver. Each day they had to travel by jeep to the Army commissary, known as Uncle Tom's Cabin, to buy the food for the following twenty-four hours. Most of the ice boxes in the Zehlendorf Area were electric, which meant they didn't operate during the hours when the current was turned off. A great many of the Berlin streets were paved with cobblestones, and when you rode a jeep over them more than your teeth rattled. Doctors refused to allow expectant mothers to ride in the jeeps, but a fine community spirit prevailed among the wives of the correspondents and if one was going to have a baby, the others rallied round, did her shopping, and helped with the housework.

David Parsons, in charge of the American Overseas Airlines (only civilian airline company to have a charter to operate into Berlin), was a tower of strength to the small isolated community of correspondents. More than one pilot stepped out of an American Airline plane at Tempelhof carrying a package containing diapers, dextro-maltose, cans of evaporated milk, boxes of vitamins and other commodities essential to the health of brand-new mothers and their brand-new babies. Dave Parsons made many friends for American Airlines during the rather unhappy summer of 1948. Parsons, quite unaware of doing so, was acting as unofficial ambassador to the correspondents and their families. Quite often around the Press Club you'd hear a rumor which, if true, would result in an important story. Invariably some correspondent would say, "I'll check with Dave Parsons on that. He'll know." Parsons spent ten or eleven hours a day at Tempelhof sweating out the arrival of his big planes. On his way home (his family had a house at Wannsee) he'd often stop at our place with his attractive wife, Barbara. I learned a great deal from him about Berlin that I hadn't known.

Why do I spend so much time talking about a man who is in charge of a commercial airline in Berlin? For this reason: I've been working abroad on and off since 1933, and I've never been particularly impressed with the type of American businessman one meets abroad. As a rule, he is a selfish, opinionated person who makes no attempt to conceal his contempt for the people of the country in which he is stationed. He is frequently unprincipled and patronizing in his dealings with them and they quite naturally think of him as a symbol of America. Big Business (like the British Foreign Office) always seemed to export its worst human products. Any foreign correspondent can name you a dozen second-raters they have seen in relatively important business jobs in Europe. It seems different now. Business firms seem to be sending their best men abroad or it may be that positions in Europe are attracting a better type of American.

Dave Parsons, for instance, would make a fine American ambassador to any country in Europe. In representing American Airlines in Berlin, he felt a certain responsibility. In a sense, he was representing American industry in Berlin; virtually everyone else was representing government or the military. And in Parsons, American industry was well represented. General Clay, Colonel Howley, every member of the American press, and the men and women who worked for him at Tempelhof all had great respect for Dave Parsons. I never had occasion to ask Parsons a favor, so this is not sweet talk to pay off for anything he or American Airlines ever did for me. I had known Parsons for nearly a month when he said casually, "Did you run across my brother in Paris?"

"Who is your brother?" I asked in surprise.

"Geoff—Geoff Parsons," he said. "I thought you and he were old friends."

"We are," I exploded. "But I never knew you were his brother. What's more important, I never knew you were the son of Geoff Parsons, Senior."

"The old boy is quite a person, isn't he?" Dave said with quiet pride. "Quite a person."

"He's quite a person," I agreed. Everything was explained. Naturally, a son of Geoffrey Parsons, Senior, had to be a stand-out.

Colonel Howley had some very bright men working for him. Men like Louis Glaser, Chief of Civil Administration and the Political Affairs Branch and Fred Shaw, who acted as Liaison between Colonel Howley and the German press. Shaw, an Air Force veteran, young, attractive, had temporarily given up newspaper work to act as one of Howley's aides. Shaw owned a 1935 Opal, the worst automobile I have ever seen. Its top speed was about twenty miles an hour; it had no brakes and no spare tire, and because it had no ignition key, you couldn't lock it.

"I should have known better than to buy this," Shaw would grumble. "I bought it from Marguerite Higgins. Now let's face it, Maggie Higgins is the smartest gal in town. When she said I could have this for five hundred dollars, I should have smelled a rat. What sold me was the fact that she said it would go about fifty miles on a gallon of gas. She was right on that. But otherwise, it's no good."

"Won't she take it back?"

"Listen, I drove it up in front of her house and left it there," Shaw said. "She had it towed back to my house. But Maggie had it insured for a thousand dollars. I kept up those premiums. I haven't even a key for it. But no one would steal it. All over Berlin they steal cars, but not this one. I have no garage. I leave it out all night. I practically plead with people to steal it, but no one will. I'm stuck with it."

Shaw and I made several evening forays into the Russian sector in his dilapidated crate. One night we had dinner at the Intourist Restaurant on Friedrichstrasse. This was a good restaurant and the Russians were very proud of it. They even advertised it in the Berlin papers, saying in English, "All that you can eat and drink. You can also take along. In the best quality." There was one catch to dining at the Intourist. They would only accept Swiss francs, Swedish kronen, British pounds or American dollars. They would not accept marks or the American script we used in the American sector. I found fourteen one-dollar bills in my brief case and Shaw and I went to the Intourist. The waiters were German and the few customers were Russian officers. There were very few Swiss francs, Swedish kronen, American dollars or British pounds left in Berlin, our waiter told us, so business had fallen off. We began our meal with caviar and vodka, ignored a thin, tasteless version of borscht, and had beef Strogonov, a bottle of German champagne (a fairly distant relative of French champagne) and French-fried potatoes. The bill came to thirteen dollars.

When we left the restaurant, two Russian G.I.'s were looking at Fred's car intently, but with no larceny in their eyes. We drove down Unter den Linden and then back again. The moonlight was bright and the ragged outlines of the wrecked buildings were etched sharply against the night. Once I'd known this section of town well. Here was the Bristol Hotel and across the street H. R. Knickerbocker's office. Here, a pile of rubble and debris, was the U. P. office, and this grotesque-looking broken façade was once the immaculate front of the Adlon Hotel. We drove around for an hour and nobody bothered us. You could spend days and nights in the Soviet sector without being questioned or stopped and then some dumb Russian G.I. might grab you and take you to the clink. This had happened often.

We drove under the Brandenburger Tor and through the desolate waste that was once the Tiergarten. We headed toward our part of town. It was about 1 A.M. now, and we seemed to be the only ones awake in the city. Not a light showed. Fred spun the car into Potsdammer Chausee and then gave a yell of warning. Four girls were standing in the middle of the street calling for us to stop. They stood there, not knowing about our lack of brakes. Fred swung the car toward the curb and stopped. The four girls came running toward us.

"Cigaretten? Chok-o-lot?" they pleaded.

"Wie alt sind sie?" Shaw asked.

"Eighteen," they answered in chorus.

"Look at them," Freddie said. "I doubt if any one of them is more than sixteen. Got any cigarettes left?"

I handed him a pack and he divided it among the squealing girls. Two of them started to climb into the car. Fred shook his head and, reluctantly, they stepped back. We drove on.

"You can hate Germans all you want," Freddie said. "But a thing like that can only make you feel sick. Four fifteen- or sixteen-year-old kids out on the prowl at one in the morning looking for men. And the best they can hope for is a candy bar or seven or eight cigarettes. It isn't pretty to think about, is it?"

"Dr. Kinsey ought to send a talent scout over here," I told him.

"You don't get it," Fred said, shaking his head. "These kids aren't nymphomaniacs or tarts at heart. Most of them are helping to support their families. Since the blockade, thousands of men have been thrown out of work. With the cut in electric power, fewer men are needed to run street cars and public utilities. These kids are in business because it is the only way most of them can survive. The cigarettes and candy they get mean coal and wood and food and clothing for them and their families. Mind you, there are hundreds (maybe thousands) of professional tarts in Berlin who would be tramps under any conditions. But you can't sell me the idea that these kids we just saw are tramps by choice."

"What's the answer?" I asked him.

"God knows," Fred said gloomily. "If we had Berlin to ourselves, I know damn well Clay and Howley would find an answer. But the horrible economic conditions in our sector are the result of what happens in the Russian sector. If there was no blockade and if there was some kind of industry here to keep people working, these kids would be leading some kind of normal life."

We passed the huge American Army Hospital on Unter den Eichen. There were two M.P.'s on guard at the gate and two others in a jeep. "Look at that sign." Fred pointed to a

282

large poster which said in German, "Loitering in This Vicinity Strictly Prohibited."

"That's why those M.P.'s are there," Fred said. "To keep German girls from sneaking into the hospital. They've even climbed that picket fence in order to slip into the hospital. There are an awful lot of V.D. cases in there, but that doesn't bother these kids. They're so desperate for the few cigarettes they'll get, that they'll even try to sneak into a V.D. ward. That's Berlin, chum. Talk to Reuter and Frau Schroeder and Suhr and you get enthusiastic about a new decent democratic Germany. Then drive around at night, and you see the other side of the picture. It's—it's unclean. I sound like a Boy Scout," Fred added apologetically, "but a couple of years around here gets you down."

Drew Middleton and his wife, Stevie, gave a cocktail party for three visiting *New York Times* executives. Giving a cocktail party in Berlin presented all of the difficulties attendant upon giving a housewarming in the Antarctic. Liquor of all kinds was strictly rationed, but an occasion like this was semi-official. Drew managed to get an extra bottle or two from the Press Club and the commissary. General Clay and Colonel Howley were present, and it was typical of Howley that he sent along a few bottles of German champagne. Both Howley and Clay had imposed the same rationing rules upon themselves that governed all military, civilian and newspaper personnel.

Clay and Howley were always frank with the correspondents and this is one reason why a newspaper reader in New York or Chicago or, for that matter, Waterloo, Iowa, today knows as much about Berlin as anyone working and living in the city. The talk at the party centered on the Soviet efforts to get America out of Berlin. The hub-hub grew as one opinion after another was tossed into the air.

David Nichol turned to me and said quietly, "Do you notice that the three men in the room who worked in Moscow are the only three who haven't tried to explain Marshal Sokolovsky and the Soviet policy here? You, Drew and I are apparently the only ones who don't know a thing about Russia and we are the only ones who worked there."

"I'm one of those who guessed wrong," I told Nichol. "I remember writing a piece in Moscow during the war. I wound up by saying, 'The Russians are going to be easy to do business with after the war.' That sentence haunts me in my sleep."

"We all thought that," David said. "We were in pretty good company. Wendell Willkie, Averell Harriman, Dean Acheson, Eric Johnston, Harry Hopkins, and most of the British thought the same. There were fourteen British and American correspondents in Moscow then, remember? Not one of us was a Communist or even a fellow-traveler. Yet, I don't remember one man who thought that Russia would be tough to deal with when peace came. I'm sure we were right, too. What they did was to change their policy sometime in 1945."

Drew had joined us. "I agree. As long as the Kremlin boys felt secure, as they did during the war, they were all for co-operation with us. They needed us to help rebuild their cities and to furnish them with consumers' goods. But when their troops went into Europe and saw that the standard of living in the poorest capitalistic countries was higher than their own they got a bit restless. They started to ask themselves questions. The Kremlin boys got a little nervous. So they switched their policy. They sold the people the idea that American and British imperialism was trying to dominate the world and that Russia was in great danger. That's all the people ever heard on their radios and all they read in *Pravda* and *Izvestia*."

"How can we understand people who deliberately break promises, who deliberately lie to your face?" David said gloomily. "They not only lie to us, they lie to their own people."

"Well, anyhow," Drew laughed, "everybody understands them but us. It's too bad we ever went to work in Moscow.

284

If we had never lived there we could talk about the Russians with authority."

"Drew," his wife interrupted, "please entertain our guests. Circulate a little, honey. Besides, I want to ask Quent something. Tell me what kind of a year Joe DiMaggio is having? The *Paris Herald Tribune* is so tiresome. It only prints the standings of the teams. It never gives you the real baseball news."

Stevie Middleton is in many ways the world's most unique baseball fan. She is tiny and beautiful and has lovely soft brown eyes and, all in all, she and Drew are as perfectly matched a pair as you'll find anywhere. Drew met Stevie in London during the war. He carried on a strange courtship with the young Welsh girl. Others would take Stevie to the theatre or to night clubs or send her flowers—not Drew.

"Drew would phone around to various American Army bases," Stevie explained, "and when he found a camp that was going to have a baseball game, he'd take me to see it. Drew was putting me through a test. If I didn't like baseball, he was all set to brush me off. But I loved baseball from the beginning, and so Drew asked me to marry him. Then we went to Moscow. Naturally, we went to the ballet a lot. What else is there to do in Moscow?"

"Nothing," I said. "But what has that to do with baseball?"

"Well, I'll tell you," Stevie said quite seriously. "From Moscow we went to New York and, naturally, the first day we arrived we went to the Yankee Stadium. Now that I think of it, that's about all of New York I ever saw," Stevie said. "Anyhow, when I saw Rizzuto and Stirnweiss working around second base, all I could think of was the ballet in Moscow. They whirled, pirouetted and did everything that good ballet dancers do—only they were even more graceful. We were in New York four days and saw the Yankees play six times."

"In four days you saw six games?"

"There were two double-headers," Stevie explained. "And Joe DiMaggio was wonderful. He made three home runs in those games and he made the most impossible catches. I think," she said, with the conviction that only comes to the dyed-in-the-wool baseball fan, "Joe is the greatest baseball player of all time and I don't care what Drew says. In fact," she added, "that is the only argument we have ever had."

"He's still holding out for the Babe?" I'd argued this point myself with Drew in several countries over the course of the years. Drew joined us at this point with the maniacal gleam in his eyes which characterizes the devout fan. "DiMaggio is a nice outfielder," he conceded generously. "He has a fine arm, and I will admit that he is one of the few base runners I know who can go from first to third on an infield single. But, you must remember that Babe Ruth led the league in hitting home runs twelve times; in his lifetime he batted in 2,209 runs, and led the American League six years in this department. Everybody knows he hit sixty home runs in 1927, but do you know he walloped 714 home runs in his lifetime? Has DiMaggio ever approached that? For eleven years Babe led the league in getting bases on balls; one year they walked him 170 times. Do you know he played in twelve World Series and in six of those series he hit better than .300? And he hit fifteen home runs in World Series play. And do you know," Drew's usually quiet voice was raised now, and neither Stevie nor I had a chance to interrupt, "that the Babe pitched 29 and 2-3 consecutive scoreless innings in a World Series game?"

"Now let me tell you about Joe DiMaggio," little Stevie stormed, but Drew smiled aloofly and said, "You told me to circulate, darling," and walked off, leaving us both furious.

There was, of course, only one thing to do. I'd have to phone New York to get some ammunition or life would be unbearable in Berlin henceforth. I went back to Ken's house and by telling the operator that this was an official call for Colonel Downs, managed to place a call to Toots Shor's restaurant, unofficial baseball headquarters in New York. Four hours later, the phone rang and I recognized the familiar voice of Mr. Toots Shor. Mr. Shor's whole world is bounded by baseball. Like myself, he is first of all a Giant fan, but because we are great DiMaggio admirers, we have to give some of our allegiance to the Yankees. Mr. Shor once said that his idea of heaven would be a place where the Giants and Yankees met every year in the World Series. If it were truly heaven, Joe would hit two home runs in every game, steal four bases, make two or three of those miracle catches only he can make, and, despite all this, the Giants would win each series in four straight.

I told Toots my difficulty. I wanted some of Joe's records to confront Drew with the next day. "The bum is here for dinner. I'll put him on." And the next moment, I was talking to DiMaggio. I told him my difficulty. "You two must be nuts," DiMaggio said. "Everyone here is worried stiff about what the Russians are going to do in Berlin, and you two are arguing about baseball. Why, we were even arguing about Berlin in the dressing room today before the game."

"What kind of day did you have?"

"Fair." I could almost see Joe shrugging his shoulders. "I got three for four."

I asked him about some of his records, but he didn't know what they were. "Listen," he said seriously, "you're out of line. Drew Middleton is right. When the Big Guy was going good nobody could touch him."

"Put Toots on!" I was disgusted. I wanted facts—not modesty.

"The bum had a fair day, he says," Toots chuckled. "He only hit two home runs, the last one with the bases full and we beat Cleveland. You want some of Joe's records? Tell Mr. Drew Middleton about that 56-game-hitting streak Joe had in 1941. During that streak he batted in 55 runs, made 91 hits, and batted .408. That streak won the pennant for the Yankees. Tell Mr. Drew Middleton that Joe won the Most Valuable Player Award three times—that's all—three times. In his very first year up he made 206 hits and then . . ."

I made notes as Mr. Shor talked. I got hold of Stevie and

briefed her on Joe DiMaggio's records. Life was much pleasanter in Berlin after that, though I did notice that any time Drew and I met, everyone else, bored by our perpetual argument, moved away in disgust. We'll be arguing this one for the rest of our lives.

There weren't many important Nazis or high-ranking officers left in Berlin. The Russians took pretty good care of thousands of them during their two months of Berlin occupation, and then, when the French took over their sector, they did a thorough job of "eliminating" any who had ever been connected with either the S.S. or S.A. or who had been ranking officers. The British and ourselves didn't go in for the "direct" method to such a great extent, but it is a fact that you seldom saw a man of military age in any part of Berlin. You saw literally hundreds of amputees any time you drove along Unter den Eichen or Potsdammer Chausee and you saw a great number of blind war veterans. It was seldom that you found anyone who admitted that he had ever been a Nazi. There were plenty of them in Frankfort and thousands in the Russian zone who had merely switched their allegiance from Fascism to Communism without finding the transition too painful. The Nazi spirit is far from dead in Germany and, if Hitler were to reappear, millions would undoubtedly hail him with the same fervent devotion they had once given him.

Now and then I managed to woo Tony away from Marie (quite an operation) for a walk. Tony loved to chase cars. One day he lit out after a jeep. He didn't pay any attention to my yelling, but finally stopped to investigate the potentialities of a German *Fräulein* (Boxer by breed) who had darted out of a gate. Although Tony had neither cigarettes nor soap nor chocolate, he seemed to be doing all right with his fraternizing. A short blond man limped out through the gate, and that is how I came to meet Hans Heydte.

Heydte took care of three gardens on Wildenow Strasse. In his fairly good English he told me that he was having bad luck with his plums. I boasted of the fine plums we were getting in our garden and asked him to come along and see for himself. He often walked past our house with his Boxer who turned out not to be a *Fräulein* at all—merely a young half-grown playboy who acted girlish. More than once I asked him into our garden (by now, of course, I was thinking of this as my house and of Ken and Marie-Therese as my guests). I offered him a cigarette, but instead of putting it in his pocket, he actually lit and smoked it. I had never seen a Berliner smoke an American cigarette. Cigarettes were currency—not casual luxuries to be dissipated in smoke.

In 1932, Hans Heydte had been a student at the University of Göttingen. He had become an enthusiastic member of the Nazi party. "All of us did at college. It was the thing to do and it was exciting to join something which promised positive action." Gradually he told me the rest of his story. In civilian life he had been a chemist. In 1938 he had joined the German Army. Now he saw another war coming. Was there a way I could help him to join the American Army? War with Russia was inevitable, he thought, and he could be useful to the American Army. Bacteria warfare, that was the coming thing, he said earnestly. He had been a very minor cog in the chemical warfare branch and his specialty had been methods of extending the range of a flame thrower. But he had heard things about the real bacterial weapons which Germany had been afraid to use. Why?

"Roosevelt warned Hitler that if he ever used bacteria as weapons, he, Roosevelt, would immediately destroy the civilian population of Germany with the same or more deadly germs than we had developed," Hans said. "That, at least, is the story we heard. That Roosevelt was tough and cruel."

"Thank God," I said fervently. When I told him I didn't have enough influence to help him join even the Salvation Army, he accepted it without protest.

"My record from your viewpoint is very bad," he said quite dispassionately. "I joined the Nazi party when I was nineteen. In time, I came to realize that National Socialism and Communism were pretty much the same, but you couldn't resign from the party. I joined the Army and fought in France, and then fought three years in Russia. I got out of Russia alive and, finally, during the last days of the war, I was captured by the Americans.

"I said my record was bad. No denazification board would ever clear me. Now I work as a gardener. My old profession is closed to me. Well, I have no quarrel with that. I made a mistake and should be made to pay for it. But I am a trained soldier. I have a great many friends like myself. When you go to war against Russia, your Army should allow us to fight on your side."

Hans Heydte was a completely disillusioned man who felt that his life as an independent citizen was over. When Hitler came to power he was twenty years old and had been well indoctrinated in the tenets of Nazism. He, more than anyone I met in Germany, was a complete product of the corrupt age of National Socialism. He was not intrinsically evil in himself. I imagine that, like millions of others in Germany, he at first merely drifted along with the Nazi tide, not caring one way or another about politics, and then, gradually, became a participant. He was drawn into the pattern of glory woven so skilfully and eloquently by Hitler and Goebbels and Rosenberg and, eventually, he came to believe. I am not trying to excuse him but to explain him. His only criticism of Hitler now was—Hitler had failed. For this he could never forgive Hitler.

"What do you think of Reuter, Frau Schroeder, Dr. Suhr and the others?" I asked.

"They are fine," he said enthusiastically. "They are not afraid to stand up to the Russian swine. They are real fighters."

"But how do you feel about their democratic principles?"

The chemist-turned-gardener shrugged his shoulders. "I don't know. We used to sneer at democracy. It was weak. Well, you must admit that your country did nothing but make speeches for the first few years of the war. You wouldn't be in the war yet if those damn fool Japs hadn't attacked you. But when you did come in we were surprised to find that you could fight fairly well. You beat us by force of numbers and material. We never thought you had that much strength. Well, if democracy can be that strong, maybe we ought to try it here. Perhaps it will be strong enough to beat the Russians. But you should allow men like myself to help.

"You know," he said quite earnestly, "you Americans and ourselves should always have been natural allies."

"What in God's name have we in common?" I asked, really surprised.

"Many things," he said earnestly. "I was always amused at your criticism of the way Hitler treated Jews. You treat your Negroes the same way. This I have read in books written by Americans. You Americans treat your Communists just as Hitler treated our Communists. The people I work for are American families. I read their newspapers, hoping to improve my English. Well, it does improve. So does my knowledge of your country."

"What surprises me," I said to him, "is the fact that you're running around loose. How come the Russians or French didn't grab you? After all, you were a German officer. How come the Americans allow you to work for them?"

"I'm harmless enough," he said. "I'm a cripple." He picked up a heavy brass ash tray that was lying on a table. He took it and slammed it against his left leg. There was a metallic clang.

"I've only got one leg," he laughed. "Your American Army doctors did a good job on me and found me a new leg that fits pretty well."

That's Hans Heydte—take him or leave him. Neither he nor his kind will ever be much help in bringing democracy to Germany. But happily the Reuters and the Frau Schroeders far outnumber the Hans Heydtes—at least in Berlin.

hey'll be talking about this one fifty years from now. It will become a legend in Air Force circles, just as the supply line over the Hump during the war years has already become a legend. They'll be talking of how a handful of American and British planes kept two and a half million people of Berlin alive during the year 1948. They'll be telling how we beat the Russians without firing a shot in the hottest cold war ever fought between nations.

The greatest air-supply operation in history began with a phone call on the morning of June 27, 1948. General Lucius Clay in Berlin was calling General Curtis E. LeMay in Wiesbaden. It was a short and rather unhappy conversation, and a great many things were left unsaid by both men. Clay told LeMay that Berlin would have to be fed by air and that he, LeMay, would be in charge of the operation.

Neither man mentioned the fine four-laned Autobahn that stretched from Frankfort right across the Russian zone almost to Berlin. Neither mentioned the railroad which the Russians had closed to make "necessary repairs." Things moved fast during the next few hours. Clay phoned Washington and told Marshall that LeMay would need a lot of C-54's. Marshall, General Omar Bradley and General Hoyt Vandenberg went into an immediate huddle. Within a few moments, teletype messages were flying to Hawaii, to Alaska, to Texas, to Panama.

Because of the time difference, it was only ten in the morning at Bergstrom Field down in Austin, Texas, where the 48th Troop Carrier Squadron was based. An hour before this a C-54 had landed from Guam, and Lieutenant Colonel Forrest Coon, pilot of the ship, had climbed down from the cockpit. He'd been away two and a half years, in the Philippines and on Guam, and now at last he was home.

It was a hot day and he joined a group of the pilots who were cavorting in the pool. Coon had a long leave coming and he'd go home and get acquainted with his family again.

His thoughts were interrupted by an order over the loud-speaker: "All personnel report immediately to Operations."

A few moments later, Coon and the others were listening to Colonel Raphael Baez telling them that they would be off for Berlin immediately. The whole squadron would go. That meant forty-eight officers and eighty-eight enlisted men. The fliers smiled. Even Coon was happy. Germany? Brother, this might be it!

The 54th Troop Carrier Squadron was at its home base, Elmendorf Field, Anchorage, Alaska, that Sunday morning. This outfit has flown more bad-weather missions than perhaps any other in the Air Force. When Colonel Thomas Mosely received the message to get his boys to the Rhein-Main airport at Frankfort he, too, acted quickly.

Lieutenant Colonel James Samouce, the squadron leader, and his forty-one officers and 169 enlisted men heard the news with joy. Germany! They wouldn't need their snowshoes, standard equipment for Alaska-based planes, but they brought them along anyhow. (And hung them on the wall of their Operations room at Rhein-Main.) Within ten hours the squadron was on its way.

Hickam Field, base for the 19th Troop Carrier Squadron, is at Honolulu. When Colonel Davidson, C. O. at Hickam, received the order from Washington that morning, one of his aircraft crews was at Brisbane, Australia. He told his squadron leader, Major E. Cresswell, to hurry to Frankfort with his eleven planes and their ground crews.

Before the last plane had left, a teletype message had reached Lieutenant Michael Pashkevich and his crew in Brisbane, where they had just landed with a load of supplies. In usual cryptic Air Force terminology the message merely read: "Return Hickam immediately." Pashkevich and his crew of nine climbed right back into their big ship and headed for Hickam. They were there only long enough to have their motors checked and they too joined the migration to Germany.

American Army planes kept streaming into Frankfort. They came from Westover Field in Massachusetts, from Albrook Field in Panama, and LeMay, chewing on his unlighted cigar, put them right to work. The boys found it a lot tougher than they had expected. They hadn't known that the C-54's would be lifting ten tons and that the two-engined C-47's would be carting 8,000 pounds of coal and flour. This overloading is called a "calculated risk" in Air Force language. No commercial plane would be allowed to leave an airport carrying such loads. But this was an emergency operation, and the rules of war were applied.

The boys hadn't known that many of them would be flying 140 hours a month and they hadn't known about Tempelhof, the Berlin airport. Tempelhof was designed for the use of relatively short-range planes, like the Junkers. The runways had to be lengthened; new strips had to be built, but the chief disadvantage of Tempelhof was (and is now) the row of two-story houses which surround the field.

Until these planes arrived, the 10th, 11th, and 12th Squadrons of the 60th Troop Carrier Group bore the brunt of the operation. They had been stationed at Kauebeuren, some sixty miles southeast of Munich. They were the very first to arrive at Wiesbaden. When General LeMay talks of the beating these boys took during the early days of the operation he forgets the cigar in his mouth and his eyes light up with admiration. They were all making three trips a day along the Rainbow Route to Berlin. These were the first planes the Berliners saw. Incidentally, these pilots, now incorporated in the 317th Group, are still at it. They were the pioneers—these crews of the original 60th Troop Carrier Group.

During the first month of Operation Vittles, there were only seven really good days for flying. Most of the time it was done by instrument. Bringing heavily loaded planes into Tempelhof under a two-hundred-foot ceiling takes a lot of careful and expert guidance, and those houses around the field added to the hazards. The boys hadn't known about the YAK's and the PE-2's which the Russians have been flying in the "corridor" every day just to make life more difficult for them. You never can know when a speedy YAK will streak out of a cloud to brush wings with you.

But the air lift was established, and the people of Berlin did not starve. More important in many ways is the fact that the thin line of aircraft landing or taking off every three minutes has enabled the United States to maintain its foreign policy.

It has cost us one and a half million dollars a week to support the life line. This has been the price of retaining our dignity as a nation. The Russians have done everything (short of shooting) to make us leave Berlin. General Clay declared in July, 1948, that the Soviets could never get us out of Berlin by anything but an act of war. The Russians thought the blockade of Berlin would eliminate us. With England and

France, we were committed to feeding the people of the Berlin Western sectors. If we had not been able to do this we would have had no alternative but to leave.

The air lift has also made it possible for us to retain the spiritual leadership of the Western nations in Europe. Had we left Berlin, the Communists in Western Europe would have chortled gleefully and would have capitalized on our weakness. Had we left Berlin, thousands in Greece, fearing that Russian domination in Europe was inevitable, would have flocked to the standard of Markos. Had we left Berlin, Togliatti in Italy, an eloquent and persuasive man, might well have doubled the already substantial strength of his Communist Party overnight, and Communists in France would have been given new strength.

As a political weapon, the air lift has been tremendously effective. Even the Russians have found no answer to it. They ridiculed it in their German-language newspapers in Berlin, but the citizens of the capital looked aloft and, seeing flour and coal coming to them on wings, laughed at the efforts of the Soviet propagandists. Only history can decide how vitally important in political terms the air lift will have been.

General LeMay, who can fly anything with wings, made a dozen trips himself, flying either a C-47 or a C-54. Even the public relations officers and the adjutants and the staff of the bases in both Wiesbaden and Rhein-Main took over the controls on week ends. LeMay wouldn't have a mess sergeant working for him unless the guy could fly.

The air lift began in June. By August 1st, the Russians had stopped ridiculing the effort. By that date, 43,224 tons of food and fuel had been flown into Berlin. There had been 8,368 flights, and the planes had covered 5,000,000 miles with only two fatal accidents. This in two months.

The air lift has rejuvenated Berlin. The policy of the Western nations had been to teach the people democracy, but the truth is that Germans at first hadn't taken very well to the teaching. They had watched the Russians take one positive, aggressive step after another while the Western nations vacillated and pussyfooted. They had begun to wonder whether "democracy" wasn't just another word for "appeasement." Then at long last, they saw democracy at work. All day and all night they heard the drone of engines. They saw trucks tearing out of Tempelhof filled with supplies for the hospitals or with food and coal which were being hurried to warehouses and then delivered to the ration shops. Americans had stopped making speeches; they were actually defying the Russians.

The air lift became the chief topic of conversation in Berlin. One day a C-47 crashed a short distance from Tempelhof, and Lieutenants Charles King and Robert Stuber were killed. This was the second fatal accident. The Russian press screamed that the overloaded planes were presenting a grave threat to the lives of the people of Berlin. Other planes would crash, they said, and Berliners would be killed. This line of reasoning aroused the people to furious anger and resentment. They held a spontaneous memorial service for the two dead pilots. Berliners crowded into a church to pray at that service.

Each day the crowds increased at Tempelhof until there were often 10,000 men, women and children on Berlinerstrasse, bordering the field. They climbed trees; they scaled the walls of ruined houses; they stood on the roofs of parked cars and trucks. They cheered as the planes roared overhead and they brought presents for the fliers.

One day I saw an M.P. stop four kids trying to slip into Tempelhof. Each carried an armful of flowers. They said they wanted to give these to the pilots. So the M.P. looked the other way, and the four kids scrambled inside looking for the pilots.

Women brought Meissenware and treasured pieces of silver, and some brought lucky charms they had knitted. These people were getting their first lesson in practical democracy, and it meant more to them than all the lectures, radio talks and editorials they had been exposed to since the Western nations took over their Berlin sectors.

At Gatow, the airport in the British sector, the same scenes were being enacted. Here the four-engined British planes were landing, and you noticed that practically every R.A.F. pilot wore one of the small knitted amulets given him by Berlin schoolchildren. Out at Lake Havel, where the huge Sunderlands landed, the shores were always crowded with people who cheered when the big ships hit the water.

If it seems that I have neglected the British participation in this great effort, let me hasten to correct that impression. The R.A.F. threw all of its resources into flying coal and flour into Berlin. Within a month after the operation began, the R.A.F. was averaging 250 flights into Berlin daily and within another month this had almost been doubled. When the R.A.F. planes couldn't absorb the tonnage required (the British have concentrated on the production of fighter aircraft since the war) the British Government hired transports from civilian airline companies. They used any type of aircraft that could raise a ton of coal off the ground; big Lanks and Yorks and Dakotas (their name for the C-47) and Wayfarers and Sunderlands. It was exciting as well as nostalgic to walk into an R.A.F. mess at Hanover or at Gatow, and meet the same kind of men you'd met at bomber stations during the war and to know that once again we were united in a common cause and that the same magnificent spirit of co-operation existed.

"Reminds you of that Indian operation," a husky pilot laughed. "Just as you Americans had the supply lift over the Hump, we had the India-Pakistan run. These chaps set out to liquidate each other and we had to fly refugees out of both places. But I'd rather haul coal or flour. You can pile that up and know it isn't going to shift all over the place. You couldn't pile those refugees on top of each other and you couldn't make them stay in one place."

"Seems funny," another said, "bringing people in Berlin food and coal. I used to make this Berlin flight a lot during the war, but I'd be bringing blockbusters."

I never met one British or American pilot who resented the

fact that he was risking his neck (weather and landing conditions as well as overloading presented the risk) helping to feed former enemies. All of their resentment was reserved for the Russians whose policy had made this operation necessary.

The Berlin newspapers not dominated by the Russians kept what amounted to a box score which told the previous day's haul. You'd go to the snack bar at Tempelhof for breakfast, and your waitress would beam and say, "We broke the record yesterday. Five hundred and seventy American and British planes came to Berlin."

For the first time since the end of the war, priests and ministers found their churches filled with people who had come to give thanks for the miracle of the flour and the coal. The air lift has done more than keep the people of Berlin alive. It has given them something they hadn't had before; courage to face the horribly uncertain future. It gave Reuter, Frau Schroeder, Neumann, and other democratic leaders actual instead of merely theoretical ammunition.

It must be remembered that there are very few men in Berlin between the ages of twenty and forty. A great portion of the ablebodied male population was killed during the battle for the German capital. When the Soviets took over they rounded up most of the rest and sent them to Russia to rebuild the cities the German Army had ruined. These never came back. So today Berlin is pretty much a city of women and children, old men and amputees. The two months during which Russia had Berlin to itself (June and July, 1945) instilled a great terror in the hearts of the surviving Berliners. The success of the air lift has, to a great extent, dissipated this terror. The people now believe that Clay meant it when he said we would never leave Berlin short of an act of war.

Washington, Moscow, London—every capital in the world— thought of the air lift in diplomatic terms as they once thought of Lend-Lease or the Atlantic Charter. The people of Berlin thought of it in different terms. The air lift to them was something that was helping them solve the fundamental problem of living. Whenever they felt a touch of warmth from a stove; whenever they picked up a piece of bread or saw their children drinking a glass of powdered milk—they thought automatically of the air lift. Conversely, when they were in a hospital for an operation and they heard a doctor say apologetically, "Sorry, we are short of ether, we'll have to use a local anesthetic," they knew the shortage of ether was caused by the Russian blockade; ether is too inflammable to be carried safely at high altitudes and therefore it was banned from the air lift. So were other commodities badly needed but impossible to transport by plane except by accepting an "uncalculable risk." Our Air Force was quite willing to accept the "calculated risk," but LeMay, a man who always thinks in human terms (that was his war reputation as a B-29 leader), quite rightly refused to gamble with the lives of his crews by loading their planes with commodities apt to explode in the air.

The air lift, by September, 1948, was beginning to dominate the lives of two and a half million citizens of Berlin. It became a part of our lives, even those of us who were transient visitors. Night after night we'd hear the drone of engines overhead. Planes coming into Berlin from Frankfort or British bases flew prescribed paths; planes leaving Berlin airfields flew different paths. No matter where you lived in the city you heard the incessant sound of motors.

One night in September we had a horrible storm in Berlin. In the morning even our placid Marie seemed worried. She hadn't been able to sleep all night, she admitted. The storm? Oh, no, she hadn't noticed that. But the planes weren't flying. The silence had kept her awake. It had kept Downs (an old First Division combat man) awake and had kept Marie-Therese awake and it had kept me awake, too, and we discussed it at breakfast. It was, as far as I knew, the only night during the summer and fall of 1948 that the air lift was silent. The silence that night was frightening. It was as though a tube feeding you a blood transfusion had suddenly snapped.

I found an old friend named Stratford working for British Military Government. He, his wife and three children lived in a rambling old house in Grunewald, and whenever I could wangle a jeep I'd make the trip out there. It was always rewarding. Mrs. Stratford always had the latest London magazines: the brilliant *Economist* and the always interesting *New Statesman and Nation,* both of which I received regularly in New York. One afternoon I found Mrs. Stratford radiantly happy.

"Anna gave me that horrible phial of poison she has always carried with her," she said.

"What have you done with it?" I asked.

"I've put it in a safe place," she said, with a sigh of relief.

"Just in case?"

The usually calm Mrs. Stratford became a little flustered. "Well, I don't know. . . . Anyhow, I have it hidden."

Just then Anna Suess, her maid, came into the room bearing a tray with tea and some of those wonderful Fortnum and Mason cookies from London. Anna, a good-looking, dark-haired German girl of about twenty, was smiling. We heard echoes of laughter from the kitchen.

"Are you girls teasing your aunt again?" Mrs. Stratford tried to look severe but she was finding it difficult.

"Yes." Anna exploded with laughter. "Aunt Hilda is so funny."

"Hilda comes once a week to do mending," Mrs. Stratford explained to me. "Hilda is sixty-seven and she had a very horrible experience during the Russian occupation of Berlin. But the girls joke about it. Anna, tell us the story."

Anna needed no prompting. Her mother had died when she was very young and when her father was killed on the Russian front she had gone to live with Aunt Hilda. Aunt Hilda was a very strict Catholic. She seldom allowed Anna to go out with boys. When Berlin was filled with soldiers on leave Aunt Hilda always kept Anna off the streets. When the Russians entered Berlin, Anna was sixteen. Aunt Hilda was frantic.

She knew that wholesale rape was the order of the day. She was over sixty; she had no fears for herself but she prayed for guidance as to how to best protect her young niece. Finally she thought of something. She tied a bandage around Anna's neck and spotted it with red ink. Anna's father, before he was killed, had sent her a small German-Russian dictionary issued to men who were sent to the Eastern Front. Aunt Hilda coached the young girl on what to say. Finally the Russians (four of them) burst into their small apartment on Bruckenalle, one of the nicest streets in Berlin. Anna merely pointed to the bandage on her neck and said one Russian word. The word was *rak*, which meant cancer. They shrank away from the young girl and looked with appraising eyes at Aunt Hilda. Evidently they hated the thought of climbing three flights of stairs for nothing.

"So they made Aunt Hilda take all her clothes off," Anna said, choking with laughter, "and all four of them raped her. I know I shouldn't laugh, but it was so funny. Aunt Hilda always boasted that no man had ever touched her. She thought it was awful for any girl to have anything to do with a man. And now four men made love to her."

"Now, whenever Aunt Hilda comes to the house, young Anna here and the cook always laugh at her," Mrs. Stratford said. "It is very cruel of them."

"I tell Aunt Hilda that she really didn't put up any fight at all against the four Russian soldiers," Anna said, and then added with some contempt, "They never would have taken me alive. But my bandage worked. They thought that cancer was contagious."

"But where does the capsule of poison come into the story?" I asked, puzzled.

"My father was an officer," Anna said proudly. "Many officers carried capsules of strychnine with them to use if they were captured. They feared that otherwise they might be tortured into revealing military secrets. Anyhow, before he died my father sent me one of the capsules. He was very fond of me and I think he knew we were losing the war and that the Russians would come to Berlin some day. So he sent me the capsule."

"I have been trying to get it away from Anna for nearly a year now," Mrs. Stratford said. "But she was afraid that the Americans and British would be forced out of Berlin, leaving the Russians here alone. Rather than endure what her aunt went through, she was going to swallow the capsule."

"Now I know the Americans will never move out," Anna laughed. "So I gave Frau Stratford the capsule. We watch hundreds of planes go over here every day and hear them every night, and we no longer fear the Russians. Now we laugh at them when we meet them."

That is what the air lift meant to one German girl.

The one question still being debated hotly in Berlin and Frankfort is, "What would have happened in June, 1948, if we had ignored the Russian blockade and gone right down the Autobahn with a convoy of trucks supported by tanks and air cover?" General Lucius Clay, usually completely frank with correspondents, shrugged the question off when I asked him. He also smiled when I asked who made the decision not to risk an incident by sending a convoy through, and reminded me that in addition to being an army officer he was also responsible for carrying out State Department policies. Clay had two bosses: General Omar Bradley, Chief of Staff, and Secretary of State Marshall, and, quite understandably, he couldn't answer certain questions that it was their prerogative to answer. Clay, in fact, is often caught right in the middle.

However, most correspondents in Berlin felt sure that Clay, finally at the end of his patience, was ready to give General Huebner and General LeMay orders to start truck convoys from Frankfort immediately. They also said that Clay had come very near resigning when Washington overrode his proposed tactics.

Colonel Howley had no qualms about discussing the question. "Why, goddamn it, man, how much can we take from these jokers? We knew their excuse for the blockade was a lie. We should have risked what you call an 'incident.' If the Russians really want trouble we have to know it sooner or later. I'm getting tired of letting them call the shots."

It may be this frankness that has kept Howley from getting the Brigadier star which he so richly deserves. No man ever carried on the best traditions of the United States Army under such impossible conditions as has Colonel Frank Howley.

Every American I knew in Berlin agreed with Howley's view. Had we driven a convoy down the road, every ethical and moral precept involved would have been on our side. When the quadripartite occupation of Berlin was agreed upon at Yalta, we didn't bother to make the Russians put in writing a provision that we would have free access to Berlin. Any lawyer (we had good lawyers at Yalta, including a former Supreme Court Justice) would agree that this was an implied provision necessary to carry out the quadripartite agreement. Quite obviously we couldn't maintain a large administrative and police staff in Berlin unless we fed and supplied them.

Would the Russians have fired on a convoy traveling down the Frankfort-Berlin road? Most correspondents in Berlin thought not. But if they had, the whole issue would have been resolved; we would have known where we stood. Are the Russians enemies or mere obstructionists? That question would have been answered. In any case, no one can blame Clay for the decision. Clay, I believe, gets blamed for a great many State Department decisions. Personally, I think Clay, Howley and Huebner form the smoothest working trio since the immortal Tinker to Evans to Chance combination. You don't hear much about General Huebner. If a shot is ever fired at an American in anger you'll hear a lot about Huebner.

I'd had enough of Germany. You might assert that I've treated the whole problem of Germany rather superficially. That's true enough. I haven't gone into the big question of decentralization of industry or how the Germans feel in the Russian zone. I haven't discussed the happy, well-satisfied Negro troops in Frankfort whose only fear is that one day they will be sent home, nor have I told of our jet planes which sit on German and British air fields—just waiting. But I warned you in the beginning that this was to be a book about people—not issues. However, the correspondents in Berlin have considered these and fifty other pertinent questions carefully in their newspaper reports. I'd like to repeat that any time you see a story with a Berlin dateline on it you can believe it.

A careless, unauthenticated story out of Berlin might conceivably inflame millions to white-hot anger, and even if the story was disproved a day later the first impression would remain. I've seen Drew Middleton and Maggie Higgins sit on a story for twenty-four hours because although it seemed certain to stand up they refused to put it on the cable until they were 100 percent satisfied that there wasn't a hole in it. This is true, too, of men like Emmett Hughes (*Time*) and John Thompson (*Newsweek*).

It is also true of a man named Demaree Bess of the *Saturday Evening Post*. He arrived in Frankfort a few days before I was due to leave. We have been very good friends in many countries during the past fifteen years. During the war we often teamed up when one of us could wangle a jeep, and traveled together. When I met him in Frankfort I had just received a cable from *Collier's* telling me how much they liked a story I'd sent them from Berlin. Naturally, I showed it to Bess. We were having dinner together that night when another cable arrived from *Collier's*. It said, "Unfortunately *Saturday Evening Post* came out today with story by Demaree Bess so similar to your cabled Berlin story that we must kill your story; sorry. Regards." I handed Demaree the cable.

"You're nothing but a pickpocket," I told him bitterly. "I had that story sold and your piece killed it. That is like stealing money out of my pocket."

"I'm sorry," Demaree said, and, to give him his due, he sounded sincere. "There's a pretty good story in Norway, Quent, why don't you go up there?"

"You've probably done it already," I grumbled.

He shook his head. "No, but I just did a piece on Sweden. I heard a lot in Stockholm about Norway, though. It seems that . . ."

He told me of a country that seemed to be unafraid of anything. It sounded good. So that afternoon I hopped a plane for Norway.

CHAPTER SEVENTEEN

I *arrived* in Oslo just before midnight on a Friday. I headed confidently for the Grand Hotel. I dropped my heavy bag, typewriter and trench coat on the lobby floor. I had forgotten that damn Sten gun distributed in the pockets. It clanked on the marble floor and half a dozen lobby sitters looked up, startled. The desk clerk was about the best-looking man I'd ever seen.

"I am sorry," he said dolefully. "You cabled for a reservation, but we are all booked."

"Well," I said, still confident, "would you mind phoning some other hotel? I don't care what accommodations I get. I just want somewhere to sleep."

"I am sorry," he repeated, even more dolefully. "I have phoned everywhere. There is not an empty bed in Oslo. Let me try again."

The clerk picked up a phone and talked in rapid Norwegian. For some obscure reason, I had always thought that Norwegian and German were pretty much alike. But I couldn't follow a word he said. However, I did like the note of urgency in his voice. He was certainly giving it the old college try, but finally, after half a dozen calls, he turned to me unhappily.

"The Savoy Hotel will put a cot in one of its bathrooms," he said. "That is the best I could do. It is most unfortunate," he shook his head sadly, "that Oslo is so crowded. It is because of the Olympic Games."

"But they're being held in London," I protested.

"They are all over," he reminded me. "But the American soccer football team and track team are here to meet Norwegian teams and they have taken all available rooms."

In Germany no one had been interested in the absurd nationalistic orgy known as the Olympic Games. I had seen American and R.A.F. pilots in their clubs turn the radio off when the dreary description of races and pole vaults began and when some announcer with a catch in his voice started to describe the "colorful" ceremonies of flag waving and the playing of national anthems. Even the *Stars and Stripes* (read religiously daily by every American G.I., officer, government employee and correspondent in Germany) had finally realized that its columns of Olympic news from London were being ignored by most of its readers and they had cut the Olympic news to a minimum. As far as I know, the Olympic Games have never done anything but contribute to ill-feeling among nations and to set up absurdly false standards. And the spectacle of seeing well-fed American lads competing against youngsters who had been through a war and who were still living on scanty rations sadly lacking in proteins was hardly one to stir pride in any American breast. The fact that Avery Brundage, once prominent as an America Firster, was in charge of the American team seemed to be quite logical. He has always represented that kind of nationalism that once flourished in Germany and if the Olympic Games stand for anything at all, they stand for this kind of obscene nationalism. Now I had an additional reason to dislike the institution: Olympic athletes had usurped the hotel rooms of Oslo. I will admit that there was no logic in my attitude, but when you find yourself in a strange city without a hotel room, who but a saint could maintain an objective calm?

"I have no Norwegian money," I said to the clerk. "Could you change some travelers checks?"

He would be glad to do that, he said. I reached for my folder of checks and then realized that I had cashed the last one a few days before in Frankfort. I went through my pockets and found I had only a few scrip dollars good only in the American zone in Germany. I did, however, find one British pound note. I remembered that I had accepted this some weeks before in Frankfort from a British correspondent who had been the loser in a poker game. The clerk accepted the pound note and gave me a handful of Norwegian kronen for it. A krone, I discovered, was about twenty cents. In the morning I'd go to the American Embassy and cash a check. Each of our embassies abroad has a press attaché, and they are usually understanding, helpful characters to stranded correspondents. So I climbed into a cab and headed for the Savoy Hotel.

It was a nice little place and the blond clerk behind the desk was the best-looking man I had ever seen. Later I was to find out that almost every man I met in Norway was the best-looking man I had ever seen. They were all blond, all slim, and all had good teeth. This clerk was almost weeping with unhappiness because all he had was a cot in a bathroom. I comforted him as best I could, gave him a package of American cigarettes to show that the incident had in no way disrupted the friendly relations between our respective countries and headed for my room.

It was a nice enough bathroom, if you wanted a bath. It was literally a bathroom in the European manner, with nothing in it but a basin and a huge tub. I threw my bag, typewriter and trench coat on the floor and once again the heavy gun clanked loudly.

"I bought some Meissen china in Berlin," I told the clerk, who had raised his eyes at the noise. "I carry it in the coat."

"Aren't you afraid it will break?" he said.

"Meissen china is unbreakable, didn't you know?" I tried to appear amused at his ignorance, but it was a poor effort.

There were sheets and blankets on the cot and I found that I had no trouble at all sleeping in a bathroom, although it was my first experience. I was awakened the next morning in the most pleasant way imaginable. The sounds that cut through the veil of sleep were pleasant. A woman's voice was singing softly, and this was backed (as we say in radio) by even pleasanter sounds; the happy laughter of a child and the noise of water splashing. At first I thought it was all part of a dream, but as sleep was gradually replaced by wakefulness, I realized that this was all happening here in my room at the Press Center in Frankfort. Frankfort? But I'd left Frankfort the day before and I was in Oslo. And then I realized with a shock that I was in a bathroom in Oslo and someone was using the bathtub. I opened my eyes.

Someone was indeed using the bathtub, a golden-haired, rosy-cheeked little girl of about ten. Her mother, an older replica, was soaping her and the kid was gurgling with pleasure. When the little girl stood up to be dried, I thought it was time to announce my presence with a cough. The mother turned and said a cheerful "Good morning" and the little girl laughed and said "Hello." I wanted to get out of there but suddenly realized that I'd been too tired to unpack the night before and I wasn't wearing pajamas. The little girl kept laughing at me and saying "Hello."

"She learns English," the mother said proudly.

"You, too," I said.

"A little," the mother laughed, rubbing the child briskly. "My husband was in English Air Force during war. Say good-bye, Ingrid."

"Good-bye," the youngster laughed, and then her mother put a robe around her.

"We go now," the mother beamed and they left.

I hopped up and locked the door. I took the quickest bath anyone ever took and was half-dressed when there came an insistent knocking on the door. I opened it and a maid pushed cheerfully by me with an armful of towels. She said something in Norwegian, but when I looked blank, she switched to German. *"Es geht spät,"* she said cheerfully. I looked at my watch. It was 7 A.M., hardly *"spät"* in any language. Two women came into the bathroom and looked at me coldly.

"Tell them," I turned to the German-speaking maid, "that I'm leaving. They can have this room all to themselves."

"No hurry," the maid said, but I grabbed my shirt, put on a tie, and fled. There was a new clerk on duty and he was, of course, the best-looking man I had ever seen. The hotel only served breakfast, he said, so I had breakfast. It consisted of fish sandwiches, a kind of salami, some black goat's cheese, and a glass of milk. Then I walked to the American Embassy. It was closed. It would not be open until Monday morning. There was a porter in charge and he gave me the home phone number of the Press Attaché. I phoned him only to be told that he was on his vacation. The prospect of spending a weekend in a strange city with less than four dollars in my pocket was not an alluring one. There were plenty of movie houses in Oslo and I walked around until one of them opened. I sat through half of a very tired old English picture and then decided that the only thing I could do consistent with my financial status was to walk. I walked for what seemed to be three or four hundred miles and then turned back to the center of the city. I decided to get half a dozen books (inexpensive paper editions are sold all over Europe) and hole up in my bathroom until Monday. But it was mid-afternoon now, and all the stores were closed. I walked into the lobby of the Grand Hotel to see if the noble athletes had left yet, but the same clerk I had met the night before told me his hotel was still crowded.

"Americans often stay here," the clerk said. "We keep a list of American and English films which are playing in Oslo. You might be interested."

He pointed to a bulletin board which advertised night clubs, the theatre and moving pictures.

"I saw one of those last night at the Bergen," the clerk said. "Very good, too. It is an American picture called *Scarface*. It stars Paul Muni."

The picture had been following me around for nearly six months. I did go to see it and found it as exciting as it had been when I'd first seen it years ago. I smiled when I saw "Original Screen Play by Ben Hecht," and then recalled that this was one of Ben's greatest triumphs over a producer. For many years Hecht has been one of Hollywood's highest-salaried screen writers. During all these years he has carried on a one-man battle with producers, and he has often out-smarted himself in these jousts.

He began losing to them (on his own terms) back in 1931, when a little-known producer named Howard Hughes offered him the then substantial sum of $35,000 to write an under-world script for him. Shrewd, canny Mr. Hecht took a look at Howard Hughes' frayed shirt cuffs, at his baggy sports coat, at the worried look on his face, and said to himself, "This character probably hasn't got to eat. He could never come up with thirty-five thousand real dollars." So Ben Hecht made a counter-proposition. He would write the script and he would charge Mr. Hughes $1,000 a day, payable in cash at six o'clock each evening. Mr. Hughes was slightly startled by this un-usual request, but agreed. Ben went right to work. Each day at six he would go into Hughes' office and collect his ten one-hundred-dollar bills. The fastest writer since Dumas, he handed Hughes a complete shooting script in fourteen days. And it turned out to be *Scarface,* one of the most successful pictures ever made. Hughes made several millions out of it. Hecht made $14,000. Some time after he had finished the script, Hecht discovered that the financial standing of Mr. Hughes was on a par with that of the Bank of England—in the days when the Bank of England was doing pretty well. Anyhow, here it was in Oslo still making money for Howard Hughes.

That night I found I still had about ten kronen left, so I blew it for a good meal at the Grand and walked back to my bathroom at the Savoy. Sunday I ate the herring and the cheese I'd passed up the day before. Sunday was a long day and the only way I could kill it was to open the portable and get to work. So I wrote a piece for *Collier's*. On Monday I went to the American Embassy and within an hour I was no longer the Oslo dead-end kid with his nose pressed hungrily against a baker's window. I met Ambassador Charles Ulrich Bay and he waved a magic wand and I found my luggage moved from the Savoy to a splendid room at the luxurious Grand Hotel; I found money in my pocket, and I found myself on the terrace of his lovely house at No. 28 Nobelsgate eating a beautiful lunch with Bay and his charming wife, and Oslo began to look pretty good, after all. It looked especially good from the terrace because Mrs. Bay had raised a garden with only red, white and blue flowers, rather fitting for the garden of an American Ambassador.

Ambassador Bay turned me over to Charles F. Baldwin, economic adviser to the Embassy, and Baldwin, who has the knack of explaining economic problems in layman's language, gave me a thorough briefing on the financial difficulties faced by Norway. It was evident that the Ambassador, Baldwin, Ted Olson, John Lund and other members of the Embassy staff all had great admiration and sincere affection for Norway and its people.

One morning my phone rang early and a familiar voice began to abuse me affectionately. The voice belonged to an old friend, Bernt Balchen, the man most pilots think to be the greatest of them all. Dirty weather has always been the business of Bernt Balchen. Although he is an American citizen, he is also president of the Norwegian Airlines. He told me he had just received orders to return to Washington and active service in the American Air Force. Bernt and his tall, striking blonde Norwegian wife, Inger, lived on a mountaintop some twenty miles from Oslo. From his windows you could see the city of Oslo circling the half moon of the Oslo fjord. I've never met Balchen without learning something worthwhile from him and this time was no exception. Balchen also gave me the use of his planes and pilots and invited me to fly anywhere in the land I wished.

I took full advantage of his offer, but I was always glad to return to Oslo and to his amazing house that clung to the precipitous side of a mountain. The three of us would talk for hours after dinner and Bernt told wonderful stories of his flight to the South Pole with Byrd; of his flights during the war when he kept resistance fighters in Norway supplied with guns and ammunition and food; of great fliers he had met. And one night he told of a shooting contest he had held with Hermann Goering.

"It was in 1938," Bernt said, "and I was in Berlin. It was some kind of convention of commercial aviation people. One night I was standing at the bar at the Adlon when someone in back of me said, 'The drinks are better at my house.' It was Ernst Udet, the German acrobatic pilot. I had known him for many years; he had often come to the Cleveland Air Races. So I went to his home, a large apartment near the Tiergarten. We had a drink and started talking of old times and it grew late and then there was a knock on the door. Udet opened it and there stood Goering. He had a drink too, and we talked of flying. No, not politics, good heavens, we were three pilots. What interest had we in politics?

"I did learn a little, however," Bernt said shyly, "about the German Air Force. Goering drank a frightening drink. He took a water tumbler and half filled it with brandy. Then he added an equal amount of benedictine. Udet always had the same drink—plain brandy. He, too, drank from a water tum-

314

bler. I have seen him stay up all night at Cleveland and then, without sleep, drink a tumbler full of brandy and then get into an airplane and do the most amazing stunts.

"So we talked very late, Udet and Goering and I, and somehow the name of Hitler came up," Balchen went on. "I did not bring it up. Hell, I was Udet's guest and we were talking of flying only. I think Goering brought it up, and the two of them laughed at Hitler. This was 1938, mind you. They talked very freely about Hitler and it was as though they were talking of a clown. Of course, this was very late, and it may have been the brandy talking. Well, Goering began to boast of how he could shoot. He and Udet had a big argument as to which was the best shot. So Udet got out some pistols. In his apartment there was a long hall and he hung a target up at one end of it. They made me enter their contest, though I said I was better with a rifle than with a pistol. Then I remembered it was four in the morning, and I said, 'This will make one hell of a lot of noise. Won't someone object?'

"Big, fat Goering looked at me as though I was crazy and said, 'But who would dare to object?' So he poured another drink of brandy and benedictine and we began."

"What did you drink, Bernt?" I asked, for Balchen was never a man for having more than one or two drinks.

"If you are born in Norway, it doesn't matter much what you drink," he said indifferently. "For some strange reason, liquor does not bother Norwegians much. I drank a Scotch and soda now and then while we shot at the target."

"Who won?"

"It was no contest." Bernt roared with laughter. "Little Udet was one of the best shots in the world with a pistol. He turned his back toward the target, picked up a mirror, and took aim that way. He had drunk maybe a bottle and a half of brandy that night, but he could not miss the bull's-eye. That is a long, dull story," Balchen said apologetically. "I'm sorry."

Bernt Balchen, American citizen and Colonel in the American Air Force was (with the possible exception of King Haakon) the most popular man in Norway. Balchen has all the attributes we usually associate with the ancient Viking: courage, gentleness, terrific strength and a robust laugh. I met many others like him in less exalted positions—men like Arvid Nilsen, for instance.

Arvid Nilsen and his wife, Ingrid, live in a pleasant three-room flat in Oslo. Arvid is thirty-five, a mechanic, and he has the high cheekbones, the tanned skin, the blue eyes and the fair hair of the typical Scandinavian. He has six pieces of shrapnel in his hard, lean body, too, mementos of April 9, 1940, the day the Germans smashed their way into Norway. Arvid's left leg from the ankle to the knee looks as though rats had been gnawing at it, but Arvid slaps the ugly scar hard and tells you that the leg is as good as new.

You can remind Arvid that Russia has a mighty army, a tremendous air force and a fleet of submarines (including the German-type Schnorkel) that would have no trouble penetrating deep into those long fingers which the sea extends into Norway and which the Norwegians call fjords. You can remind Arvid Nilsen that Norway is a country of only 3,000,000 and that she is desperately short of steel, food and all war equipment, but Arvid only shrugs his shoulders impatiently.

"That was all true of the Germans in 1940, but we managed to hold them sixty-three days before they established military superiority by sheer weight of numbers," he says. "I might add that Denmark didn't fight at all; Holland held out only four days; Belgium fell after nineteen days and France fell after thirty-nine days. And we learned a lot during the occupation. All of us who worked in the resistance movement and who survived are still available and ready. We will not make the mistakes we made last time. This time we will know who our enemies within the country are. Mind you, not all Norwegian Communists are enemies of Norway. Many members of the party are enemies, however, but we know them

316

and they will be taken care of quickly. We know their names and where they are to be found."

"That is true," Ingrid said earnestly. "We will fight, all of us, and hold out until help arrives. We are not Swedes, you know," she added with contempt.

You can travel as far north as Narvik and west to Bergen and south to Stavanger and even to the smaller places bearing names like Dirdal or Byrkjedal or Gloppedal or Hundalen (where the Germans met their first organized resistance in 1940) and you'll find a thousand men who speak as Arvid Nilsen speaks and a thousand women like Ingrid who are readying to fight. Norway today is perhaps the only country in Europe that does not live with fear, and yet Norway knows that should the Russians finally decide to engage in a flirtation with atomic paradise by making the cold war a hot one, Norway will be the first logical target. The citizens of Norway know this, accept it calmly, and go about their increasingly difficult job of maintaining their home economy and bolstering their military defenses. Although Norway has a king, it also has a constitution and a Storting (parliament) composed of 150 members. Even the ever-present threat of danger from her huge neighbor has not resulted in hysteria or witch-hunting. Ten percent of the members of the Storting are Communists, and the party has considerable strength in the industrial centers, like Bergen, but not even the most conservative members of the Storting have ever suggested that the Communist Party be banned or its members be denied the protection of the constitution.

In 1945, just after he had made his famous Fulton, Missouri, speech, Winston Churchill was invited to speak in Oslo. The Russian Foreign Office, smarting under the criticism leveled at the Soviet policy by Mr. Churchill at Fulton, put considerable pressure on the Norwegian government to withdraw the invitation to Churchill. Russia said that his presence in Norway would be considered to be an unfriendly act on the part of Norway, and the invitation was withdrawn. For three years

Norway's monarch, King Haakon VII, brooded on what he felt to be a discourteous gesture toward Mr. Churchill, and last May he invited the former war leader to Norway as his private guest. Churchill went to Norway, was presented an honorary degree by the University of Oslo and was given the greatest personal ovation ever given a foreign visitor in Norway. The whole country roared its approval at what King Haakon had done. It was more than a welcome for Churchill; it was a cry of defiance toward Russia and a reminder to Russia that this little country, the size of Southern California, would not submit to pressure from any outside sources.

For the past two years, traditionally neutral Sweden has been trying desperately to persuade Norway to join Denmark and herself in what amounts to a neutrality pact. Sweden would like to think that if a war between Russia and the Western powers developed, the Scandinavian countries could maintain a polite aloofness and be untouched by the conflict. The Norwegians believe that such a policy has no relation to reality at all. They know that if war comes all of Scandinavia will immediately become involved and will immediately have to make a choice between the Eastern and Western blocs. Norway long since made that choice. Norway feels much closer to England than she does to her close neighbor, Sweden. Norway feels a kinship for America that she has never felt for Russia, even though Northern Norway borders on the Soviet Union. Norway speaks English and thinks along democratic lines. To date, Norway has made no formal commitment to the Western bloc, but her Prime Minister, her King, and her people have made no secret as to how they stand.

Norway's bitter anti-Russian feeling is perhaps the first tangible sign that Jan Masaryk did not die in vain. Masaryk was well liked in Norway and the people of Norway had a great admiration for Czechoslovakia, the only democracy with strong and virile traditions in the Slav world. Jan Masaryk was a frequent visitor to Oslo and the Norwegians often heard him declare that he believed that his country could co-operate with Russia without losing her national integrity. His suicide (or murder) was, in effect, an admission that he had been wrong. The Czechoslovakia coup taught Norway the lesson that "co-operation" and "democracy" are two words which the Soviet Union interprets in its own peculiar way. Whenever you discuss Soviet-Norway relations, whether it be with private citizen Arvid Nilsen or with brilliant Foreign Minister Halvard M. Lange, the name of Jan Masaryk comes up and the story of Czechoslovakia's death as a democracy is retold.

And you hear, too, of the Russian ship which went aground at Christensen in the winter of 1948. It was the third Russian ship to go aground in a month, and, by what Norwegians thought to be a significant coincidence, each "accident" occurred in or near ports of strategic importance. A large Russian salvage crew promptly appeared to refloat the ship whose nose was buried in a mud bank in the Christensen harbor. The crew labored for two weeks trying to refloat the vessel. An editorial in the *Arbeiderbladet*, official organ of the controlling Labor Party, suggested sarcastically that a dozen Norwegian seamen be given the task of floating the ship. They could do it, the editorial said dryly, in a matter of hours. The whole country roared with laughter. That night the hitherto inept Soviet salvage crew showed surprising efficiency. The ship was floated and sailed out of the harbor.

The Norwegian Labor Party, until the time of the Czech coup, was a strong advocate of friendship and understanding toward Russia. After all, Russia had helped to liberate Norway and had scrupulously observed the agreement to evacuate the country, once the war was over. During its tenure in Northern Norway as a liberating force, the Red Army behaved in an exemplary manner. The Labor Party also remembered the fact that Russia had never broken an agreement made with Norway. The death of Jan Masaryk changed the attitude of the Labor Party almost overnight.

Immediately it sponsored a bill in the Storting (only the eleven Communist members opposed it) calling for a sum of

319

twenty million dollars to supplement the already appropriated defense fund. It also authorized Minister of Defense Jens Hague to mobilize the Home Guard, the reserves, and to hold intensive maneuvers for all armed forces. All summer Norway was virtually in a state of mobilization. Practically every able-bodied man in the country went through a hard ten days' refresher course. I spent a few days with one unit which was training a few miles outside of Oslo. Nearly all of these men in uniform had been resistance fighters during the occupation. Their physical condition was amazing. They would come into camp after a fifteen-mile forced march over rugged terrain, drop their heavy packs and then choose up sides for a soccer game.

Lieutenant Torborg Lavik, a highly intelligent graduate of Oslo University, talked of these men he was helping to train, and he couldn't keep the pride out of his voice. These were not perfunctory, casual maneuvers to Lavik or to the other officers. Lavik, like so many Norwegians, was convinced that war with Russia is inevitable.

"Do you not agree that war is inevitable?" he asked.

"Of course not," I said more impatiently than politely. "Nothing evil is inevitable. To accept such an idea is to allow your reason to abdicate."

"You of the strong democracies appease Russia too much," he said.

"That may be," I admitted, "but you should see the air lift working in Germany. That is hardly an instrument of appeasement."

"Had you ignored the blockade," he smiled, "and sent trucks down the big highway to Berlin the day after the blockade was announced by the Russians it would have been the positive answer which they would have understood."

I found myself nodding in agreement. "But Roosevelt is dead," I said, half to myself, and he muttered, "Yes, Roosevelt is dead. If he had lived we wouldn't have this conflict now. Here in Norway we have to proceed on the assumption that war is coming. We didn't the last time. We deluded ourselves and we were almost destroyed. But the prospect of war doesn't frighten us. Nothing could be worse than the years of occupation."

Lavik talked of those horrible days. He had been sentenced to death three times by the Germans and each time he had escaped to continue to fight with the resistance forces. His eyes lit up when he talked of the work and fighting that Balchen had done (this is a story still untold). He told of suicide raids made by the British Navy (five British destroyers crept into the Ofoten Fjord in April, 1940, to attack a huge German naval force and although only one of the destroyers escaped, this little force sunk eleven ships).

"Our men don't march like West Pointers," he smiled, watching a group of gray-clad men filing into camp. "But we aren't concerned much with how they march. You know we Norwegians spend half our lives on skis, and when we can't ski, we walk. If Russia attacks us we will fight a delaying action. Mobility, not massed static defense, is the keynote of our military strategy. We were not well organized or trained back in April, 1940, and we were taken by surprise. We only had about 200,000 men available for defense then. Today we have nearly that many in our Home Guard alone. And we will not be taken by surprise. We have plans to defend all key spots."

"Like Sola?" I suggested.

The General Staff of every army in the world knows about Sola. Sola is the Stavanger airport, and you can bet that every map of Norway hanging on the wall of the huge map room in the Kremlin has a circle around the word Sola. You can bet that any time General Montgomery or Air Marshal Tedder looks at a map of Norway in the British War Office in Whitehall, their eyes automatically drop to that spot thirteen miles from Stavanger called Sola. You can bet that General Omar Bradley and our air chief, General Hoyt Vandenberg, both know everything there is to be known about the airport known as Sola. And yet Sola is nothing but a commercial airport in Southwest Norway. I hitchhiked there on one of Bernt Balchen's planes.

You only have to fly over Sola to realize its importance. Four long, white, gleaming concrete runways stretch out below you. The sea was kind enough to push its way right to the perimeter of the air field, and so Sola is also used as a seaplane base by the Norwegian Airlines. The nearest hills are some miles away. Sola was a good airport in 1940; so good that the Germans landed three hundred troop-carrier planes there in two hours. During the occupation the Germans lengthened the runways; during the past year Norway lengthened two of them to such an extent that today any military aircraft in the world can land or take off from Sola.

In case of war, Sola would be indispensable to both sides. Russia would want to use it as a base from which to attack near-by England and North Sea shipping routes. England would have to have Sola not as an offensive air base, but merely to insure that it wouldn't be used as such by Russia. Standing up in the control tower watching an occasional Scandinavian Airline plane casually take off for Rio or New York, it seemed hard to believe that some day men might die attacking or defending the four strips of concrete shining in the sun. Just three miles from Sola (and connected beautifully by a taxi strip) is the military airport of Forus. Consider the two airports as one and you have one of the greatest air bases in Europe.

"A nice airport," the Norwegian pilot who had flown me down said. "Never snows this far southwest—the Gulf Stream takes care of that. Never any fog. Very seldom have any storms here—just nice peaceful weather."

"But where are the defenses for Sola?" I asked, puzzled.

"Defenses?" The pilot smiled. "I don't know. Why not ask the R.A.F. chaps or your own Air-Force people? I'm sure they'd know. But me—I'm just a commercial pilot. That is," his smile disappeared, "until it starts. I still have my R.A.F. commission."

When the war ended, Norway counted her dead, totaled up her economic losses, and then settled down grimly to an austere, rigid regime of self-denial that was necessary for her economic survival. Norway has always lived by shipping, fishing and the export of wood pulp. The war destroyed two-and-a-half million tons of her shipping (660 ships). During the occupation, the Germans literally destroyed all of Northern Norway and even today there is hardly a town or village north of Namsos that is self-supporting. Germany used Norway as a reservoir which she drained of coal, raw materials, machinery, machine tools and livestock.

Despite the heavy loss in shipping, her merchant fleet continued to operate all during the war, and the result was a tidy amount of dollar and sterling credit. The Labor Government acted realistically. It decreed that this foreign credit be used exclusively for long-term benefits and not as a temporary palliative. Orders were placed for new ships and today both England and America are filling those orders. The foreign exchange was used to import steel, machine tools, agricultural machinery, and other absolute necessities.

You can stay in Oslo for a month without ever seeing an egg or a piece of meat. They have to be imported and the government will not spend its dwindling foreign reserves for food. The people understand, tighten their belts and continue their fish diet. Thousands of Norwegian families live entirely on fish, bread, milk and cheese.

The housing situation in Norway is desperate. In Oslo the government reluctantly took drastic measures to help remedy it. The Norwegians are an independent, strong-willed people who won't be pushed around even by their own government, but they are also a people who think realistically and they know that there is no alternative to the stringent housing regulations imposed by their leaders. There are many fine houses on the outskirts of Oslo, owned and occupied by well-to-do shipowners or bankers. If a family of three occupied a ten-room house the government requisitioned seven of the rooms and moved in seven homeless people. In the workers' section of Oslo, a man and his wife occupying a four-room flat would have to take in two additional boarders to live with them. No one likes this disruption of family life, but no one grumbles about it. They accept it as they accepted starvation and the life of the hunted during the occupation—with patience and courage. They know that overcrowding and monotonous, strictly rationed food are not due to the whim of an irresponsible government but are conditions necessary for their eventual economic recovery.

The Norwegians have great confidence in their monarch and in their Labor Government, which holds seventy-six seats in the Storting. It is a government of young, dynamic men and the people believe that these men have avoided many of the mistakes made by the Socialist Government in England. The Conservative members of the Storting were worried when the Labor Party took over in 1945, lest it immediately socialize the great shipping industry. Prime Minister Einar Gerhardsen, who spent three years in a German concentration camp, immediately set their minds at rest by declaring bluntly, "Our shipping has always been run by private industry. It has been built up by the enterprise, ingenuity and courage of individual shipowners, who have shown that they can conduct the shipping industry far better than any government could run it. There will be no government ownership or interference with Norway's shipping."

Norwegians like their thirty-two-year-old Minister of Defense, Jens Hauge, one of the most revered heroes of the resistance. They greatly admire their Foreign Minister, Halvard Lange, a man who combines the suavity of an Anthony Eden with the toughness of a Bernt Balchen. I sat in his office, which overlooks the lovely Oslo fjord, and he talked of the problems his country faces. Minister Lange began by questioning me.

"You've been here a couple of weeks now," he said in the

English of a cultured European. "You've been all over the country. What do you think of us?"

"I think you're the toughest people I ever met," I told him with complete honesty. "I've been in almost every country in Europe these past six months. Quite often in these countries you get a feeling of uneasiness, insecurity and fear of the future. Here in Norway, where you might have real reason to fear the future, no one is uneasy or insecure."

"It's not in the Norwegian nature to tremble when a storm approaches," the Minister smiled. "We've been fighting storms for a thousand years. During the occupation we lost more than 10,000 of our best men. The Germans tried to make slaves of us, but they failed. They only occupied Norway; they never conquered Norway. Today, through a mere accident of geography, we find ourselves in a rather delicate position. We cannot be indifferent to the ideological struggle between democracy and totalitarian government. Economically, culturally and spiritually Norway is a part of Western Europe. We are and will continue to be a Western democracy. We are realists. We recognize the danger of this stand and are prepared to accept that danger. The refusal of the Soviet Union and the Communists everywhere to co-operate in the economic reconstruction of Europe has not deterred us from wholeheartedly accepting the Marshall Plan. The generous help which the United States is now giving Europe is entirely in accord with the best traditions of your Western democracy."

Today Norway stands alone in Scandinavia. When Finland signed the so-called Russo-Finnish Friendship Pact she wrote herself off as an independent nation. Unhappy Denmark is as vulnerable as a bear in a tree, and although her whole spirit is in revolt against accepting Sweden's concept of neutrality, she feels that she has no alternative. Sweden is committed to a do-nothing, hope-for-the-best policy, although her people show increasing signs of impatience toward the weasel-minded policy of their government. Only Norway is tough enough to defy any attempt to compromise her sovereignty.

"We've had salt on our pillows before," Arvid Nilsen, the mechanic, said to me, voicing an old Viking proverb. "But we don't cry in public. We don't want war now any more than we wanted it in 1940, but if we are forced to choose between war and the loss of our national integrity, there is no question as to our choice. If war comes a lot of us will die, but," he added, "in church our ministers tell us that we can't get to heaven without dying. And there are worse things than death."

The national anthem of Norway, written by the Reverend Björnstjerne Björnson nearly a hundred years ago is called *Ja Vi Elsker Dette Landet* (Yes, We Love This Country). It is a militant hymn which tells of the fight against the Roman Empire by King Sverre. When the Norwegians sing that song they mean it.

They are stubborn, uncompromising people when they believe they are right. If there is one thing they hate above all, it is regimentation. They believe that their kind of socialization is akin to our kind of democracy, and they are right. Their unions are tremendously strong but they are not obstructive. Their labor leaders have a strong sense of responsibility; first to Norway, secondly to the labor organizations they head. There are no labor "czars" in Norway, no arrogant labor leaders who seek domination and power. Such men wouldn't last very long.

Norway has only two real industries—fishing and shipping. These cannot bring her the foreign exchange she needs to buy steel and wheat and other necessary and scarce commodities. She knows that ERP is her only real hope, but she would sacrifice every benefit she would receive from the United States if she had to compromise her integrity or to yield one iota of her sovereignty. But she hasn't been asked to do this and, finally, the sorely needed materials are arriving in her harbors.

The Norwegians are not the somber gloomy characters their great dramatists and novelists have pictured. At night their restaurants and theatres and night clubs are jammed with cheerful-looking men and women who are quite obviously enjoying themselves. Food is monotonous and drinks horribly expensive, but they shrug off such minor annoyances and live twenty-four hours a day.

One day I dropped into the American Embassy to see if any New York newspapers had arrived. I found a *New York Times* only two days old. I read it from beginning to end but when I reached the sports pages I received a rude shock. I read that the Yankees, the Red Sox and the Cleveland Indians were all closely bunched, fighting it out for the American League Pennant. It was not that which shocked me; the crusher came when I read that the World Series was only a week away. Time had crept up on me. I hadn't been looking at calendars. I ran to Bernt Balchen's office and told him it was urgent that I get home at once.

"We'll get you out quick," Bernt assured me. "Let's see now. We can make room for you in the plane leaving a week from today."

"That'll be too late, Bernt," I said desperately. "I got to get back for the World Series."

"That's different," Bernt snapped. "Why didn't you say so? There is a plane out tonight for New York. We'll transfer someone to a later plane. Go to your hotel and get your bags."

Within four hours I was in a big Scandinavian Airline DC-6 headed toward the World Series. But it wasn't easy to forget Norway, or Bernt Balchen or Charles Ulrich Bay. The Ambassador was tremendously popular in Norway. He was of Norwegian descent; he knew the language and he sailed his own sloop through the Norwegian fjords. In addition, he was an expert fisherman. A month after he had arrived to take over his post he and his wife had adopted two Norwegian war orphans. They tried to do it anonymously but the news leaked out and it strengthened the affection the people had for the American Ambassador. But it wasn't this which made me think of Bay as the big plane slid smoothly over the North Sea. It was something that had happened when we were fishing together. With us was Ole Hanson, renowned for fifty years as a great hunting and fishing guide. The Ambassador's luck was very bad this day.

"You and I are old friends, Ole," he said reproachfully to the guide. "But today you are letting me down badly. Why are the fish so inhospitable? Perhaps they just don't like America. You know, Ole, a thing like that could cause an international incident. It might even cause war."

The old guide nodded sagely. "*Ja, ja*. Maybe. It would be a great pity if we Norwegians ever had to go to war against America. We are very fond of your country." He busied himself with some fishing tackle for a moment and then looked up at the Ambassador and said emphatically, "But if it ever does come to war, no matter against what country, always remember this: we Norwegians will win."

Ambassador Bay chuckled and slapped the old man affectionately on the shoulder. Then he turned to me. "That's Norway speaking," he said.

The Ambassador was right. That was Norway speaking. I'm glad they're on our side.

CHAPTER EIGHTEEN

Events have a nasty habit of contradicting even the most carefully thought-out, logical conclusions. You return from six months in Europe with very definite ideas as to where Europe is heading and you can present substantial evidence to support your conviction. Then a trigger-happy kid may shoot a gun, the fourteen men in the Politburo may decide to reverse their policy completely, a persuasive spellbinder may suddenly arise to mesmerize a whole country—and all of your carefully collected evidence can immediately be tossed into the discard.

I returned from Europe a complete optimist, convinced that the people themselves are showing an increasing and impatient desire for the kind of democracy we enjoy here. I returned convinced that people are weary of being regimented in thought and action and that they are finally realizing that Communism is a religion that demands absolute obedience from its converts and imposes horrible penance upon those who question or deviate from the rigid dogma. I am still convinced that this is true, but I recognize that events may contradict my judgment.

Being an optimist these days is a lonely pastime. I am writing this in January, 1949, a time of the year traditionally set aside by editorial writers and columnists for a glance backward. During the past week you could almost hear the mighty sigh of relief arising from the editorial pages of the newspapers. It is as though the sigh said, "Well, 1948 was a horrible year but somehow we managed to get through it without war. Yeah, we just made it."

I think, on the other hand, that 1948 was a glorious year and that some time in the future historians may write, "It was in 1948 that the first signs appeared in Europe of the breakdown in Communist influence and that we saw a definite rebirth of the democratic spirit." Posterity will record the confusions and alarms of 1948, but it will also note that the tools which shaped history in 1948 were for the most part the tools of peace, and if they did not build a permanent structure it is because mankind is a little unaccustomed to using these tools. Democracy has not combated Communism in Europe with the traditional weapons of war, but with the relatively new weapons of ideas and the material fruits of democracy, and I believe that these weapons are proving more efficacious than guns or bombs could ever be. During the last nine months of 1948 we sent five billion dollars to Europe as part of the Marshall Plan, and I believe that this was a more damaging blow to Communism than five hundred atomic bombs would have been.

I believe that 1948 will be known as the year during which, for the first time, we embarked on a positive program as contrasted with our traditional program of negative opposition. During the two years following the war we did an awful lot of shouting about how horrible Communism was, and always there was the implied threat that if the Russians didn't look out we'd drop our little bomb on them. We did a lot of boasting about our still serviceable B-29's, our wonderful new B-50's,

330

our jet planes, our strategic bases, our unlimited ability to produce unlimited supplies of weapons—but all this boasting apparently didn't scare anyone or give the people of Europe a more fervent appreciation of democracy. Then we stopped rattling our nuclear sabers, lowered our voices and began to sell the positive virtues of democracy. Also, we backed up our sales campaign with performance.

A year ago Europe was sick, mentally and physically, and even the patient had about given up hope. The patient was so desperate that he was willing to try any nostrum offered by the first persuasive medicine man who came along. The medicine men of the Kremlin were there with their bogus panaceas, and the patient was in the position of a hopeless invalid who, in desperation, cries out, "I'll try anything!"

Then the Marshall Plan came along to treat the patient. With the caution typical of a careful doctor, ERP promised no quick cure, no miracle, but did promise that a five-year adherence to a certain rigid and difficult regime of diet and exercise might help. After nine months of treatment, the patient is far from being cured, but at least he is showing definite signs of confidence in his doctor and a willingness to co-operate. Human nature being what it is, the patient occasionally grumbles; he occasionally shows signs of irritation, doubt and impatience, but these are all symptoms common to any patient who is told that his convalescence will be a long and tedious one.

It would be difficult to point to one European community to show the tangible benefits it has received under ERP. The Marshall Plan has not been in operation long enough for such concrete manifestations to be evident, but one can say without fear of contradiction that during the past year we have seen the word "recovery" replace the word "relief" in the European dictionary. If the actual recovery has not as yet been spectacular, it has been substantial. And ERP has given hope, new confidence and the incentive to resist Communism to the people of Europe.

The year 1948 will mark the first time in history that representatives of nineteen European communities sat down to plan an economic program based on joint operations. From Crete to Narvik a realization grew that the economy of each country depended upon the economy of all. A common fear brings countries together in wartime. This is the first time in history that countries have been brought together in peacetime not by fear, but by hope. This would have been impossible a few years ago. During the 1930's each country had an exaggerated idea of the importance of its sovereignty. Each country felt it could work out its own destiny alone. The war proved that this comforting, pleasant philosophy was absurd as long as there were predatory forces at work in the world. A great deal of Europe was destroyed before the predatory force of German Fascism was halted.

Today the people of Western Europe realize that the grave economic problems they face are common problems which can only be solved by common understanding and common effort. The people of these countries realize finally that only the Marshall Plan offers them any chance of security and eventual economic recovery. The Russians were the first to realize that ERP could eventually restore prosperity to Europe, a condition which would stymie their own aggressive aspirations. They immediately organized the Cominform, began a desperate propaganda offensive against ERP and did their best to hinder economic rehabilitation in Europe. By now the Russians expected to be in control of Italy and close to it in France. There is no doubt that the Marshall Plan was the dominant factor in frustrating their hopes.

Averell Harriman has been consistently honest in his appraisal of what ERP can and cannot do. He has never been over-optimistic. He says frankly that Europe, even assuming that the most favorable conditions exist, will reach 1952 with still a big deficit in the dollar area and that present estimates of the increase in production are too high. He sees no immediate improvement in European standards of living. This does not mean that he thinks the Marshall Plan will fail. He is merely being realistic about conditions and conservative as to anticipated progress.

No single government or combination of governments can succeed in making the Marshall Plan work. Only the people themselves can do this. Harriman and his assistants in various European capitals have faith in the people and have confidence in their willingness to sacrifice and work their way out of their present condition. Harriman learned a great deal about the strength of the people during the war years. England was in a bad way and hoping for a miracle when Churchill made his famous "blood, sweat and tears" speech. That single speech made the people of England realize that no miracle was in the offing; their salvation could only be carved out laboriously, painfully, by themselves. The people responded by superhuman efforts and these efforts were rewarded.

Today the people of Western European countries realize that there is no miracle on the agenda; the production which will mean full employment, foreign exchange, and eventual stability can only come as a result of laborious, back-breaking work and personal sacrifice. I believe they are willing to accept this program. If they do, there is no doubt that by 1952 they will have achieved at least a basis on which to build a permanent economic security.

There are many obstacles in the way of real economic achievement in Europe. France, for instance, has made very little progress during the past year because she (at this writing) is so politically unstable. It seems to be an economic axiom that economic progress can only follow political stability.

The people of France are getting very tired of the great gap between wages and prices. It is an over-simplification to say that the many strikes among miners and factory workers during the past year were Communist-inspired. Most of them were ordered by Communist labor leaders, but there is plenty of evidence to support the viewpoint of many capable correspondents in France, who say that the primary cause for the labor unrest is economic rather than political; workers and miners just cannot feed their families on their scanty wages. In the various 1948 elections the popular vote in France ran 18 percent Socialist, 29 percent Communist, and 53 percent center-and-right. Up to now the Socialists, the Communists and a large section of the moderate center have been in violent opposition to De Gaulle, but that is all they have had in common. However, ERP has given the various moderate groups time to consolidate their forces. It has given them hope and a determination to fight the extremists of either right or left. No party or group as yet has had courage enough to insist that the voters face the facts of life and prepare to share the sacrifices that lie ahead.

The coalition government of De Gasperi had the courage to do this in Italy, and the people accepted the stern, unpalatable truth. That is why Italy is so far ahead of France in advancing toward recovery. It is because the people themselves have not been afraid to swallow the tough medicine poured down their throats by the men they elected to office. Until the people of France accept the years of hard work and sacrifice ahead, wages and prices will remain out of line, the hoarding of dairy products and all produce will continue, and France will continue to lag.

I have said that in the main the tools which shaped history in 1948 were the tools of peace. These tools were not used in all troubled spots. The fighting continues in Greece and not even the military leadership of General van Fleet has been able to resolve the issue. When I was in Greece I felt that it was a country under sentence of death, and nothing has happened during the past six months to change my opinion. The people of Greece still have no voice in the affairs of their country. Until the silent thousands find a way to articulate their hopes and their ambitions, Greece will continue to be a battlefield which can furnish no one anything but a Pyrrhic victory. The dakas fly gnaws away at the olive crop each year, so infecting it that the fine oil which was once produced is now of such inferior grade that it can be used only for lubrication. And the politicians of both left and right gnaw away at the once-healthy body of Greece and gradually the country becomes weaker and weaker as its vitality is drained. If the world would leave Greece to the Greek people, perhaps they might find their salvation, but geographic circumstances have made the country a key point in the fight between Western and Eastern ideology, and the bewildered, unhappy people are caught right in the middle.

Nor has the world used the tools of peace to smother the Middle Eastern conflagration. The whole question of Israel will always have to be remembered as the first great failure of the United Nations. The UN had the machinery to stop the fighting in Israel but apparently it didn't have the will. On November 29, 1947, the UN adopted a partition resolution settling the borders of the Jewish State. Ernest Bevin immediately, in effect, declared war on Palestine. When Israel was born, May 15, 1948, Great Britain encouraged the Arab governments to launch full-scale military invasions of the country. The attack was led by the Trans-Jordan Arab Legion, a military force completely equipped, financed and officered by Great Britain. Great Britain maneuvered ceaselessly and skillfully in the Security Council to keep the Arab states from being punished as aggressors. Senator Warren Austin denounced the Arab states as being guilty of international aggression, but Great Britain induced the Security Council to refrain from taking the action so clearly indicated.

Finally the people of Israel performed the greatest military miracle of our age to repel the invaders. Then Great Britain immediately led a campaign for a truce and actually attempted to impose sanctions against Israel for successfully defending her own territory. At this writing Great Britain is threatening unilateral military action against the new nation.

Some of the guilt must be borne by us because of our own American policy. When Bernadotte was assassinated, the whole world was shocked and nowhere was there more anger shown against his murderers than in Israel itself. Here in America the unforgivable crime is that of killing the umpire. We can criticize him, disagree with him, boo him to our heart's content, but that is the limit of our protest. Bernadotte was an umpire. After his horrible death, his plan for Israeli boundaries was revealed, and it is no reflection on him or his character to say that his decision was one that was outrageously unfair to Israel. Months after his death, the United Nations, prodded by Great Britain, attempted to revise the Bernadotte Plan, and the United States meekly abstained from voting, a cowardly expedient hardly consistent with the courage of what we like to think of as our ideals. And because of this indecisive attitude of ours the hostilities continued.

It seems incredible that a tiny nation of 750,000 should have survived not only the armed might of five sovereign Arab nations but the diplomatic front led by Great Britain. The answer is simple. It can be given in one word—people. The people of America provided the funds and the people of Israel provided the blood. Today Israel is a strong little nation which has earned the same respect from the world we gave to England during the early days of the war. Once again the people (acting within the framework of democracy) prevailed, even though the tools of war were used against them. And Israel kept her promise to absorb those who came to her shores. Since the country became a nation a quarter of a million new citizens have reached Israel and have settled there.

Holland, too, resorted to the tools of war in attacking the Indonesian Republic. Her representatives gave fervent lip service to the UN, declaring repeatedly that its decisions would be considered the highest law by the Dutch Government. Meanwhile, Holland ignored a "cease fire" order and continued its aggression against the republic. Moscow, of course, gleefully arose to appoint itself a defender of the rights of colonial people and undoubtedly signed up many recruits for its cause in Indonesia. Events seem to have borne out the rumors prevalent in Holland when I was there in September, to the effect that the real reason for the abdication of Queen Wilhelmina was her refusal to go along with what she felt to be a betrayal of Indonesia and a repudiation of her promises to the republic.

During the past six months the democratic people of Germany have won further victories. It can well be argued that this sign of German unity is a symbol of an emergence of German nationalism and that this is a sign of potential danger. However, all signs point to the fact that this growth of what appears to be nationalism is not as unhealthy as it might appear. The Berlin population has shown that it is quite willing to run any risk to back the Western policies and to oppose either the Fascist or Communist type of totalitarianism. There is no doubt that the success of the air lift has sparked this growth of democracy. And there is no doubt that the people themselves, after closely observing the policies and tactics of Eastern and Western powers, are wholeheartedly on our side. They have not been frightened or intimidated by the threats or by the actual violence of the Soviet (and German Communist) leaders. The people themselves are groping toward democracy. During their years under Hitler the word "ersatz" became more and more important in their language. They had "ersatz" rubber, "ersatz" tobacco, "ersatz" sausage, "ersatz" leather, and "ersatz" coffee. Nazi leaders used to boast that there was an "ersatz" for everything, but it begins to look as though a great many of the German people are beginning to believe that there is no "ersatz" for democracy.

This surprising and almost unbelievable resurgence of the democratic spirit in Europe is not confined to Germany. Czechs who have managed to slip out of their country insist that 75 percent of the population retains its democratic spirit and is merely waiting for a chance to express it militantly. I found refugees from Soviet totalitarianism in Tel Aviv, Athens, Rome, Paris, Amsterdam, Brussels, Berlin and Oslo. Slowly but inexorably democracy seems to be gathering strength in Europe, and wherever it gains there is a corresponding weakening of

Communism. Cracks (to use our most overworked cliche) are really beginning to appear in the Iron Curtain.

During the past year the Kremlin has been no end embarrassed by such incidents as the failure to capture Trieste, the loss of the Italian election, the deviation of Tito from the sacred Kremlin line, the defiant attitude of the marchers in the Sokol parade in Prague, the parliamentary walkouts in Budapest, the peasant resistance in Poland and Yugoslavia and the refusal of newly born Israel to give Kremlin overtures anything but polite and skeptical attention.

The Italian Federation of Labor (C.G.I.L.) has always been Communism's sharpest weapon in Italy, but this weapon has been blunted by "infiltration" of democratically minded labor leaders. In September, 600,000 Catholic C.G.I.L. workers resigned to set up a new labor organization with Communists barred. Thousands of Socialists and anti-Communists of all parties followed the exodus, and today the membership of the C.G.I.L. is probably half what it was two years ago. Italian workers are realizing that the Marshall Plan offers them a great deal more than does the Moscow Plan, and this makes the Kremlin very unhappy. Since the Marshall Plan went into operation Soviet borders in Europe have not been extended one mile.

A great many people are selling democracy short in Europe, but after six months of traveling on the continent I feel that democracy is a pretty good investment; certainly worth the investment represented by the Marshall Plan.

Last July a reader of the European edition of the *Herald Tribune* wrote a letter to the editor asking for a definition of democracy. The letter was printed and a deluge of answers from a dozen countries swamped the editorial staff of the *Tribune*. One definition of democracy which came from London seemed to me to make sense.

"Democracy," the definition read, "is an institutional framework that permits reform without violence and which insists upon the use of reason in political matters."

Soviet propagandists have made a grotesque mockery of the word "democracy," but if there is confusion over the definition there can be no confusion about the aims of our brand of democracy. Former Secretary Marshall said (June 5, 1947, at Harvard): "Our policy is not directed against any country or doctrine but against hunger, poverty, desperation and chaos." Russia and her satellite states were all offered the benefits of the Marshall Plan, and had the Kremlin accepted, the Eastern and Western nations by now might have joined in making a pretty secure and peaceful world for us all to live in.

It was the late General Andrei Zhdanov who answered for the Kremlin. "The Soviet Union will make every effort to see that the Marshall Plan is not realized," he said bluntly in a speech made in Warsaw (October 5, 1947). And the war between totalitarianism and democracy intensified. The Marshall Plan (unlike the Truman Plan) was not conceived primarily as a weapon against Russian expansion, but the Soviet refusal to accept it automatically converted it into a weapon that is proving to be increasingly powerful in this ideological war.

There is no doubt that democracy lost the first few rounds in this fight, but six months in Europe has convinced me that democracy, having survived those tough early rounds, is now coming fast and is well ahead on points. Our poor showing in the earlier stages of the battle was, I believe, due to our own complacency and reluctance to combat the intensified propaganda war Russia was waging against democracy in Europe and our reluctance to take the fight directly to the people.

Democracy in Europe is just about the livest corpse ever to pick up its shroud and walk. It is so alive that Moscow Communist propaganda during the past year has been directed toward identifying Communism with democracy. Soviet apologists have blandly ignored the fact that the struggle in Europe is a fight between political democracy and political totalitarianism and insist that it is a battle between capitalism and collectivism. Ever since the war ended they have thundered that capitalism was very sick and that it was only a matter

339

of weeks before a gigantic economic depression in America would give capitalism its deathblow. Pick up practically any back issue of *La Voix Ouvrière* (Geneva), the *Taegliche Rundschau* (Berlin), *L'Humanité* (Paris), *L'Unita* (Rome), the *Daily Worker* (London), or any other Communist newspaper or magazine published in Europe and you'll find the same dire prophecy, yet today American economy, despite the great strain on it, seems to be about the healthiest animal of its kind in the world. Whether you call it "capitalism" or "free enterprise" or plain "democracy," it is healthy enough to give a badly needed economic blood transfusion to sixteen exhausted, anemic countries in Europe and to three German communities.

Go to Amsterdam or Brussels or Stockholm or Oslo or Paris or Rome or Tel Aviv and you'll find that if the accents seem strange, the people talk the language of democracy. Today democracy can with complete truth serenade Stalin with the Irving Berlin song, "Anything you can do I can do better; I can do anything better than you." Today democracy is selling itself to Europe on performance as well as salesmanship. It seems to me that, on the whole, the people of Europe are eager customers.

Democracy dead? I seriously doubt if it is dead even in Russia. It is certainly very much alive in every country I visited in 1948. People like to think for themselves, and democracy is the only political system yet devised that guarantees them that privilege. Religion and democracy have always been two targets at which the dictators have leveled their sights. But one by one the dictators and the tyrants passed, and faith and democracy remained.

I know that this is a minority report, but I believe that the spirit of democracy in Europe is stronger, more active and militant, than ever before. Democracy is too tough to kill.

Communism in Europe had its chance in the postwar years. It seemed to offer millions the only hope of escape from intolerable conditions. It had relatively small appeal in countries

340

which had decent standards of living and real political and civil liberty. It only made headway in countries which had been bypassed, ignored or exploited by Western civilization or in countries where we mistakenly underwrote outworn empires or a decaying feudalism which had already been rejected by the mass of the people.

Today, in nineteen European countries (most of which still suffer from intolerable conditions and low standards of living) we have offered an alternative to Communism and other desperate and doubtful remedies. It is a decent alternative which allows the individual to retain his independence and, although it doesn't promise pie in the sky, it does promise an ultimate hope of bread on the table and a pay check every week. We might eventually wind up with a pretty decent world—if we'll just leave it to the people.